AIRFRAME & POWERPLANT MECHANICS

POWERPLANT TEST GUIDE
Written, Oral, and Practical

ALIGNS WITH

FAA-H-8083-32B & FAA-H-8083-32B-ATB
Airframe & Powerplant Mechanics Powerplant Handbook

2024 EDITION

Aircraft Technical Book Company
72413 US Hwy 40 - Tabernash, CO 80478-0270 USA
(970) 726-5111
www.actechbooks.com

DON'T HAVE SKYPREP YET?

If you purchased this Test Guide without SkyPrep, you may add SkyPrep at any time for this version of Test Guide for $21.95. To order SkyPrep visit this URL https://www.actechbooks.com/skyprep.html and place your order. Your activation code will be emailed to you within (1) one business day.

2 YEARS OF UNLIMITED SKYPREP PRACTICE EXAMS FOR $21.95

PURCHASED SKYPREP OPTION

If you purchased this Test Guide with the SkyPrep option, your activation code is located on the inside front cover of this book.

LOCATE THIS STICKER ON THE INSIDE FRONT COVER TO FIND YOUR ACTIVATION CODE	SKYPREP ACTIVATION CODE XXXXX-XXXXX

Enhance your test preparation with SkyPrep online exam practice. With SkyPrep, you can take practice exams in the same format as you will take your FAA written tests. SkyPrep allows you to practice your exams in three useful ways:

1. Practice all questions in all topics in random order.
2. Practice only those questions in a particular topic.
3. Take a simulated timed practice exam just as you would for the FAA.

After completing any of the above formats, SkyPrep will give you your score for that session including corrections, explanations, and references within the 8083-ATB Handbooks for any questions answered incorrectly. SkyPrep keeps track of your progress so you can see your improvements over multiple testing sessions. Your unlimited SkyPrep subscription remains valid for two years after the first login.

Getting Started With SkyPrep
Access SkyPrep with any online device by scanning the QR code or visit the following URL
https://actechbooks.skyprepapp.com/users/enrol?course_id=198055
Complete the registration process along with your activation code.

HOW TO USE THIS TEST GUIDE

This book is designed to help you pass your FAA knowledge exams. But even more important, it is designed to help reinforce your understanding of the subjects which you have been studying in the classroom and shop. However, rather than this being the first book you pick up, it should be the last. When you take that route, you will find the questions in this book both easy and an excellent reinforcement to your studies.

The chapters in this test guide are organized to follow those of the FAA 8083-32B Powerplant Handbook, which can be found here: www.actechbooks.com/ap-textbooks.html. Thus, the process we suggest is this: Beginning with Chapter 1, first learn from the handbooks and in the classroom. Only when you feel comfortable with each subject, is it time to prepare for your exam. This is the best time to open this Test Guide to confirm what you have learned or to reopen the Handbook to review those topics for which you need reinforcement. You will see that every question in this Test Guide includes its reference pages to that subject in the Handbook to make that process easy. Following this, is then the best time to use SkyPrep and take simulated practice exams for further confirmation that you are ready for the FAA Exam. See page ii for further information about SkyPrep.

ABOUT THE QUESTIONS
In 2011 FAA made the decision to no longer publish the actual test questions. Previous test guides where one could memorize the same questions as would be on your test are no more. Instead, questions in this and other available Test Guides are only examples of the type of question you will receive on your actual test.

Questions in this book are derived from two sources. Some are practice questions provided by FAA, for which we have added the answer, an explanation, and a reference to the 8083 Handbooks. However, most are instead written by ATB authors to cover other topics from the 8083 Handbooks for which FAA samples did not exist.

AIRMAN CERTIFICATION STANDARDS (ACS)

As of August 2023 FAA has adopted the Airman's Certification Standards, replacing the older Practical Test Standards. The ACS identifies each topic which you are required to learn subdivided by knowledge, risk management, and practical skills. Each subject is given a learning code found in the ACS. The codes for each question are referenced in this book next to the question number. The complete list of codes is provided in the ACS, which can be downloaded for free below.

Free Download - www.actechbooks.com/test_standards/amt_acs.pdf

Or, if you prefer a printed copy of the ACS, please visit the following link.

Print Copy - www.actechbooks.com/0427-ASA-B.html

ISBN: 978-1951275747

9 781951 275747

VERSION 1

TABLE OF CONTENTS

AIRCRAFT ENGINES

Types of Engines, Connecting Rods, Piston Rings, Firing Order,
Valves and Valve Operating Mechanisms, Bearings, Propellers, and Efficiencies

CHAPTER
1

1-1 AM.III.B.K4
Based on the criteria of efficiency of an engine's weight
to the power it produces, which type of engine is the best
choice for an aircraft operating at speeds of 300 mph at
altitudes between 20,000-25,000 feet?
  A. Reciprocating Engines
  B. Turbofan Engines
  C. Turboprop Engines

1-2 AM.III.A.K5
An aircraft engine has 9 cylinders. From this information
alone we can deduce that
  A. it contains both master and articulating rods.
  B. its firing order is 1-3-5-7-9-2-4-6-8.
  C. it is water cooled.

1-3 AM.III.A.K4
The crankcase of an aircraft engine
  A. houses the valve operating mechanism and the
     engine cylinders.
  B. is lightweight and primarily used as a reservoir for the
     engine oil.
  C. is the foundation of the engine containing crankshaft
     bearings and cylinder pads.

1-4 AM.III.A.K4
The cylinders of an aircraft engine are mounted on cylinder
pads that are machined onto the crankcase. The common
method of attachment of the cylinders to the crankcase is
  A. by studs mounted in threaded holes in the crankcase.
  B. by bolts into locking helicoils mounted in the crankcase.
  C. by heating the crankcase and cooling the cylinder for
     an interference fit.

1-5 AM.III.A.K4
The crankpin is
  A. used to ensure the crankshaft does not shift in
     the crankcase.
  B. a solid, heavy journal to withstand crankshaft
     shock loads.
  C. hardened by nitriding and is hollow to reduce weight.

1-6 AM.III.A.K5
Which statement is correct about radial engine crankshafts?
  A. Movable counterweights serve to reduce the torsional
     vibrations in an aircraft reciprocating engine.
  B. Movable counterweights serve to reduce the dynamic
     vibrations in an aircraft reciprocating engine.
  C. Movable counterweights are designed to resonate at
     the natural frequency of the crankshaft.

AIRCRAFT ENGINES

ANSWERS

1-1 Answer C
In the cruising speed range of 180-300 mph, the turboprop engine delivers more power per weight than the reciprocating engine. Below this speed and altitude reciprocating engines provide the greatest efficiency based on cost. At higher speeds and altitudes, the turbofan engine provides the greatest efficiency. Turbo jet engines and low bypass turbofans are the only type capable of speeds higher than Mach 1.
Ref: Powerplant Handbook H-8083-32B-ATB Chapter 1 Page 3, 4

1-2 Answer B
All radial engines contain an odd number of cylinders with firing orders starting with consecutive odd number cylinders followed by consecutive even cylinders. Articulated rods exist only on multiple row radial engines. This would not be possible with a 9 cylinder engine. Generally, radial engines are air cooled.
Ref: Powerplant Handbook H-8083-32B-ATB Chapter 1 Page 5, 16

1-3 Answer C
The cast or forged crankcase is the foundation of the aircraft engine. It contains the bearings which support the crankshaft. Cylinders are bolted to the crankcase and the crankcase provides the attach points for the engine to be secured to the airframe. As such it must be very strong to receive the many variations of mechanical loads and forces from these components while keeping the crankshaft stable. The crankcase does act as a reservoir for the engine oil, but with all of its other functions and relatively heavyweight construction, this is not the crankcase's primary function.
Ref: Powerplant Handbook H-8083-32B-ATB Chapter 1 Page 5

1-4 Answer A
Several studs are installed into the crankcase around the circumference of each machined cylinder pad.
These are used to mount the cylinders securely to the crankcase with nuts. The inner portion of a cylinder pad may be chamfered or tapered to permit the installation of a large rubber o-ring around the cylinder skirt. This seals the joint between the cylinder and the crankcase pad against oil leakage.
Ref: Powerplant Handbook H-8083-32B-ATB Chapter 1 Page 6

1-5 Answer C
Crankpins are the machined journals on the crankshaft to which the piston connecting rods are attached. They are off center from the main journal. The two crank cheeks and the crankpin together make a "throw". When the force of combustion is applied to the crankpin, it causes the crankshaft to rotate. Crankpins are hardened by nitriding to resist wear and are hollow to keep the total weight of the crankshaft as light as possible. The hollow crankpin also permits the passage of oil as it turns in the crankcase.
Ref: Powerplant Handbook H-8083-32B-ATB Chapter 1 Page 8

1-6 Answer B
Vibration occurs as the crankshaft rotates due to the forces of combustion acting on the pistons, connecting rods, and crankpins. These power impulses cause even a statically balanced crankshaft to vibrate. Movable counterweights are dynamic dampeners are located in the counterweight lobes of the crankshaft. Using pendulum motion, the dampeners oscillate out of time with the crankshaft vibration thus reducing overall vibration.
Ref: Powerplant Handbook H-8083-32B-ATB Chapter 1 Page 8, 9

1-7 AM.III.A.K5

Master rod bearings are generally what type of bearing?
- A. Plain
- B. Roller
- C. Ball

1-8 AM.III.A.K4

Cam ground pistons are installed in some aircraft engines to
- A. provide a better fit at operating temperatures.
- B. act as a compensating feature so that a compensated magneto is not required.
- C. equalize the wear on all pistons.

1-9 AM.III.A.K4

Full-floating piston pins are those which allow motion between the pin and
- A. the piston.
- B. the piston and the large end of the connecting rod.
- C. the piston and the small end of the connecting rod.

1-10 AM.III.A.K4

How is oil collected by the piston oil ring returned to the crankcase?
- A. Down vertical slots cut in the piston wall between the piston oil ring groove and the piston skirt.
- B. Through holes drilled in the piston oil ring groove.
- C. Through holes drilled in the piston pin recess.

1-11 AM.III.A.K4

Which is the primary factor in ensuring a gas tight joint between a cylinder barrel and the cylinder head?
- A. An initial precision fit.
- B. Cylinder head gaskets.
- C. Proper torque procedures.

1-12 AM.III.A.K4

Which is the typical firing order on an 4 cylinder opposed aircraft engine?
- A. Opposed cylinders from the rear to the front.
- B. Opposed cylinders from the front to the rear.
- C. Opposed cylinders and opposed diagonal.

AIRCRAFT ENGINES

ANSWERS

1-7 Answer A

The master rod bearings refer to the bearing located on the crankpin end and the piston end of the master connecting rod commonly found in radial engines. Whether of solid or split design, plain bearings are used to mate with the crankpin journal of the crankshaft. The piston pin end of the master rod uses a plain bearing usually called a bushing to mate with the piston pin.

Ref: Powerplant Handbook H-8083-32B-ATB Chapter 1 Page 22

1-8 Answer A

Modern engines use cam ground pistons that have a larger diameter perpendicular to the piston pin. This larger diameter keeps the piston straight in the cylinder as the engine warms up from initial start. As the piston heats up during warm up, the part of the piston in line with the piston pin has more mass. It expands more than the piston area perpendicular to the piston pin making the piston completely round at operating temperature.

Ref: Powerplant Handbook H-8083-32B-ATB Chapter 1 Page 12

1-9 Answer C

The piston pins used in modern aircraft engines are the full-floating type, so called because the pin is free to rotate in both the piston and in the connecting rod piston pin bearing which is the small end of the connecting rod. As such, full floating piston pins must be held in place to prevent the pin ends from scoring the cylinder walls. This is accomplished with soft aluminum plugs on each end of the piston pin.

Ref: Powerplant Handbook H-8083-32B-ATB Chapter 1 Page 13

1-10 Answer B

Oil control rings are located just below the compression rings but above the piston pin on the typical aircraft piston. They regulate the thickness of the oil film on the cylinder wall. This keeps excessive oil from entering the combustion chamber past the compression rings. To allow the surplus oil to return to the crankcase, holes are drilled in the bottom of the oil control piston ring grooves or in the lands next to these grooves.

Ref: Powerplant Handbook H-8083-32B-ATB Chapter 1 Page 13

1-11 Answer A

While all three play a role in producing a gas tight fit, ensuring a perfect and tight fit upon construction plays the greatest. At initial assembly, a heated cylinder head is joined to a chilled cylinder body. When the head then cool (contracts) and the cylinder warms (expands) a gas tight fit is created.

Ref: Powerplant Handbook H-8083-32B-ATB Chapter 1 Page 15

1-12 Answer A

To minimize vibration, cylinders fire from one side to the other from rear to the front. Typically 1-4-2-3 or 1-3-2-4.

Ref: Powerplant Handbook H-8083-32B-ATB Chapter 1 Page 16

1-13 AM.III.A.K4
What is an advantage of using metallic sodium filled exhaust valves in aircraft reciprocating engines?
    A. Increased strength and resistance to cracking.
    B. Reduced valve operating temperature.
    C. Greater resistance to deterioration at high valve temperature.

1-14 AM.III.A.K4
What is the purpose of the stem keys installed on the valve stems?
    A. To hold the valve guide in position.
    B. To hold the valve spring retaining washer in position.
    C. To prevent valves from falling into the combustion chamber.

1-15 AM.III.A.K4
What is the purpose of installing two or more springs on each valve in an aircraft engine?
    A. To equalize side pressure on the valve stem.
    B. To eliminate valve spring vibration or surging.
    C. To help equalize valve face loading.

1-16 AM.III.A.K5
Cam rollers, cam rings, and cam tracks are a part of the valve operating mechanisms of which engine type(s)?
    A. Radial engines.
    B. Opposed engines.
    C. Both Radial and Opposed engines.

1-17 AM.III.A.K4
Excessive valve clearance in a piston engine
    A. increases valve overlap.
    B. increases valve opening time.
    C. decreases valve overlap.

1-18 AM.III.A.K4
Valve clearance changes on opposed-type engines using hydraulic lifters are accomplished by
    A. adjusting the rocker arm.
    B. replacing the rocker arm.
    C. replacing the push rod.

AIRCRAFT ENGINES

ANSWERS

1-13 Answer B
Some intake and exhaust valves are hollow and partially filled with metallic sodium. This material is used because it is an excellent heat conductor. The sodium melts at 208°F. The reciprocating motion of the valve circulates the liquid sodium, allowing it to carry heat away from the valve head and into the stem, where the heat is dissipated through the valve guide to the cylinder head and the cooling fins. Operating temperature of a sodium filled valve may be reduced as much as 300°F to 400°F.
Ref: Powerplant Handbook H-8083-32B-ATB Chapter 1 Page 17

1-14 Answer B
The valve stem acts as a pilot for the valve head and rides the valve guide installed in the cylinder head. The stem is surface-hardened to resist wear. A machined groove near the tip of the valve stem opposite the valve head receives the split-ring stem keys. These stem keys form a lock ring to hold the valve spring retaining washer in place.
Ref: Powerplant Handbook H-8083-32B-ATB Chapter 1 Page 17

1-15 Answer B
Valve springs which slip over the stem of the valves are held in place by the valve spring retaining washer and stem key. The springs hold the valves closed when not forced open via the valve operating mechanism. Any single spring will surge at certain engine speeds, allowing a less that tight seating of the closed valve. By using two or more valve springs on each valve stem, while one spring may be surging at a certain engine RPM, the other(s) will not, due to variation in mass and construction. Thus oscillations are dampened with the added protection of one or more extra springs should one of the springs break.
Ref: Powerplant Handbook H-8083-32B-ATB Chapter 1 Page 21

1-16 Answer A
The geometry and so the number of moving parts are greater on a radial type engine than an opposed engine. On an opposed engine, the pushrod is in direct contact with the camshaft lobe.
Ref: Powerplant Handbook H-8083-32B-ATB Chapter 1 Page 19

1-17 Answer C
Reciprocating aircraft engines that use solid lifters or tappets generally require that the clearance between the rocker arm and the valve tip is adjusted to ensure that the valve can fully close. If the clearance is too great, the valve operating mechanism must span this distance which causes the valve timing to be late. The valve will open late and close early. Valve overlap refers to the time period when both the intake and exhaust valve are open. Late opening and early closing of the valves reduces valve overlap.
Ref: Powerplant Handbook H-8083-32B-ATB Chapter 1 Page 20

1-18 Answer C
Hydraulic lifters are normally adjusted at the time of overhaul. They are assembled dry (no lubrication), clearances checked, and adjustments made by using pushrods of different lengths. A minimum and maximum valve clearance is established in this dry condition. Any measurement between these extremes is acceptable, but a pushrod that creates a clearance halfway between the minimum and maximum extremes is desired. Once assembled with the engine running, the hydraulic lifters are filled with oil; this removes the clearance and provides a quiet, lubricated, low maintenance valve operating mechanism.
Ref: Powerplant Handbook H-8083-32B-ATB Chapter 1 Page 21

AIRCRAFT ENGINES

QUESTIONS

1-19 AM.III.A.K5
Which of the following is a characteristic of a thrust bearing used in most radial engines?
- A. Tapered Roller
- B. Double-Row Ball
- C. Deep-Grooved Ball

1-20 AM.III.A.K2
What is the primary advantage of using propeller reduction gears?
- A. To enable the propeller RPM to be increased without an accompanying increase in engine RPM.
- B. To enable the engine RPM to be increased with an accompanying increase in power and allow the propeller shaft to remain at a lower RPM.
- C. To enable the engine RPM to be increased with an accompanying increase in propeller RPM.

1-21 AM.III.M.K7
On a smaller aircraft engine with a keyed propeller shaft, to what is the keyway aligned with during installation of the propeller?
- A. Number 1 cylinder at bottom dead center.
- B. Number 1 cylinder at top dead center.
- C. The magneto firing point for the number one cylinder.

1-22 AM.III.A.K2
During the power stroke of a four stroke engine, which are correct positions of the valves?
- A. Intake valve is open, exhaust valve is closed.
- B. Intake valve is closed, exhaust valve is open.
- C. Both the intake and exhaust valves are closed.

1-23 AM.III.A.K2
On which stroke are both valves on a four-stroke cycle reciprocating engine open?
- A. Power and exhaust.
- B. Intake and compression.
- C. Intake and exhaust.

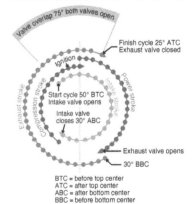

Valve timing chart.

AIRCRAFT ENGINES

ANSWERS

1-19 Answer C
Special deep-grooved ball bearings are used to transmit propeller thrust and radial loads to the engine nose section of radial engines. This type of bearing can accept both radial and thrust loads with minimal friction.
Ref: Powerplant Handbook H-8083-32B-ATB Chapter 1 Page 22

1-20 Answer B
Increased brake horsepower of an engine results partially from increased crankshaft RPM. However, increasing crankshaft RPM without regard to propeller speed can cause propeller inefficiency-as propeller tip speed approaches the speed of sound, the prop becomes less efficient. Reduction gearing allows the engine RPM to be increased to extract maximum power while rotating the propeller at a slower speed than the crankshaft.
Ref: Powerplant Handbook H-8083-32B-ATB Chapter 1 Page 23

1-21 Answer B
The propeller shaft of most low power engines is tapered and with a milled slot so that the propeller hub can be keyed to the shaft. The keyway position is in relation to the top dead center position of the number 1 cylinder.
Ref: Powerplant Handbook H-8083-32B-ATB Chapter 1 Page 23

1-22 Answer C
The four-strokes plus the ignition event are the five events of a four-stroke cycle engine. In order of occurrence, the 5 events are: The Intake Stroke, The Compression Stroke, Ignition, The Power Stroke and The Exhaust Stroke. During the intake stroke, the crankshaft rotates and the piston moves down away from the top of the cylinder. As it does, it draws in a gaseous fuel/air charge through an open intake valve. As the piston nears the bottom of the cylinder, the intake valve closes and the piston reverses direction to begin the compression stroke. The fuel/air charge, trapped between the piston and the cylinder walls, compresses as the piston moves upward toward the cylinder head. Just before top center of the stroke, the spark plug fires which lights off the compressed charge. The energy released by the burning of the fuel air mixture forces the piston down toward the bottom of the cylinder during the power stroke--the heat energy is thus transferred to the crankshaft. The exhaust valve opens and the burnt gases are forced out of the cylinder as the piston returns to the top of the cylinder during the exhaust stroke.
Ref: Powerplant Handbook H-8083-32B-ATB Chapter 1 Page 25

1-23 Answer C
The valve timing chart below (Figure 1-37 of FAA-H-8083-32) illustrates when the valves open during the four stroke of the engine and upon what strokes both valves are open at the same time, which is known as valve overlap. On a typical reciprocating engine, the intake valve opens just before the piston reaches TDC (top dead center) on the exhaust stroke. The exhaust valve opens just before the exhaust stroke begins and stays open until a little after the exhaust stroke is complete. This means the exhaust valve is open as the intake stroke begins, so both valves are open during a part of the exhaust stroke and a part of the intake stroke.
Ref: Powerplant Handbook H-8083-32B-ATB Chapter 1 Page 26

One complete actual cycle of a four-stroke cycle reciprocating engine

Valve overlap 75° both valves open

Finish cycle 25° ATC
Exhaust valve closed

Ignition

Exhaust stroke
Compression stroke
Intake stroke
Power stroke

Start cycle 50° BTC
Intake valve opens

Intake valve
closes 30° ABC

Exhaust valve opens

30° BBC

BTC = before top center
ATC = after top center
ABC = after bottom center
BBC = before bottom center

Valve timing chart.

1-24 AM.III.A.K2

If fuel/air ratio is proper and ignition timing is correct, the combustion process should be completed

A. 20° to 30° before top center at the end of the compression stroke.

B. when the exhaust valve opens at the end of the power stroke.

C. just after top center at the beginning of the power stroke.

1-25 AM.III.A.K2

The actual power delivered to the propeller of an aircraft engine is called

A. friction horsepower.

B. brake horsepower.

C. indicated horsepower.

1-26 AM.III.A.K2

The compression ratio of an engine is equal to

A. the volume of the cylinder multiplied by the manifold pressure.

B. the volume of the combustion chamber multiplied by the manifold pressure.

C. the volume of the cylinder with the piston at BDC divided by the volume of the cylinder at TDC.

1-27 AM.III.A.K2

During a 4 stroke cycle, which of the following event occurs at about 60° BDC?

A. The exhaust valve opens.

B. Ignition occurs.

C. The intake valve closes.

1-28 AM.III.A.K2

How many of the following are factors in establishing the maximum compression ratio limitations of an aircraft engine?

1. Detonation characteristics of the fuel used.

2. Design limitations of the engine.

3. Degree of supercharging.

4. Spark plug reach.

A. 4

B. 2

C. 3

1-29 AM.III.A.K2

The horsepower developed in the cylinders of a reciprocating engine is known as the

A. shaft horsepower.

B. indicated horsepower.

C. brake horsepower.

AIRCRAFT ENGINES

ANSWERS

1-24 Answer C
The time of ignition varies from 20° to 30° before TDC (depending upon the requirements of the specific engine) to ensure complete combustion of the charge by the time the piston is slightly past the TDC position.
Ref: Powerplant Handbook H-8083-32B-ATB Chapter 1 Page 26

1-25 Answer B
Indicated horsepower is the term used to describe the theoretical output of an engine. The total horsepower lost in overcoming friction (friction horsepower) must be subtracted from the indicated horsepower to arrive at the actual horsepower delivered to the propeller by the engine. This is known as brake horsepower.
Ref: Powerplant Handbook H-8083-32B-ATB Chapter 1 Page 31

1-26 Answer C
All internal combustion engines must compress the fuel/air mixture to receive a reasonable amount of work from each power stroke. The fuel/air charge in the cylinder can be compared to a coil spring. The more it is compressed, the more work it is potentially capable of doing. A comparison of the volume of the cylinder at Bottom Dead Center (BDC) and at Top Dead Center (TDC) of a stroke describes the amount of compression developed. Compression ratio is a controlling factor in the maximum horsepower developed by an engine.
Ref: Powerplant Handbook H-8083-32B-ATB Chapter 1 Page 29

1-27 Answer C
The intake valve is timed to close at about 50-75° past BDC on the compression stroke to allow the momentum of the incoming gases to charge the cylinder more completely. The exhaust valve opens at about 135° on the exhaust stroke. Ignition occurs at approximately 20° before TDC of the compression stroke.
Ref: Powerplant Handbook H-8083-32B-ATB Chapter 1 Page 25-26

1-28 Answer C
Manifold pressure is the average absolute pressure of the air or fuel air charge supplying the engine. Combined with the compression ratio, the total pressure inside the combustion chamber of the engine is determined. Design limitations prevent unlimited pressure inside the engine. Since supercharging affects manifold pressure and fuels have various characteristics which affect their ability to be compressed without exploding, these three factors limit the maximum compression ratio that can be developed by an engine. The reach of the spark plug will affect the ignition of the compressed charge in an engine that has already been designed with the other three factors taken into consideration, however it does not affect maximum compression ratio.
Ref: Powerplant Handbook H-8083-32B-ATB Chapter 1 Page 29

1-29 Answer B
The indicated horsepower produced by an engine is the horsepower calculated from the indicated mean effective pressure and other factors which affect the power output of an engine. Indicated horsepower is the power developed in the combustion chambers without reference to frictional losses of the engine. This horsepower is calculated as a function of the actual cylinder pressure recorded during engine operation.
Ref: Powerplant Handbook H-8083-32B-ATB Chapter 1 Page 30

1-30 AM.III.A.K7
Friction horsepower
  A. is insignificant when considering the actual power output of an engine.
  B. is not included in the calculation of brake horsepower.
  C. may be as high as 10-15% of the indicated horsepower on a modern aircraft engine.

1-31 AM.III.A.K7
What is defined by the equation:
_____ = PLANK/33,000
  A. Brake Horsepower
  B. Indicated Horsepower
  C. Thrust Horsepower

1-32 AM.III.A.K7
The thermal efficiency of an engine
  A. affects the fuel consumption of an engine.
  B. is a fixed amount directly related to the heat energy of the fuel.
  C. results in less of the heat energy in the fuel being used.

1-33 AM.III.A.K7
Which of the following will decrease volumetric efficiency in a reciprocating engine?
  1. Full throttle operation.
  2. Low cylinder head temperature.
  3. Improper valve timing.
  4. Sharp bends in the induction system.
  5. High carburetor air temperatures.
  A. 2, 4, and 5
  B. 3, 4, and 5
  C. 1, 2, 3, and 4

1-34 AM.III.A.K7
Propulsive efficiency
  A. can be maximized through the use of a fixed pitched prop.
  B. is a ratio of thrust horsepower to the length of the prop.
  C. is maximized through the use of a constant-speed prop.

1-35 AM.III.B.K2
Most modern airliners that fly in the .8 mach speed range are fitted with
  A. turbofan engines.
  B. turboprop engines.
  C. turboshaft engines.

AIRCRAFT ENGINES

ANSWERS

1-30 Answer C
Friction horsepower is the indicated horsepower minus brake horsepower. It is the horsepower used by an engine in overcoming friction of moving parts, drawing in fuel, expelling exhaust, driving oil and fuel pumps, and other engine accessories. On modern engines, this power loss through friction may be as high as 10 to 15 percent of the indicated horsepower.
Ref: Powerplant Handbook H-8083-32B-ATB Chapter 1 Page 32

1-31 Answer B
Indicated horsepower is the power developed in the combustion chamber without deducting friction losses in the engine. The acronym PLANK refers to those variables within the basic construction of the engine as:
  P = mean effective pressure in psi
  L = length of the stroke in feet
  A = area of the piston head in square inches
  N = power strokes per minute : RPM/2
  K = number of cylinders
33,000 foot/pounds is the constant used to define horsepower
Ref: Powerplant Handbook H-8083-32B-ATB Chapter 1 Page 30

1-32 Answer A
Each quantity of fuel contains a finite amount of heat energy which can be extracted by the engine for mechanical work. The ratio of useful work done by an engine to the heat energy of the fuel it uses, expressed in work or heat units, is called the thermal efficiency of the engine. High thermal efficiency results in an engine producing the greatest amount of power with minimal excess heat reaching the valves, cylinders, pistons and cooling system of the engine. It also means low specific fuel consumption, therefore less fuel for a flight of a given distance at a given power setting.
Ref: Powerplant Handbook H-8083-32B-ATB Chapter 1 Page 33

1-33 Answer B
Volumetric efficiency is a ratio expressed in terms of percentages. It is a comparison of the volume of the fuel/air charge inducted into the cylinder to the total piston displacement of the engine. Since piston displacement is unaffected by external factors, volumetric efficiency is a measure of external factors that reduce the total volume of the fuel/air charge inducted into the engine. Some of these factors are: part throttle operation, long intake pipes of narrow diameter, sharp bends in the induction system, high carburetor air temperature, high cylinder head temperature, incomplete scavenging, and improper valve timing. Full throttle operation and low cylinder head temperatures would increase the volume of the induction charge.
Ref: Powerplant Handbook H-8083-32B-ATB Chapter 1 Page 35

1-34 Answer C
Propeller efficiency affects propulsive efficiency which is defined as the ratio of thrust horsepower to brake horsepower. A constant-speed propeller maximizes propeller efficiency by changing the propeller blade angle to the most efficient angle for the power produced by the engine. This increases thrust horsepower which, by definition, increases propulsive efficiency.
Ref: Powerplant Handbook H-8083-32B-ATB Chapter 1 Page 36

1-35 Answer A
Differently constructed turbine engines are suited for various aircraft and flying conditions. Most modern airliners use turbofan engines that have at the front of the engine a relatively large diameter fan section. This accounts for the name – turbofan. This type of engine is relatively quiet and has better fuel consumption at the average cruising speed of airline flight. Turboprop engines have greater efficiency at 300-400mph. Turboshaft engine are found on helicopters and Auxiliary Power Units (APUs).
Ref: Powerplant Handbook H-8083-32B-ATB Chapter 1 Page 36

1-36 AM.III.B.K3
Accessories such as electric generators and hydraulic pumps on turbine powered aircraft are
  A. Driven directly off the turbine shaft.
  B. Driven at the same speed as the engine using a tower shaft.
  C. Driven at reduced speed from the high pressure compressor via a reduction gear box.

1-39 AM.III.B.K3
What is the primary purpose of stator vanes in the compressor of an axial flow turbine engine?
  A. Increase air velocity.
  B. Create swirl of the oncoming air ahead of the compressor rotors.
  C. Increase air pressure.

1-37 AM.III.B.K3
The primary function of the compressor on a gas turbine engine is to
  A. cool the engine.
  B. supply air in sufficient quantity for combustion.
  C. supply the pressure for cabin environmental purposes.

1-40 AM.III.B.K3
What is the function of the inlet guide vane assembly on an axial-flow compressor?
  A. Directs air onto the first stage rotor blades at the proper angle.
  B. Converts velocity energy to pressure energy.
  C. Converts pressure energy to velocity energy.

1-38 AM.III.B.K3
What is meant by a double entry centrifugal compressor?
  A. A compressor that has two intakes.
  B. A two-stage compressor independently connected to the main shaft.
  C. A compressor with vanes on both sides of the impeller.

1-41 AM.III.B.K3
Which component of a centrifugal flow compressor performs the most similar work as does the rear stator vanes in an axial flow compressor?
  A. Diffuser
  B. Impeller
  C. Guide Vanes

AIRCRAFT ENGINES

ANSWERS

1-36 Answer C
The accessory section of a gas turbine aircraft has various functions. One of these includes driving accessories concerned with the operation of the aircraft such as electrical generators and hydraulic pumps. The rotational speeds of a turbine engine and its shafts are much greater than the optimum speed for driving rotating accessories. Therefore, turbine engine accessory sections incorporate a series of gears to reduce the speed of the various drives provided for accessories. The gear train is driven by the engine's high pressure compressor through an accessory drive shaft gear coupling.
Ref: Powerplant Handbook H-8083-32B-ATB Chapter 1 Page 38

1-37 Answer B
The compressor section of a gas turbine engine has many functions. Its primary function is to supply air in sufficient quantities to satisfy the requirements of the combustion burners. Specifically, to fulfill its purpose, the compressor must increase the pressure of the mass of air received from the air inlet duct, and then discharge it to the burner section in the quantities and pressures required. Cooling the engine and supplying air for cabin environmental functions are secondary purposes of the compressor.
Ref: Powerplant Handbook H-8083-32B-ATB Chapter 1 Page 38

1-38 Answer C
The impeller in an engine with a centrifugal compressor may be of two types – single entry or double entry. The principal differences between the two types of impellers are size and ducting arrangement. The double entry type has a smaller diameter and is usually operated at higher rotational speed to ensure sufficient airflow. Its impeller has vanes on both sides (i.e. front and back) but requires more complex ducting to have intake air reach both sides. The single entry impeller has simple, conventional inlet ducting but the impeller is of a larger diameter, which increases the overall dimensions of the engine.
Ref: Powerplant Handbook H-8083-32B-ATB Chapter 1 Page 39

1-39 Answer C
The stationary stator vanes increase the pressure of air between each compressor stage and also help control the direction of air to each rotor stage to obtain the best possible compressor blade efficiency.
Ref: Powerplant Handbook H-8083-32B-ATB Chapter 1 Page 40

1-40 Answer A
The first stage rotor blades on an axial-flow compressor can be preceded by an inlet guide vane assembly that can be either fixed or variable. The guide vanes help direct the airflow into the first stage rotor blades at the proper angle and establish a swirling motion for the air entering the compressor. This preswirl, in the direction of engine rotation, improves the aerodynamic characteristics of the compressor by reducing drag on the first stage rotor blades. The inlet guide vanes are curved steel vanes usually welded to steel inner and outer shrouds.
Ref: Powerplant Handbook H-8083-32B-ATB Chapter 1 Page 40

1-41 Answer A
Both the rear stator vanes of an axial flow compressor and the diffuser of a centrifugal flow compressor have the job of stabilizing the direction of airflow prior to entering the combustion chamber. Guide vanes are not a part of a centrifugal flow compressor.
Ref: Powerplant Handbook H-8083-32B-ATB Chapter 1 Page 39-40, 43

1-42 AM.III.B.K1
The compression ratio of an axial flow compressor is a function of the
A. number of compressor stages.
B. rotor diameter.
C. air inlet velocity.

1-43 AM.III.B.K3
What is referred to as blade profile of a turbine engine compressor blade?
A. The leading edge of the blade.
B. A cutout that reduces blade tip thickness.
C. The curvature of the blade root.

1-44 AM.III.B.K1
What is the primary advantage of an axial-flow compressor over a centrifugal flow compressor?
A. High frontal area.
B. Less expensive.
C. Greater pressure ratio.

1-45 AM.III.B.K1
In the dual axial flow or twin spool compressor system, the first stage turbine drives the
A. N1 and N2 compressors.
B. N2 compressor.
C. N1 compressor.

1-46 AM.III.B.K1
What is the purpose of the diffuser section of a turbine engine?
A. To increase air pressure and decrease its velocity.
B. To decrease air pressure and increase its velocity.
C. To straighten the airflow prior to its entrance to the combustion chamber.

1-47 AM.III.B.K1
What turbine engine section provides for proper mixing of the fuel and air?
A. Combustion Section
B. Compressor Section
C. Diffuser Section

AIRCRAFT ENGINES

ANSWERS

1-42 Answer A
In an axial flow compressor, each consecutive pair of rotor and stator blades constitutes a pressure stage. The number of rows of blades (stages) is determined by the amount of air and total pressure rise required. The compressor pressure ratio increases with the number of compression stages. Most large engines use 16 stages or more.
Ref: Powerplant Handbook H-8083-32B-ATB Chapter 1 Page 41

1-43 Answer B
Compressor blade tips are reduced in thickness by cutouts, referred to as blade profiles. These profiles prevent serious damage to the blades or housing should the blades contact the compressor housing. Profiling also allows tighter clearances between the blade tips and the compressor case and requires the case interior surface to be lined with a relatively soft material to allow the blades to rub the surface without blade damage.
Ref: Powerplant Handbook H-8083-32B-ATB Chapter 1 Page 41

1-44 Answer C
In an axial flow engine, at each stage of compression, the air is compressed at a ratio of approximately 1.25 to 1. Each consecutive pair of rotor and stator blades constitutes a pressure stage. The compressor pressure ratio increases with the number of compression stages. Large engines utilize up to 16 stages of compression (or more), and at each stage compression is increased by a ratio of 1.25 to 1 above the previous stage. This gives an axial flow engine the ability to have a much higher overall compression ratio than a centrifugal engine which typically has one stage of compression at approximately an 8 to 1 pressure increase.
Ref: Powerplant Handbook H-8083-32B-ATB Chapter 1 Page 43

1-45 Answer B
A spool in a split spool or twin spool engine refers to a turbine section, the compressor it drives, and the interconnecting shaft between the two. Each spool is independent of the other. The first stage turbine wheel is located immediately downstream of the combustion section of the engine--it receives the most energy from the combusted gases and, therefore, drives the high pressure compressor which is known as the N2 compressor. The second stage turbine is behind or downstream of the first stage turbine--it receives less energy from the combusted gases since the gases have already passed through the first stage turbine. The second stage turbine drives the low pressure compressor, which is known as the N1 compressor.
Ref: Powerplant Handbook H-8083-32B-ATB Chapter 1 Page 40

1-46 Answer A
The diffuser is the divergent section of the engine after the compressor but before the combustion section. Its function is to increase air pressure at a slower velocity. This prepares the air for the combustion section of the engine where it is mixed with fuel and burned. A continuous burn is desired and the slower velocity air allows the flame to persist without being extinguished and prevents the combustion process from moving forward into the compressor.
Ref: Powerplant Handbook H-8083-32B-ATB Chapter 1 Page 43

1-47 Answer A
The primary function of the combustion section of a gas turbine engine is to burn the fuel/air mixture, thereby adding heat energy to the air. To do this efficiently, the combustion chamber must provide the means for proper mixing of the fuel and air to ensure good combustion.
Ref: Powerplant Handbook H-8083-32B-ATB Chapter 1 Page 42, 43

1-48 AM.III.B.K1
The air passing through the combustion chamber of a turbine engine is
  A. used to support combustion and to cool the engine.
  B. entirely combined with fuel and burned.
  C. speeded up and heated by the action of the turbines.

1-51 AM.III.B.K1
The function of the exhaust cone assembly of a turbine engine is to
  A. collect the exhaust gases and act as a noise suppressor.
  B. swirl and collect the exhaust gases into a single exhaust jet.
  C. straighten and collect the exhaust gases into a solid exhaust jet.

1-49 AM.III.B.K3
The highest heat to metal contacts in a jet engine are the
  A. burner cans.
  B. turbine inlet nozzle vanes.
  C. turbine blades.

1-52 AM.III.G.K2
The oil dampened also known as hydraulic main bearing utilized in some turbine engines is used to
  A. provide lubrication of the bearings from the beginning of starting rotation until normal oil pressure is established.
  B. provide an oil film between the outer race and the bearing housing in order to reduce vibration tendencies in the rotor system, and to allow for slight misalignment.
  C. dampen surges in oil pressure to the bearings.

1-50 AM.III.B.K1
Why are turbine blades generally more susceptible to operating damage than compressor blades?
  A. The high probability of carbon deposits.
  B. Exposure to high temperatures.
  C. Less exposure to solutions during engine pressure washes.

1-53 AM.III.G.K2
Main bearing oil seals used in turbine engines are usually what type?
  A. Labyrinth and/or carbon rubbing.
  B. Teflon® an D synthetic rubber.
  C. Labyrinth and/or silicone rubber.

AIRCRAFT ENGINES

ANSWERS

1-48 Answer A
The air entering the combustion chamber is divided into two main streams – the primary and the secondary. The primary or combustion air is directed inside the liner at the front end, where it mixes with the fuel and is burned. Secondary or cooling air passes between the outer casing and the liner and joins the combustion air gases through larger holes toward the rear of the liner, cooling the combustion gases from about 3500°F to below what the turbine section can withstand (near 1500°F on earlier engines).
Ref: Powerplant Handbook H-8083-32B-ATB Chapter 1 Page 44

1-49 Answer B
The turbine inlet nozzle vanes are located directly aft of the combustion chamber and immediately forward of the turbine wheel. This is the highest or hottest temperature that comes in contact with metal components in the engine. The turbine inlet temperature must be controlled or damage will occur to the turbine inlet nozzle vanes.
Ref: Powerplant Handbook H-8083-32B-ATB Chapter 1 Page 46

1-50 Answer B
Turbine blades are generally more susceptible to operating damage than compressor blades due to the exposure of high temperatures, extreme temperature gradients between the disk rim and inner portions of the disk, and the added rotational stresses.
Ref: Powerplant Handbook H-8083-32B-ATB Chapter 1 Page 48-49

1-51 Answer C
The exhaust cone collects the exhaust gases discharged from the turbine section and gradually converts them into a solid flow of gases. In performing this, the velocity of the gases is decreased slightly and the pressure is increased.
Ref: Powerplant Handbook H-8083-32B-ATB Chapter 1 Page 51

1-52 Answer B
The gas turbine rotors are supported by ball and roller bearings, which are antifriction bearings. Many newer engines use hydraulic bearings, in which the outside race is surrounded by a thin film of oil. This reduces vibrations transmitted to the engine and allows for slight misalignment.
Ref: Powerplant Handbook H-8083-32B-ATB Chapter 1 Page 52

1-53 Answer A
The oil seals for turbine engines are generally labyrinth or carbon rubbing-type seals. Labyrinth type seals are pressurized to minimize oil leakage along the compressor shaft. Carbon seals are usually spring loaded and are similar in material and application to the carbon brushes found in electric motors.
Ref: Powerplant Handbook H-8083-32B-ATB Chapter 1 Page 53

1-54 AM.III.B.K1
The energy to turn the propeller on a turboprop engine is typically produced by
  A. additional compressor stages.
  B. additional turbine stages.
  C. use of a flow-through combustion chamber.

1-55 AM.III.B.K2
A turboshaft engine can be defined as
  A. a gas turbine engine that delivers power through a shaft to operate something other than a propeller.
  B. a free turbine engine.
  C. a full bypass turbofan engine.

1-56 AM.III.B.K2
What is meant by a free turbine as it relates to turboprop and turboshaft engines?
  A. The compressor wheel is free turning and unconnected from the rest of the engine.
  B. The turbine wheel is not physically connected to the reduction gears and shaft.
  C. The turbine wheel is not physically connected to the compressor wheel.

1-57 AM.III.B.K1
Within the Brayton cycle of a turbine engine, in which section does air pressure remain constant and air volume greatly increases?
  A. Exhaust duct.
  B. Combustion chamber.
  C. Turbine assembly.

1-58 AM.III.B.K1
What is described by the formula:
FORCE = (MASS × ACCELERATION) ÷ GRAVITY?
  A. The Brayton Cycle
  B. Horsepower
  C. Thrust

1-59 AM.III.B.K1
The most important factors affecting thermal efficiency in a turbine engine are
  A. compressor speed and exhaust gas temperature.
  B. total air temperature and compressor speed.
  C. turbine inlet temperature, compression ratio, and the component efficiencies of the compressor and turbine.

AIRCRAFT ENGINES

ANSWERS

1-54 Answer B
Turboprops are, fundamentally, gas turbine engines that have a compressor, combustion section, turbine, and exhaust nozzle (gas generator), all of which operate in the same manner as any other gas engine turbine engine. However, the difference is that the turbine in the turboprop engine usually has extra stages to extract energy to drive the propeller.
Ref: Powerplant Handbook H-8083-32B-ATB Chapter 1 Page 54

1-55 Answer A
A gas turbine engine that delivers power through a shaft to operate something other than a propeller is referred to as a turboshaft engine. The output shaft may be coupled directly to the engine turbine, or the shaft may be driven by a turbine of its own (free turbine). The turboshaft engine's output is measured in horsepower instead of thrust because the power output is turning a shaft.
Ref: Powerplant Handbook H-8083-32B-ATB Chapter 1 Page 55

1-56 Answer C
A fixed turbine has a mechanical connection between each engine component and the reduction gear box. The free turbine has only an air link between the compressor/combustion chamber and the turbine wheel. The turbine wheel is powered only by air pressure as the fast moving air enters its inlet nozzle.
Ref: Powerplant Handbook H-8083-32B-ATB Chapter 1 Page 54

1-57 Answer B
During intake, air enters at ambient pressure and leaves with increased pressure and decreased volume. In the compressor, pressure is increased and volume is decreased. In the combustion chamber, pressure remains constant with a large increase in volume. In the turbine assembly the expanding gases are converted from velocity to mechanical energy. In the convergent exhaust duct volume expands and pressure decreases yielding the final high velocity.
Ref: Powerplant Handbook H-8083-32B-ATB Chapter 1 Page 58

1-58 Answer C
The formula shown $F = MA/G$ defines thrust. Horsepower is defines as ft-lb of force per second/550. The Brayton Cycle refers to the continuous combustion as an operating principle of turbine engines and does not have a formula.
Ref: Powerplant Handbook H-8083-32B-ATB Chapter 1 Page 58

1-59 Answer C
Thermal efficiency is a prime factor in gas turbine performance; it's the ratio of net work produced by the engine to the chemical energy supplied in the form of fuel. The three most important factors affecting the thermal efficiency are turbine inlet temperature, compression ratio, and the component efficiencies of the compressor and turbine. Other factors that affect thermal efficiency are compressor inlet temperature and combustion efficiency.
Ref: Powerplant Handbook H-8083-32B-ATB Chapter 1 Page 59

1-60 AM.III.B.K1
An engine's thrust output temporarily decreases as aircraft speed increases from static. This is overcome at higher speeds by
  A. turbine efficiency.
  B. ram air effect.
  C. exhaust nozzle pressure.

1-61 AM.III.B.K3
Which of the following acts as a diffuser in a turbine engine and converts velocity to pressure?
  A. Impeller
  B. Manifold
  C. Stators

1-62 AM.III.B.K3
The non-rotating axial-flow compressor airfoils in an aircraft gas turbine engine are called
  A. rotor blades.
  B. stator vanes.
  C. disc rims.

1-63 AM.III.B.K3
What are the three types of turbine blades?
  A. Impulse, converging, and impulse-converging
  B. Impulse, reaction, and reaction-impulse
  C. Impulse, diverging, and impulse-diverging

1-64 AM.III.B.K1
When subsonic air flows through a convergent nozzle of a turbine engine; its pressure _____ and its velocity

_____.
  A. increases; decreases
  B. increases; increases
  C. decreases; increases

AIRCRAFT ENGINES

ANSWERS

1-60 Answer B
A rise in pressure above ambient pressure at the engine inlet as a result of forward velocity of an aircraft is referred to as ram pressure. Since any ram effect causes an increase in compressor entrance pressure over atmospheric, the resulting pressure rise causes an increase in the mass airflow and gas velocity, both of which tend to increase thrust. An engine's thrust output temporarily deceases as aircraft speed increases from static, but soon ceases to decrease. Moving toward higher speeds, thrust output increases again due to the increases pressure of ram recovery.
Ref: Powerplant Handbook H-8083-32B-ATB Chapter 1 Page 60

1-61 Answer C
With an axial flow type compressor, the stator blades act as diffusers at each stage, partially converting high velocity air flow to pressure. Each consecutive pair of rotor and stator blades constitutes a pressure stage. Compressor pressure increases with the number of stages. Most engines utilize up to 16 such stages.
Ref: Powerplant Handbook H-8083-32B-ATB Chapter 1 Page 40

1-62 Answer B
An axial flow compressor has two blade types. The rotor, which turns at high speeds has rotating blades fixed on a spindle. The stator has rows of vanes which are attached inside an enclosing case. The purpose of the stator vanes are to receive air from the preceding stage and deliver it to the next stage at the correct pressure and velocity.
Ref: Powerplant Handbook H-8083-32B-ATB Chapter 1 Page 40

1-63 Answer B
The three types of turbine blades are impulse, reaction, and reaction-impulse. With an impulse blade, the stream strikes the blade and changes the direction of energy as it causes the blade to rotate. The reaction blade causes the disk to rotate by the aerodynamic action of the airstream directed past the blade at a particular angle. The reaction-impulse blade combines the action of both.
Ref: Powerplant Handbook H-8083-32B-ATB Chapter 1 Page 47

1-64 Answer C
As stated by Bernoulli's principle, when air flows through a converging passage, its pressure decreases as its velocity increases. This is similar to the function of an airfoil as well as airflow though a carburetor.
Ref: Powerplant Handbook H-8083-32B-ATB Chapter 1 Page 58

ORAL EXAM

1-1(O).   What is the reciprocating engine theory of operation?

1-2(O).   What is the basic radial engine design and how does it operate?

1-3(O).   What is firing order and how is it determined?

1-4(O).   Why are valves adjusted on a radial engine?

1-5(O).   What is the purpose of a master rod and articulating rods?

1-6(O).   What is the purpose, function, and operation of multiple springs on a valve?

1-7(O).   What is propeller reduction gearing and why is it used?

1-8(O).   What is the basic theory of operation of a gas turbine engine?

1-9(O).   What are some causes for turbine engine performance losses?

1-10(O).   What is the purpose of a turbine engine diffuser?

1-11(O).   What type of engine is a typical Auxiliary Power Unit (APU)? What is its function and how does it operate?

AIRCRAFT ENGINES

ANSWERS

ORAL EXAM

1-1(O). A reciprocating engine is an internal combustion device that converts the energy in fuel into mechanical energy. A compressed fuel/air charge is burned in each cylinder of the engine. The energy released pushes the piston down in successive cylinders so that the crankshaft, which is attached to the pistons via connecting rods, develops a rotational motion (force). This force is transferred to a propeller geared off of the end of the crankshaft to produce thrust. A camshaft is geared to the crankshaft to enable valves to open and close at precise times. The valves let the fuel/air mixture into each cylinder and, after the charge is burned, the valves let the exhaust gases out. Magnetos develop a high-tension current that is distributed to successive cylinders at the precise time it is advantageous to ignite the fuel air mixture. Most reciprocating aircraft engines are 4 stroke cycle engines. A stroke is the movement of the piston in the cylinder from top to bottom or from bottom to top. The 4 strokes are labeled to indicate their function in the cycle. They are in order of occurrence: the intake, compression, power, and exhaust strokes. Ignition of the fuel/air mixture via spark plugs in each cylinder occurs just before the piston reaches the top of the compression stroke. The force created by burning the fuel is then transmitted by the piston to the crankshaft on the power stroke.
Ref: Powerplant Handbook H-8083-32B-ATB Chapter 1

1-2(O). Radial engines are simply reciprocating engines with the cylinders arranged radially around a central crankcase and crankshaft. It operates like any other 4-stroke cycle reciprocating engine.
Ref: Powerplant Handbook H-8083-32B-ATB Chapter 1

1-3(O). The firing order of an engine is the sequence in which the power event occurs in the different cylinders. Firing order is designed to provide for balance and to eliminate vibration. It is set by the engineers of the engine. Cylinder firing order in opposed reciprocating aircraft engines is usually listed in pairs of cylinders as each pair fires across the center main bearing. On single row radial engines, the firing order is the sequential odd numbered cylinders followed by the sequential even numbered cylinders (from low number to high number each). Double row radials can be calculated by using a pair of firing order numbers that are either added or subtracted to the number of the cylinder previously fired as is possible.
Ref: Powerplant Handbook H-8083-32B-ATB Chapter 1

1-4(O). Reciprocating engines with solid lifters or cam followers generally require the valve clearance to be adjusted manually by adjusting a screw and locknut. Valve clearance is needed to assure that the valve has enough clearance in the valve train to close completely. This adjustment (or inspection thereof) is a continuous maintenance item except on engines with hydraulic lifters. Hydraulic lifters automatically keep the valve clearance at zero.
Ref: Powerplant Handbook H-8083-32B-ATB Chapter 1

1-5(O). The master rod serves as the connecting link between the piston pin and the crankpin. The crankpin end contains the master rod bearing. Flanges around the large end of the master rod provide for the attachment of articulating rods. They are attached to the master rod with knuckle pins which are pressed into the holes in the master rod flanges. The master and articulating rod assembly is commonly used on radial engines. In radial engines, the piston in one cylinder in each row is connected to the crankshaft by the master rod. All other pistons in the row are connected to the crankshaft through the master rod via the articulating rods.
Ref: Powerplant Handbook H-8083-32B-ATB Chapter 1

1-6(O). The function of the valve springs is to close the valve and to hold the valve securely on the valve seat. The purpose of having two or more valve springs on each valve is to prevent vibration and valve surging at certain speeds. The springs are arranged one inside the other and vibrate at different engine speeds. The result is rapid damping of all spring-surge vibrations. Two or more springs also reduce the danger of weakness and possible failure by breakage due to heat and metal fatigue.
Ref: Powerplant Handbook H-8083-32B-ATB Chapter 1

ORAL EXAM

1-7(O).   For an engine to develop high power, an increase in crankshaft rotational speed is required. However as propeller tip speed approaches the speed of sound, efficiency is greatly reduced. Propeller reduction gearing is used to allow the engine to turn at a high RPM while keeping the propeller speed lower and efficient. The propeller is geared to the engine crankshaft in such a way as to make the propeller not turn as fast as the engine. There are three common types of reduction gearing: spur planetary, bevel planetary, and spur and pinion.
Ref: Powerplant Handbook H-8083-32B-ATB Chapter 1

1-8(O).   A gas turbine engine is an internal combustion engine. Like a reciprocating engine, the functions of intake, compression, combustion, and exhaust are all required. The difference is that, in a turbine engine, these functions happen in dedicated sections of the engine and they happen continuously. Air is taken in at the front of the engine and is compressed in the compressor section, either axially or centrifugally. From there it is sent through a diffuser to the combustion section where fuel is discharged and combustion takes place. The energy in the fuel is released and is directed into the turbine section. Turbine wheel(s) extract the energy in the burning fuel. Depending on the engine type, the energy is converted into rotational mechanical energy to operate the engine and create thrust by turning a fan, propeller, or rotor. In turbojet engines, just enough energy is extracted to operate the engine and the remainder is directed out of the exhaust of the engine to be used as thrust.
Ref: Powerplant Handbook H-8083-32B-ATB Chapter 1

1-9(O).   The thermal efficiency of a gas turbine engine is a prime factor in performance. This is the ratio of the net work produced by the engine to the chemical energy supplied in the fuel. The turbine inlet temperature, compression ratio, and component efficiencies are the three most important factors affecting thermal efficiency. Other factors are compressor inlet temperature and combustion efficiency. A high turbine inlet temperature will result in higher efficiency and more power. However, temperature limits must be adhered to or the turbine section can be overheated and destroyed. If the efficiency of the engine components is reduced, then engine performance will reduce. So, damaged or worn components will produce performance losses. Also, if the stagnation density (a combination of airspeed, altitude, and ambient temperature) is reduced, the performance is reduced. This results from the reduced mass of air flowing through the engine.
Ref: Powerplant Handbook H-8083-32B-ATB Chapter 1

1-10(O).   The diffuser is the divergent section of the engine after the compressor and before the combustion section. It functions to reduce the velocity of the compressor discharge air and increase its pressure so that it can be combined with fuel and burned in the combustion section. The lower velocity of the gases aids in the continuous burning process. If the gases pass through the combustion section at too high of a velocity, the flame could extinguish.
Ref: Powerplant Handbook H-8083-32B-ATB Chapter 1

1-11(O).   A typical APU is a turboshaft gas turbine engine that is made to transfer horsepower to a shaft. The shaft turns the engine compressor from which bleed air for the aircraft is obtained. It also drives an accessory gearbox that rotates a generator. The generator supplies the aircraft with electrical power on the ground and in the air. The APU is often operated with no personnel on the flight deck.
Ref: Powerplant Handbook H-8083-32B-ATB Chapter 10 Page 58, Chapter 9 Page 19, Chapter 1

AIRCRAFT ENGINES

QUESTIONS

PRACTICAL EXAM

1-1(P).   Given an actual aircraft reciprocating engine or mockup, measure the valve clearance with the lifters deflated and record your findings. [Level 2]

1-2(P).   Given an actual aircraft reciprocating engine or mockup, accomplish a compression test, and record all findings. [Level 3]

1-3(P).   Given an actual aircraft reciprocating engine or mockup, inspect engine control cables for proper rigging and record your findings. [Level 3]

1-4(P).   Given an actual aircraft reciprocating engine or mockup, inspect engine push-pull tubes for proper rigging and record your findings. [Level 3]

1-5(P).   Given an actual aircraft reciprocating engine or mockup, inspect ring gap and record your findings. [Level 3]

1-6(P).   Given an actual aircraft reciprocating engine or mockup, install piston rings on a piston and record maintenance. [Level 3]

1-7(P).   Given an actual aircraft reciprocating engine or mockup, install an aircraft engine cylinder and record maintenance. [Level 3]

1-8(P).   Given an aircraft engine component and appropriate publications, inspect dimensionally and record your findings. [Level 3]

1-9(P).   Given an actual aircraft reciprocating engine or mockup, component, and appropriate publications, install the component and record the maintenance. [Level 3]

1-10(P).   Given a turbine engine compressor blade and appropriate publications, complete a repair by blending and record maintenance. [Level 3]

1-11(P).   Given an actual aircraft turbine engine or mockup, component, and appropriate publications, install the component and record the maintenance. [Level 3]

1-12(P).   Given the required information, calculate the cycle life remaining between overhaul of a turbine engine life limited component. [Level 2]

1-13(P).   Given an actual aircraft turbine engine or mockup and appropriate publications, check the rigging of a turbine engine inlet guide vane system and record your findings. [Level 3]

1-14(P).   Given an actual aircraft turbine engine or mockup and appropriate publications, measure a compressor or turbine blade clearance and record your findings. [Level 3]

1-15(P).   Given an actual aircraft turbine engine or mockup, appropriate publications, and an unknown discrepancy, troubleshoot a turbine engine and record your findings. [Level 3]

PRACTICAL EXAM

1-16(P).   Given an actual aircraft turbine engine or mockup, locate and identify various turbine engine components. [Level 2]

1-17(P).   Given an aircraft turbine component and appropriate publications, inspect turbine engine component and record your findings. [Level 3]

NOTE: AUXILIARY POWER UNITS may be tested at the same time as TURBINE ENGINES. No further testing of auxiliary power units is required.

AIRCRAFT ENGINES

PAGE LEFT BLANK INTENTIONALLY

FUEL AND METERING SYSTEMS

Basic Fuel Systems, Fuel Metering Devices, Carburetor Fuel Systems,
Fuel System Maintenance, and Turbine Engine Fuel Systems

QUESTIONS

2-1 AM.III.I.K10
If a pilot suspects the onset of vapor lock, which of the
following procedures might be helpful?
A. Enrich the mixture.
B. Increase throttle until roughness clears.
C. Turn on the auxiliary fuel pump.

2-2 AM.III.I.K1
When the stoichiometric mixture a fuel/air ratio changes from
15:1 to 16:1,
A. the energy produced by combustion increases.
B. the energy produced by combustion decreases.
C. the temperature produced by combustion decreases.

2-3 AM.III.I.K1
On a carburetor without an automatic mixture control, as you
ascend to altitude, the mixture will
A. be enriched.
B. be leaned.
C. not be affected.

2-4 AM.III.I.K1
What carburetor component limits the maximum airflow into
the engine at full throttle?
A. Throttle valve
B. Venturi
C. Main metering jet

2-5 AM.III.I.K2
If fuel is found running from the carburetor with the engine
not running, the likely cause is that the
A. float needle valve is not seated properly.
B. float level is adjusted too low.
C. main air bleed is clogged.

2-6 AM.III.I.K2
What component is used to ensure fuel delivery during
periods of rapid engine acceleration?
A. Acceleration pump
B. Engine-driven fuel pump
C. Power enrichment unit

FUEL AND FUEL METERING

ANSWERS

2-1 Answer C
Vapor lock is typically caused by low fuel pressure, high fuel temperatures, and excess agitation of the fuel. Low air pressure at higher altitudes lowers fuel pressure. Aggressive maneuvering or turbulence introduces vapor into the fuel, lowering pressure. The auxiliary fuel pump increases fuel pressure in the fuel line where vapor lock can form.
Ref: Powerplant Handbook H-8083-32B-ATB Chapter 2 Page 1

2-2 Answer B
The perfect mixture of air to fuel in a reciprocating engine is 15:1. At this mixture all the fuel and oxygen is completely burned up, so producing the greatest amount of heat and energy. If the ratio of air to fuel is increased to 16:1, there will be slight loss of power and temperature, but a more significant gain in economy of operation.
Ref: Powerplant Handbook H-8083-32B-ATB Chapter 2 Page 4, 5

2-3 Answer A
Typically, air density decreases as altitude increases. A normally aspirated engine has a fixed volume of air that it can draw in during the intake stroke. Therefore, less air is drawn into the engine as altitude increases because of the lower air density. Less air results in the fuel air mixture being more rich as you ascend in altitude. A mixture control is provided on some aircraft to lean the mixture during climbs. On some aircraft this is done manually. On other, it is automatic.
Ref: Powerplant Handbook H-8083-32B-ATB Chapter 2 Page 2

2-4 Answer B
The size and shape of the venturi is the limiting factor in determining the maximum airflow into the engine at full power. The throttle valve limits the airflow to a lesser amount from what the maximum amount which the venturi will allow, dependent on the throttle setting. The main metering jet determines full power fuel flow.
Ref: Powerplant Handbook H-8083-32B-ATB Chapter 2 Page 5

2-5 Answer A
A fuel leak when the engine is not running can indicate that fuel is rising in the float bowl to a higher level than the tip of the discharge nozzle. The most likely cause is that the float needle valve and its seat is leaking and needs to be reset or replaced.
Ref: Powerplant Handbook H-8083-32B-ATB Chapter 2 Page 10

2-6 Answer A
After a quick opening of the throttle, the fuel air mixture momentarily leans out as the normal flow can not keep up with the instant demand. This can cause the engine to accelerate slowly or stumble as it tries to accelerate. The accelerator pump momentarily sprays additional fuel into the venturi to temporarily make up for this imbalance.
Ref: Powerplant Handbook H-8083-32B-ATB Chapter 2 Page 13

2-7 AM.III.I.K2
What carburetor component measures the amount of air delivered to the engine?
   A. Economizer Valve
   B. Automatic Mixture Control
   C. Venturi

2-8 AM.III.I.K2
Where on a float type carburetor is the throttle valve positioned?
   A. Between the air inlet and the discharge nozzle.
   B. Between the discharge nozzle and the venturi.
   C. Between the venturi and the engine.

2-9 AM.III.I.K2
The fuel metering force of a conventional float-type carburetor in its normal operating range is the difference between the low air pressure acting on the discharge nozzle located within the venturi and the atmospheric pressure
   A. acting on the fuel in the float chamber.
   B. of the fuel as it enters the carburetor.
   C. air as it enters the venturi (impact pressure).

2-10 AM.III.I.K2
Which of the following best describes the function of an altitude mixture control?
   A. Regulates the richness of the fuel/air charge entering the engine.
   B. Regulates air pressure above the fuel in the float chamber.
   C. Regulates the air pressure in the venturi.

2-11 AM.III.I.K2
What is the basic function of the accelerator system of a carburetor?
   A. Increases fuel flow during rapid throttle movements.
   B. Increases air flow in high density altitude conditions.
   C. Increases fuel flow for sustained high power operations.

2-12 AM.III.I.K2
The economizer system in a float-type carburetor
   A. keeps the fuel/air ratio constant.
   B. functions only at cruise and idle speeds.
   C. increases the fuel air ratio at high power settings.

FUEL AND FUEL METERING

ANSWERS

2-7 Answer C
As the velocity of air increases to get through the narrow portion of the venturi, pressure drops. This pressure drop is proportional to the velocity and is therefore a measure of the airflow. The basic operating principle of most carburetors depends on the differential pressure between the inlet and the venturi throat.
Ref: Powerplant Handbook H-8083-32B-ATB Chapter 2 Page 5

2-8 Answer C
The throttle valve is located between the venturi and the engine. Mechanical linkage connects this valve with the throttle lever in the cockpit. By means of the throttle, airflow to the cylinders is regulated and controls the power output of the engine. As the throttle is opened, more air is admitted to the carburetor which automatically supplies enough additional fuel to maintain the correct fuel air ratios. As the volume of airflow increases, the velocity in the venturi increases, lowering the pressure and allowing more fuel to be forced into the airstream.
Ref: Powerplant Handbook H-8083-32B-ATB Chapter 2 Page 6

2-9 Answer A
The discharge nozzle is located in the throat of the venturi at the point where the lowest drop in pressure occurs as air passes through the carburetor to the engine cylinders. There are two different pressures acting on the fuel in the carburetor – the low air pressure at the discharge nozzle and a higher atmospheric pressure at the float chamber. The higher pressure in the float chamber forces the fuel through the discharge nozzle into the airstream in the venturi.
Ref: Powerplant Handbook H-8083-32B-ATB Chapter 2 Page 6

2-10 Answer A
The mixture control system determines the ratio of fuel to air in the mixture. This can be done manually with a cockpit control, or, an automatic mixture control can be built into the carburetor. As an aircraft climbs, the atmospheric pressure decreases. There is also a corresponding decrease in the weight of the air passing through the induction system. The volume, however, remains constant. It is the volume of air that determines the pressure drop across the venturi. Therefore, regardless of altitude, the same amount of fuel is metered into the engine from the discharge nozzle. Thus, with less air weight due to lower air density at altitude, the mixture tends to become too rich. The automatic or manual mixture control decreases the rate of fuel discharge to compensate for the decrease in air density.
Ref: Powerplant Handbook H-8083-32B-ATB Chapter 2 Page 7

2-11 Answer A
During rapid throttle increases, the instant rate of acceleration of incoming air is greater than can be matched by incoming fuel. Until the rate of fuel flow can catch up, the accelerator pump inserts additional fuel so that the engine's rate of acceleration can be steady.
Ref: Powerplant Handbook H-8083-32B-ATB Chapter 2 Page 13

2-12 Answer C
The economizer system in a float-type carburetor is also known as the power enrichment system. It increases the richness of the mixture during high power operation. At cruising speeds, a lean mixture is desirable for economy reasons, while at high power output, the mixture must be rich to obtain maximum power and to aid in cooling the engine cylinders. Essentially, the economizer is a valve that is closed at cruising speed and opened to supply extra fuel to the mixture during high power operation.
Ref: Powerplant Handbook H-8083-32B-ATB Chapter 2 Page 13

2-13 AM.III.I.K1
When does refrigeration icing occur in carburetors?
  A. When humidity surrounding the fuel freezes.
  B. When moisture within the fuel freezes.
  C. When water (rain or snow) present in the atmosphere freezes.

2-14 AM.III.I.K2
The fuel level within the float chamber of a properly adjusted float-type carburetor will be
  A. slightly higher than the discharge nozzle outlet.
  B. slightly lower than the discharge nozzle outlet.
  C. at the same level as the discharge nozzle outlet.

2-15 AM.III.I.K2
One purpose of an air bleed in a float-type carburetor is
  A. increase fuel flow at altitude.
  B. meter air to adjust the mixture.
  C. decrease fuel density and destroy surface tension.

2-16 AM.III.I.K2
When idling, from what source is sufficient pressure available to feed fuel into the idle circuit?
  A. From the engine.
  B. Through the venturi.
  C. From the idle air bleed.

2-17 AM.III.I.K2
Which of the following best describes the function of an altitude mixture control?
  A. Regulates the richness of the fuel/air charge entering the engine.
  B. Regulates the air pressure above the fuel in the float chamber.
  C. Regulates the air pressure in the venturi.

2-18 AM.III.I.K1
An aircraft carburetor is equipped with a mixture control in order to prevent the mixture from becoming too
  A. lean at high altitudes.
  B. rich at high altitudes.
  C. rich at high speeds.

ANSWERS

2-13 Answer A
There are three general types of icing: fuel evaporation ice, throttle ice, and impact ice. All three can form at temperatures between 30 and 40°F, however, fuel evaporation ice can form during ambient air temperature of up to 100°F. When fuel evaporates in the venturi of a float-type carburetor, temperature decreases. Any water vapor present can freeze onto the fuel discharge nozzle, throttle valve, or inside the venturi if the temperature drops below 32°F. Throttle ice is formed typically when air makes its way around a partially closed throttle valve. A pressure differential is formed around the obstruction and ice can form on the back side of the throttle when moisture is present. This condition is usually limited to temperature below 38°F. Impact ice occurs when water, snow, ice, etc., is present in the atmosphere and it contacts a cold surface of the aircraft. The carburetor screen is an especially susceptible and dangerous area for impact ice to form but it can also form inside the carburetor. This type of ice forms when temperature of the aircraft structure is below 32°F.
Ref: Powerplant Handbook H-8083-32B-ATB Chapter 2 Page 8

2-14 Answer B
A float chamber is provided between the fuel supply and the main metering system of the carburetor. This chamber provides a nearly constant level of fuel to the main discharge nozzle which is usually about 1/8" below the holes in the main discharge nozzle. The fuel level must be maintained slightly below the discharge nozzle outlet holes to provide the correct amount of fuel flow and to prevent leakage from the nozzle when the engine is not operating.
Ref: Powerplant Handbook H-8083-32B-ATB Chapter 2 Page 10

2-15 Answer C
Air bleed into the main metering fuel system decreases the fuel density and destroys surface tension. This results in better vaporization and control of fuel discharge, especially at lower engine speeds. See Figure 2-13 in FAA-H-8083-32-ATB and associated description in paragraph of same page.
Ref: Powerplant Handbook H-8083-32B-ATB Chapter 2 Page 11

2-16 Answer A
With the throttle valve closed at idling speeds, air velocity through the venturi is so low that it cannot draw enough fuel from the main discharge nozzle. However, low pressure caused by piston suction exists on the engine side of the throttle valve. To allow the engine to idle, a fuel passageway is incorporated to discharge fuel from an opening in this low pressure area near the edge of the throttle valve. This is called the idling jet or idle discharge nozzle. With the throttle open enough so that the main discharge nozzle is operating, fuel does not flow out of the idling jet. As soon as the throttle is closed far enough to stop the spray from the main discharge nozzle, fuel flows out of the idle discharge nozzle.
Ref: Powerplant Handbook H-8083-32B-ATB Chapter 2 Page 12

2-17 Answer A
As altitude increases, the air becomes less dense. Because the same volume of fuel is discharged through fuel nozzle regardless of altitude, the less dense air at altitude results in a rich mixture being delivered to the engine at higher altitudes. It is the function of the altitude mixture control to reduce the richness of the fuel/air charge entering the engine at altitude. This provides the correct amount of fuel for air of varying densities.
Ref: Powerplant Handbook H-8083-32B-ATB Chapter 2 Page 12

2-18 Answer B
The action of the venturi draws the same volume of fuel through the discharge nozzle at high altitudes as it does at low altitudes. Therefore, the fuel mixture becomes richer as altitude increases due to the low air density. This can be overcome by either a manual or an automatic mixture control.
Ref: Powerplant Handbook H-8083-32B-ATB Chapter 2 Page 12, 13

2-19 AM.III.I.K2

Mixture control systems in float type carburetors
- A. use a needle or back-suction type arrangement.
- B. are directly connected to the throttle lever.
- C. are independent of the idle system.

2-22 AM.III.I.K3

On an engine equipped with a pressure type carburetor, fuel supply in the idling range is ensured by the inclusion in the carburetor of
- A. a spring in the unmetered fuel chamber to supplement the action of the normal metering forces.
- B. an idle metering jet that bypasses the carburetor in the idle range.
- C. a separate boost venturi that is sensitive to the reduced airflow at start and idle speeds.

2-20 AM.III.I.K2

Float-type carburetors which are equipped with economizers are normally set for
- A. their richest mixture delivery and leaned by means of the economizer system.
- B. the economizer system to supplement the main system supply at all engine speeds above idling.
- C. their leanest practical mixture delivery at cruising speeds and enriched by means of the economizer system at high power settings.

2-23 AM.III.I.K3

On a pressure injection carburetor, what will happen if the vapor vent float losses its buoyancy and sinks deeper in its chamber?
- A. The amount of fuel returning to the fuel tank from the carburetor will be increased.
- B. The engine will continue to run after the mixture control is placed in IDLE CUTOFF.
- C. A rich mixture will occur at all engine speeds.

2-21 AM.III.I.K3

In a pressure injection carburetor, there is no float chamber. Fuel to the discharge nozzle is controlled by a diaphragm that uses a comparison of
- A. venturi air pressure and throttle body air pressure.
- B. fuel pump pressure and venturi air pressure.
- C. venturi air pressure and carburetor inlet air pressure.

2-24 AM.III.I.K3

What is the relationship between the accelerating pump and the enrichment valve in a pressure injection carburetor?
- A. No relationship since they operate independently.
- B. Unmetered fuel pressure affects both units.
- C. The accelerating pump actuates the enrichment valve.

FUEL AND FUEL METERING

ANSWERS

2-19 Answer A
On float-type carburetors, two types of purely manual or cockpit controllable devices are in general use for controlling fuel air mixtures. They are the needle-type and the back-suction type. Both types are operated in the cockpit by an independent mixture control lever. On the needle type, pulling the lever full aft into the idle cutoff position seats a needle in the float chamber and all fuel is cut off. On the back-suction type, the idle cutoff position of the lever connects the air in the float chamber to the extreme low pressure of the piston suction side of the throttle valve which causes fuel flow to stop.
Ref: Powerplant Handbook H-8083-32B-ATB Chapter 2 Page 10, 12

2-20 Answer C
For an engine to develop maximum power at full throttle, the fuel mixture must be richer than for cruise. An economizer is essentially a valve that is closed at throttle settings below approximately 60 - 70 percent of rated power. This system is operated by the throttle control. At cruise speed, the economizer valve is closed. Through linkages, as the throttle is advanced, the valve opens and supplies more fuel at higher power settings.
Ref: Powerplant Handbook H-8083-32B-ATB Chapter 2 Page 14

2-21 Answer C
In a pressure injected carburetor, venturi air pressure is used on one side of a diaphragm in the pressure regulator unit. This venturi pressure drop is compared to air pressure at the carburetor inlet which is ported to the other side of the diaphragm. As the throttle valve is opened, the corresponding pressure drop through the venturi as the volume of air increases causes the diaphragm move. It is connected to a valve that controls the amount of fuel supplied to the discharge nozzle from the fuel pump. Thus, the difference in pressure proportional to the airflow through the carburetor is met with the proper fuel flow.
Ref: Powerplant Handbook H-8083-32B-ATB Chapter 2 Page 14

2-22 Answer A
Under low power settings (low airflows), the difference in pressure created by the boost venturi is not sufficient to accomplish consistent regulation of the fuel. Therefore, an idle spring is incorporated in the regulator unit. As the poppet valve moves toward the closed position, it contacts the idle spring. The spring holds the poppet valve off its seat far enough to supply more fuel than is needed for idling. This potentially over rich mixture is regulated by the idle valve. At idling speeds, the idle valve restricts the fuel flow to the proper amount. At higher speeds, it is withdrawn from the fuel passage and has no metering effect.
Ref: Powerplant Handbook H-8083-32B-ATB Chapter 2 Page 17

2-23 Answer A
If the vapor vent valve sticks open or the vapor vent float becomes filled with fuel and sinks, a continuous flow of fuel and vapor occurs through the vent line. It is important to detect this condition, as the fuel flow from the carburetor to the fuel tank may cause an overflowing tank with resultant increased fuel consumption.
Ref: Powerplant Handbook H-8083-32B-ATB Chapter 2 Page 16

2-24 Answer A
The power enrichment valve in a pressure injected carburetor is completely independent of the acceleration pump. The power enrichment valve is the poppet-type which begins to open at the beginning of the power range. It is opened by the unmetered fuel pressure overcoming metered fuel pressure and spring tension. The power enrichment valve continues to open wider during the power range until the combined flow through the valve and auto-rich jet exceeds that of the power enrichment jet. At this point, the power enrichment jet takes over and meters fuel throughout the power range. This action occurs in the fuel control unit and is independent of any accelerating pump.
Ref: Powerplant Handbook H-8083-32B-ATB Chapter 2 Page 17

2-25 AM.III.I.K3
The function of the automatic mixture control on a pressure injection carburetor is
- A. to increase the amount of fuel delivered to the discharge nozzle at high power settings.
- B. to compensate for changes in air density due to temperature and altitude changes.
- C. to provide the correct fuel/air ratio during idle and slow engine speeds.

2-26 AM.III.I.K3
Which of the following causes a single diaphragm acceleration pump to discharge fuel?
- A. An increase in venturi suction when the throttle is open.
- B. An increase in manifold pressure that occurs when the throttle is open.
- C. A decrease in manifold pressure that occurs when the throttle is opened.

2-27 AM.III.I.K4
The purpose of the fuel metering section of the Bendix/ Precision fuel injection system is to
- A. regulate the flow of fuel into the airflow section.
- B. meter and control the fuel flow to the flow divider.
- C. return excess fuel to the tank.

2-28 AM.III.I.K4
The primary purpose of the air bleed openings used with continuous flow fuel injector nozzles is to
- A. provide for automatic mixture control.
- B. lean out the mixture.
- C. aid in proper fuel vaporization.

2-29 AM.III.I.K4
An aircraft engine continuous cylinder fuel injection system normally discharged fuel during which strokes?
- A. Intake
- B. Intake and Compression
- C. All (Continuously)

2-30 AM.III.I.K4
A fuel discharge nozzle on a fuel injected reciprocating engine is marked with the code 312B. What, in part, does this number mean?
- A. The cylinder for which this nozzle is designated.
- B. The manufacturer's part number.
- C. The date of its next required service.

FUEL AND FUEL METERING

ANSWERS

2-25 Answer B
The purpose of the automatic mixture control is to compensate for changes in air density due to temperature and altitude changes. The automatic mixture control unit consists of a bellows assembly, calibrated needle, and seat located at the carburetor inlet. The expansion and contraction of the bellows in response to pressure changes moves the tapered needle in the atmospheric line which controls pressure in the "A" chamber of the pressure regulator and the small bleed holes in the diaphragm therein. The result is that fuel mixture is automatically adjust as the aircraft experiences pressure changes associated with altitude and/or temperature changes.
Ref: Powerplant Handbook H-8083-32B-ATB Chapter 2 Page 18

2-26 Answer B
A single diaphragm accelerator pump such as one in a Stromberg PS carburetor, is a spring loaded diaphragm assembly located in the metered fuel channel. The opposite side of the diaphragm is vented to the engine side of the throttle valve. With this arrangement, opening the throttle results in a rapid decrease in suction (increase in manifold pressure). This permits the spring to extend and move the acceleration pump diaphragm which displaces the fuel in the acceleration pump and forces it into the discharge nozzle.
Ref: Powerplant Handbook H-8083-32B-ATB Chapter 2 Page 16, 21

2-27 Answer B
The fuel metering section is attached to the air metering section and contains an inlet fuel strainer, a manual mixture control valve, an idle valve and the main metering jet. The purpose of the fuel metering section is to meter and control fuel flow to the flow divider where it is kept under pressure and divided for delivery to the various cylinders at all engine speeds.
Ref: Powerplant Handbook H-8083-32B-ATB Chapter 2 Page 21

2-28 Answer C
The fuel discharge nozzles are of the air bleed configuration. Each nozzle incorporates a calibrated jet. The fuel is discharged through this jet into an ambient air pressure chamber within the nozzle assembly. Before entering the individual intake valve chambers, the fuel is mixed with air to aid in the atomizing of the fuel.
Ref: Powerplant Handbook H-8083-32B-ATB Chapter 2 Page 24

2-29 Answer C
The continuous fuel injection system injects fuel into the intake valve port in each cylinder head. The fuel system consists of a fuel injector pump, a control unit, a fuel manifold, and a fuel discharge nozzle. It is a continuous-flow type which controls fuel flow to match engine airflow. This permits the use of a rotary vane pump which does not require timing to the engine.
Ref: Powerplant Handbook H-8083-32B-ATB Chapter 2 Page 25

2-30 Answer A
This first digit of the code 312B (#3) which is stamped on the hex shape of the nozzle body indicates which cylinder this nozzle is for. The next group of two numbers (12) indicate the nozzles size. The final letter (B) indicates the range of calibration.
Ref: Powerplant Handbook H-8083-32B-ATB Chapter 2 Page 28

2-31 AM.III.I.K9
Prior to checking the idle mixture setting on a carbureted piston engine, the propeller control should be placed
  A. in its increased RPM setting.
  B. in its decreased RPM setting.
  C. in its normal taxi speed setting.

2-32 AM.III.I.K2
To set the idle on a new carburetor installation; with the engine at normal operating temperatures,
  A. adjust the float level, then the idle mixture setting.
  B. adjust the idle speed setting, and then its mixture.
  C. adjust the idle mixture setting and then the idle speed.

2-33 AM.III.I.K9
Fuel system inspection and maintenance
  A. does not include operation of the boost pumps to prevent flooding of the carburetor.
  B. includes the complete system except for the fuel tanks which are considered airframe components.
  C. consists of an examination of the system for conformity to design requirements and functional tests to prove correct operation.

2-34 AM.III.I.K8
It is necessary to control acceleration and deceleration rates in turbine engines in order to
  A. prevent blowout or die-out.
  B. prevent over-temperature.
  C. prevent friction between turbine wheels and the case due to expansion and contraction.

2-35 AM.III.I.K8
Which type of fuel control is used on most of today's turbine engines?
  A. Electromechanical
  B. Mechanical
  C. Hydromechanical or Electronic

2-36 AM.III.I.K8
Which of the following influences the operation of an automatic fuel control on a turbojet engine?
  A. Burner Pressure
  B. Mixture Control Position
  C. Exhaust Gas Temperature

FUEL AND FUEL METERING

ANSWERS

2-31 Answer A
Before checking the idle mixture on any engine, the propeller should be placed in its lowest thrust fine pitch position, thus yielding idle power, with no additional load on the engine.
Ref: Powerplant Handbook H-8083-32B-ATB Chapter 2 Page 29

2-32 Answer C
Before checking the idle mixture on any engine, warm up the engine until oil and cylinder head temperatures are normal. The idle mixture adjustment is made on the idle mixture fuel control valve. It should not be confused with the adjustment of the idle speed. Excessively rich idle mixture results in incomplete combustion and spark plug fouling. Excessively lean idle mixture results in faulty acceleration. After adjusting idle mixture, reset the idle stop to the idle RPM specified in the aircraft maintenance manual.
Ref: Powerplant Handbook H-8083-32B-ATB Chapter 2 Page 30

2-33 Answer C
The inspection of a fuel system installation consists basically of an examination of the system for conformity to design requirements together with functional tests to prove correct operation. It is important that the manufacturer's instructions for the aircraft concerned be followed when performing inspection and maintenance functions. Boost pumps and fuel tanks are part of the aircraft fuel system and should be fully inspected and tested for operation when performing system inspection and maintenance.
Ref: Powerplant Handbook H-8083-32B-ATB Chapter 2 Page 31

2-34 Answer A
If the quantity of fuel becomes excessive in relation to mass airflow through the engine, it could produce compressor stall and a condition referred to as rich blowout. If there is not enough fuel for the mass airflow, a lean flame-out or die-out can occur. Thus, a balanced amount of fuel and air must occur in the engine for combustion to be sustained. Rapid acceleration of deceleration are instances where fuel adjustments must be made by the fuel control to match the extreme airflow changes to prevent blowout or die-out.
Ref: Powerplant Handbook H-8083-32B-ATB Chapter 2 Page 33

2-35 Answer C
There are 3 basic types of fuel controls used on turbine engines: Hydromechanical, Hydromechanical/Electronic, and Full Authority Digital Electronic Control (FADEC). Hydromechanical controls are the original type of fuel control. An improvement over the standard hydromechanical fuel control occurred when electronic sensing was added. FADEC fuel controls are a further improvement with electronic inputs and outputs governing the system. So, regardless of how advanced the turbine engine fuel control in question, it will be Hydromechanical, Electronic, or a combination of both.
Ref: Powerplant Handbook H-8083-32B-ATB Chapter 2 Page 33

2-36 Answer A
Regardless of the type, all fuel controls schedule the fuel flow to match the power required by the pilot. Some sense more engine variables than others. Fuel controls can sense many different inputs, such as power lever position, engine RPM for each spool, compressor inlet pressure and temperature, burner pressure, compressor discharge pressure and more. There is no mixture control selector in the cockpit of aircraft powered by turbine engines as the fuel control automatically schedules the correct fuel flow given input parameters. Exhaust gas temperature is monitored on most turbine engines but more as feedback to ensure proper operation than as an input for fuel scheduling.
Ref: Powerplant Handbook H-8083-32B-ATB Chapter 2 Page 34

2-37 AM.III.I.K5
In a supervisory electronic engine control EEC, any fault in the EEC that adversely affects engine operation
  A. causes redundant back-up systems to take over and continue normal operation.
  B. usually degrades performance to the extent that continued operation can cause damage to the engine.
  C. causes an immediate reversion to control by the hydromechanical fuel control unit.

2-38 AM.III.I.K6
Within a hydromechanical fuel control system on a turbine engine, what pressure is measured by the EFCU to ultimately determine the quantity of fuel to be sent to the engine?
  A. Compressor Inlet Pressure
  B. Compressor Discharge Pressure
  C. Fuel Pump Outlet Pressure

2-39 AM.III.I.K5
A Full Authority Digital Electronic Control (FADEC)
  A. uses the hydromechanical fuel control as a back-up.
  B. combines electronic inputs with mechanical input for full control of fuel delivery.
  C. has no hydromechanical fuel control back-up.

2-40 AM.III.I.K5
An electronic engine control (EEC) is a system that receives engine operating information and
  A. adjusts a standard hydromechanical fuel control unit to obtain the most effective engine operation.
  B. develops the commands to various actuators to control engine parameters.
  C. controls engine operation according to ambient temperature, pressure, and humidity.

2-41 AM.III.I.K5
An Electronic Engine Control (EEC) in a Full Authority Digital Engine Control (FADEC) aircraft
  A. requires a second computer as back-up should the EEC fail.
  B. relies on crosstalk between channels for the best engine control output.
  C. eliminates the need for a fuel metering unit.

2-42 AM.III.I.K5
After control signals are sent from the Electronic Engine Control (EEC) to regulate fuel flow to the engine,
  A. feedback from several systems in the engine is sent back to the EEC.
  B. the fuel pump output is increased or decreased as instructed.
  C. rotary differential transformers position the metering devices as directed.

FUEL AND FUEL METERING

ANSWERS

2-37 Answer C
A supervisory EEC uses electronic control to adjust fuel flow through a hydromechanical fuel control unit. It uses numerous inputs of engine parameters to issue commands. An EEC can be thought of as the computer which calculates the correct fuel metering for the engine and then issues outputs for the hydromechanical fuel control to follow. If the EEC fails, the hydromechanical portion of the fuel control will take over.
Ref: Powerplant Handbook H-8083-32B-ATB Chapter 2 Page 33, 34

2-38 Answer B
Fuel is supplied to the fuel control through a 200-micron inlet filter screen and is metered to the engine by the servo-operated metering valve. It is a fuel flow/compressor discharge pressure (Wf/P3) ratio device that positions the metering valve in response to engine compressor discharge pressure (P3). Fuel pressure differential across the servo valve is maintained by a servo-operated bypass valve in response to commands from the EFCU.
Ref: Powerplant Handbook H-8083-32B-ATB Chapter 2 Page 34

2-39 Answer C
A Full Authority Digital Electronic Control (FADEC) controls fuel flow on most new turbine engine models. A true FADEC system has no hydromechanical fuel control back-up. The system uses electronic sensors that feed engine parameter information into the Electronic Engine Control unit. The EEC is a computer that gathers the needed information to determine fuel flow. The fuel metering valve simply reacts to the commands from the EEC.
Ref: Powerplant Handbook H-8083-32B-ATB Chapter 2 Page 36

2-40 Answer A
During normal turbine engine operation, the EEC (same as EFCU) performs the functions of thrust setting, speed governing, and acceleration and deceleration in response to the pilot's power level inputs. Basically in automatic mode, the EEC is in control of metering fuel. In manual mode, a hydromechanical control takes over.
Ref: Powerplant Handbook H-8083-32B-ATB Chapter 2 Page 34, Figure 2-51

2-41 Answer B
The EEC is a two channel computer that controls every aspect of engine operation. Each channel, which is an independent computer, can completely control the operation of the engine. The processor(s) do all of the control calculations and supply all the data for the control signals to torque motors and solenoids. Cross-talk logic compares data from channels A and B and uses the cross-talk to find which EEC channel is best to control the output driver for a torque motor or solenoid bank. The EEC controls the metering valve in the FMU (fuel metering unit) to supply fuel flow for combustion.
Ref: Powerplant Handbook H-8083-32B-ATB Chapter 2 Page 38

2-42 Answer A
The EEC controls the metering valve in the fuel metering unit to supply fuel flow for combustion. The EEC also sends a signal to the minimum pressure and shutoff valve in the fuel metering unit to start or stop fuel flow. The EEC receives position feedback for several engine components by using rotary differential transformers and linear variable differential transformers. It also receives thermocouple signal inputs. These sensors feed engine parameters information from several sources back to the EEC.
Ref: Powerplant Handbook H-8083-32B-ATB Chapter 2 Page 38

2-43 AM.III.I.K5
On a FADEC system aircraft, the EEC (Figure 2-56)
  A. manages only engine parameters and fuel flow.
  B. lacks the mechanical outputs to control the variable stator vanes.
  C. controls many engine subsystems as well as the FMU.

2-45 AM.III.I.K8
Generally, the practice when trimming an engine is to
  A. turn all accessory bleed air off.
  B. turn all accessory bleed air on.
  C. make adjustments (as necessary) for all engines on the same aircraft with accessory bleed air settings the same – either on or off.

2-44 AM.III.I.K8
When trimming a turbine engine, the fuel control is adjusted to
  A. produce as much power as the engine is capable of producing.
  B. set idle RPM and maximum speed or EPR.
  C. allow the engine to produce maximum RPM without regard to power output.

2-46 AM.III.I.K8
The main engine-driven fuel pump on a turbine engine
  A. is a variable displacement pump.
  B. produces adequate capacity at all operating conditions and has excess capacity over most of the range of operation.
  C. is a single stage pump.

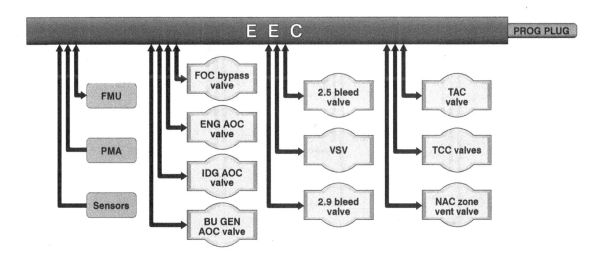

Figure 2-56. Systems controlled by EEC.

FUEL AND FUEL METERING

ANSWERS

2-43 Answer C
The EEC uses a torque motor driver to control the position of the metering valve in the fuel metering unit. The EEC uses solenoid drivers to control the other functions of the FMU. The EEC also controls several other subsystems of the engine through torque motors and solenoids as shown in Figure 2-56. Some of these subsystems are: fuel and air oil coolers, bleed valves, variable stator vanes, turbine cooling air valves, and the turbine case cooling system.
Ref: Powerplant Handbook H-8083-32B-ATB Chapter 2 Page 39, Figure 2-56

2-45 Answer A
After the engine has started and run until stabilized, a check should be made to ensure that the compressor air bleed valves have fully closed. All accessory drive air bleed for which the trim curve has not been corrected must be turned off. Then, a comparison can be made of the observed and computed turbine discharge pressure Pt7 (or EPR) to trim as necessary. The engine fuel control is then adjusted to obtain the target turbine discharge pressure Pt7 or EPR.
Ref: Powerplant Handbook H-8083-32B-ATB Chapter 2 Page 40, 41

2-44 Answer B
During engine trimming, the fuel control is checked for idle RPM, maximum RPM, acceleration and deceleration. In general, the procedure consists of obtaining the ambient air temperature and the field barometric pressure immediately preceding the trimming of the engine. Using these readings, the desired turbine discharge pressure or EPR reading, computed from charts published in the maintenance manual, should be attained.
Ref: Powerplant Handbook H-8083-32B-ATB Chapter 2 Page 40

2-46 Answer B
Main fuel pumps deliver a continuous supply of fuel at the proper pressure and at all times during operation of the aircraft engine. They are positive displacement pumps so, often, when fuel requirements are low during a flight segment, a pressure relief valve bypasses excess fuel back to the pump inlet. A centrifugal, variable displacement pump often discharges into the inlet of the positive-displacement second stage pump which produces the pump outlet fuel flow.
Ref: Powerplant Handbook H-8083-32B-ATB Chapter 2 Page 41, 42

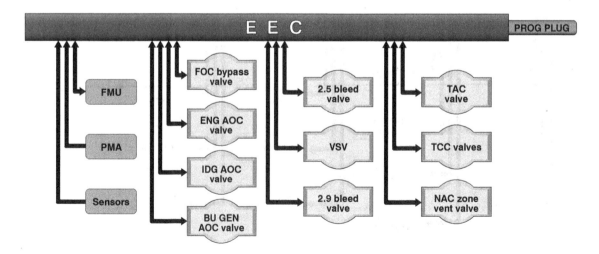

Figure 2-56. Systems controlled by EEC.

FUEL AND FUEL METERING

2-47 AM.III.I.K11
The temperature of turbine engine fuel is often kept above 32°F
A. by fuel heaters located in the wing and main fuselage tanks.
B. to ensure rapid combustion in the engine.
C. so that ice crystals do not form in the filter and block fuel flow.

2-48 AM.III.I.K7
Hot spots can burn a hole in the combustion section liner on a turbine engine. This is caused by
A. a misaligned fuel nozzle resulting in a flame that is not centered in the flame area.
B. insufficient fuel flow to the fuel nozzles.
C. excessive fuel flow to the fuel nozzle which cannot be fully combusted.

2-49 AM.III.I.K7
What is the purpose of the flow divider in a turbine engine duplex fuel nozzle system?
A. Allows an alternative flow of fuel if the primary flow clogs or is restricted.
B. Creates the primary and secondary fuel supplies.
C. Provides a flow path for bleed air which aids in the atomization of fuel.

2-50 AM.III.I.K14
What is the purpose of a dump valve as used with fuel on a gas turbine engine?
A. It cuts off the fuel flow to the engine fuel manifold and dumps the manifold fuel into the combustor to burn just before the engine shuts down.
B. It drains the engine manifold lines to prevent fuel boiling and subsequent deposits in the lines as a result of residual engine heat (at engine shutdown).
C. It dumps extra fuel into the engine in order to provide for quick acceleration during rapid throttle advancement.

2-51 AM.III.I.K11
Which of the following types of heat exchangers is used to regulate the fuel temperature?
A. The bleed air type is called an air-to-liquid exchanger and the oil type is known as a liquid-to-liquid heat exchanger.
B. The bleed air type is called an air-to-air exchanger and the oil type is known as a liquid-to-liquid heat exchanger.
C. The bleed air type is called an air-to-liquid exchanger and the oil type is known as a liquid-to-air heat exchanger.

2-52 AM.III.I.K9
Prior to performing engine trimming, you should
A. call the control tower to obtain current sea level barometric pressure and temperature.
B. observe the reading on the aircraft Outside Air Temperature (OAT) gauge.
C. obtain a true temperature reading comparable to that of the air that enters the engine.

FUEL AND FUEL METERING

ANSWERS

2-47 Answer C
Gas turbine engine fuel systems are every susceptible to the formation of ice in the fuel filters. When fuel inside the aircraft fuel tanks cools to 32°F or below, residual water in the fuel tends to freeze, forming ice crystals. These ice crystals can become trapped in the fuel filter and block fuel flow to the engine.
Ref: Powerplant Handbook H-8083-32B-ATB Chapter 2 Page 42

2-48 Answer A
The fuel nozzles inject fuel into the combustion area in a highly atomized, precisely patterned spray so that burning is completely even, in the shortest possible time, and in the smallest possible space. It is very important that the fuel be evenly distributed and well centered in the flame area within the liners. This is to preclude the formation of any hot spots in the combustion chambers and to prevent the flame burning through the liner.
Ref: Powerplant Handbook H-8083-32B-ATB Chapter 2 Page 43, 44

2-49 Answer B
Fuel nozzle types vary considerably between engines, although for the most part, fuel is sprayed into the combustion area under pressure through small orifices in the nozzles. The two types of fuel nozzles generally used are the simplex and the duplex configuration. The duplex nozzle usually requires a dual manifold and a pressurizing valve or a flow divider for dividing primary and secondary (main) fuel flow. A flow divider creates primary and secondary fuel supplies that are discharged through separate manifolds, providing two separate fuel flows.
Ref: Powerplant Handbook H-8083-32B-ATB Chapter 2 Page 45

2-50 Answer B
Drain valves are units used for draining fuel from the various components of the engine where accumulated fuel is most likely to present operating problems. The possibility of combustion chamber accumulations with the resultant fire hazard is one problem. A residual problem is the deposit of lead and/or gum, after evaporation, in such places as fuel manifolds and nozzles. In some instances, fuel manifolds are drained by an individual unit known as a drip or dump valve. This type of valve may be operated by pressure differential or it may be solenoid operated.
Ref: Powerplant Handbook H-8083-32B-ATB Chapter 2 Page 45

2-51 Answer A
One method of regulating fuel temperature is to use a fuel heater which operates as a heat exchanger to warm the fuel. The heater can use engine bleed air or engine lubricating oil as a source of heat. The bleed air type is called an air-to-liquid exchanger and the oil type is known as a liquid-to-liquid heat exchanger.
Ref: Powerplant Handbook H-8083-32B-ATB Chapter 2 Page 42

2-52 Answer C
Prior to trimming, care must be taken to obtain an true temperature reading in the proximity of the engine and comparable to the air which will enter the engine. A good practice prior to trimming is to place an accurate thermometer in a shaded place near the engine intake such as a wheel well or a shaded location within the nacelle.
Ref: Powerplant Handbook H-8083-32B-ATB Chapter 2 Page 40, 41

ORAL EXAM

2-1(O).   Name two maintenance or inspection tasks performed during routine fuel system inspection and maintenance.

2-2(O).   What checks of a fuel system can be made to verify proper operation?

2-3(O).   What is the function and operation of a fuel boost (booster) pump?

2-4(O).   What is the function of a fuel selector valve?

2-5(O).   What is done to inspect an engine driven pump for leaks and security?

2-6(O).   What is the function and operation of engine fuel filters on a turbine engine fuel system?

2-7(O).   What is vapor lock and how can it be avoided or remedied?

2-8(O).   What is a possible reason for fuel running out of a carburetor throttle body?

2-9(O).   What are some indications that the mixture is improperly adjusted?

2-10(O).   What is the procedure for checking idle mixture adjustment on a reciprocating engine?

2-11(O).   What are possible causes of poor engine acceleration, engine backfiring or missing when the throttle is advanced?

2-12(O).   What are three types of fuel metering systems used on reciprocating engine and how do they operate?

2-13(O).   Name the fuel metering system components in a float type carburetor.

2-14(O).   What is the purpose of the part power stop on some engines when accomplishing engine trim procedure?

2-15(O).   Explain the operation of a fuel flow indicating system and where it is connected into the engine.

2-16(O).   What is the operation of a manifold pressure gauge?

FUEL AND FUEL METERING

ANSWERS

ORAL EXAM

2-1(O).   Drain sumps, change or clean filters, check linkages for smooth stop-to-stop operation, check fuel lines for cracks and hoses for deterioration, leak check, check pump operation and motor brush wear, check selector valve for wear, check fuel tanks for corrosion and leaks, check fuel quantity and pressure gauges for proper operation, check vents for obstruction, check function of warning system.
Ref: Powerplant Handbook H-8083-32B-ATB Chapter 2

2-2(O).   A fuel system should have no external leaks. Make sure all units are securely attached. Drain plugs and valves should be opened to clear any water or sediment. The same is true for the filter, screen, and sump. Filter screens and auxiliary pumps must be clean and free from corrosion. Fuel system controls should move freely, lock securely, and should not rub or chafe. Fuel vents must be in the correct position and free from obstruction. Overall engine performance checks give insight into proper fuel system operation. If engine input (manifold pressure) results in the correct power output (engine RPM), the engine performance is acceptable and it is likely the fuel system is operating properly. Check all fuel system related gauges for indications of fuel system operation. Carburetor air temperature, fuel flow, fuel pressure, and cylinder head temperature indications can all indicate potential fuel system problems. An idle mixture check can also be performed.
Ref: Powerplant Handbook H-8083-32B-ATB Chapter 2, and Chapter 10

2-3(O).   A fuel boost pump is designed to provide positive fuel pressure to the engine fuel system. The boost pump forces fuel through the selector valve to the main line strainer. During starting, the boost pump forces fuel through a bypass in the engine-driven fuel pump to the carburetor or fuel injection system. Once the engine driven pump is up to speed, it takes over and delivers the fuel to the metering device.
Ref: Powerplant Handbook H-8083-32B-ATB Chapter 2

2-4(O).   A fuel selector valve is controlled on the flight deck to select the tank from which tank fuel will be delivered to the engine.
Ref: Powerplant Handbook H-8083-32B-ATB Chapter 2

2-5(O).   If booster pumps are installed, they should be energized to check the fuel system for leaks. (During this check, an ammeter can be used to insure all boost pumps pull roughly the same amperage.) The drain lines of the engine drive pump should be free of traps, bends, or restrictions. Check for leaks and the security of the engine driven pump mounting bolts. Check the vent and drain lines for obstructions.
Ref: Powerplant Handbook H-8083-32B-ATB Chapter 2

2-6(O).   The function of the engine fuel filters is to remove micronic particles that may be in the fuel so they do not damage the fuel pump or the fuel control unit. Typically, a low-pressure filter is installed between the supply tanks and the engine fuel system. An additional high-pressure fuel filter is installed between the fuel pump and the fuel control. Three kinds of filters are used: micron, wafer screen, and screen mesh. The micron has the smallest particle filtering capability. It requires a bypass valve because it could be easily clogged. Many filters have a bypass indicator. Periodic servicing and replacement of filter elements is imperative. Daily draining of fuel tank sumps and low pressure filters eliminates much filter trouble and undue maintenance of fuel pumps and fuel control units.
Ref: Powerplant Handbook H-8083-32B-ATB Chapter 2

2-7(O).   Fuel should be in the liquid state until it is discharged in the intake air stream for combustion. Under certain conditions, the fuel may vaporize in the lines, pumps, or other units. The vapor pockets formed restrict fuel flow through the units to the fuel-metering device. The partial or complete interruption of fuel flow is called vapor lock. The three general causes of vapor lock are low pressure on the fuel, high fuel temperatures, and excessive fuel turbulence. Fuel systems are designed to avoid vapor lock. The most significant remedy for vapor lock is the use of boost pumps which pump the fuel from the storage tank to the metering devise under pressure so it cannot vaporize prematurely.
Ref: Powerplant Handbook H-8083-32B-ATB Chapter 2

ORAL EXAM

2-8(O).   The float level and fuel level in the float chamber of the carburetor must be below the level of the discharge nozzle or fuel will leak from the nozzle when the engine is not operating.
Ref: Powerplant Handbook H-8083-32B-ATB Chapter 2

2-9(O).   Carbon deposits on the spark plugs and spark plug fouling are signs that the idle mixture is not properly set. Also, faulty acceleration may be an indication of an excessively lean mixture.
Ref: Powerplant Handbook H-8083-32B-ATB Chapter 2

2-10(O).   To check the idle mixture on a warmed up engine, move the mixture control slowly toward the idle cutoff position. Observe the tachometer for a slight RPM rise (10 – 50 RPM) before the engine cuts out. If this does not occur, adjust the idle mixture until it does.
Ref: Powerplant Handbook H-8083-32B-ATB Chapter 2

2-11(O).   A lean mixture is the most like likely cause. A cracked distributor block or high-tension leak between two ignition leads can also cause these symptoms and backfiring.
Ref: Powerplant Handbook H-8083-32B-ATB Chapter 2, and Chapter 10

2-12(O).   Float-type carburetors, pressure carburetors, and fuel injection systems are all used on reciprocating aircraft engines. A float type carburetor uses the volume of air moving through a venturi to cause a suction that meters the fuel. A pressure carburetor uses a closed, pressurized fuel system. The venturi serves only to create pressure differentials that control the quantity of fuel to the metering jet in proportion to the airflow to the engine. The fuel is discharged under positive pressure. A fuel injection system is a continuous flow system that measures engine air consumption and uses airflow forces to control the fuel flow to the engine. Fuel is injected into the airstream on a float type carburetor just before the throttle valve, just after the throttle valve on a pressure carburetor and directly into the cylinder head on a fuel injection system.
Ref: Powerplant Handbook H-8083-32B-ATB Chapter 2

2-13(O).   The main metering system components include the throttle, the venturi, the discharge nozzle, and the float and float valve in the float chamber. The idling system components include the idling jet and the idle mixture adjustment. The mixture control system includes either a needle valve or a back-suction line, the acceleration system including a piston/pump and the economizer system including the economizer needle valve.
Ref: Powerplant Handbook H-8083-32B-ATB Chapter 2

2-14(O).   The engine is operated at full power or at the part power control trim stop for a sufficient amount of time to ensure it has completely stabilized. This is usually at least 5 minutes. Follow all manufacturer's instructions.
Ref: Powerplant Handbook H-8083-32B-ATB Chapter 2

2-15(O).   A fuel pressure gauge, calibrated in pounds per hour fuel flow, is used as a fuel flow meter with the Bendix/ RSA fuel injection system for reciprocating aircraft engines. This gauge is connected to the flow divider and senses the pressure being applied to the discharge nozzles. This pressure is in direct proportion to the fuel flow and indicates engine power output and fuel consumption.
Ref: Powerplant Handbook H-8083-32B-ATB Chapter 2

2-16(O).   The manifold pressure gauge indicates the pressure in the induction system of a reciprocating aircraft engine. The pressure is measured in the intake manifold downstream of the throttle valve. It is displayed on the flight deck in inches of mercury (Hg) and is directly proportional to the power output of the engine.
Ref: Powerplant Handbook H-8083-32B-ATB Chapter 2, and Chapter 10

FUEL AND FUEL METERING

PRACTICAL EXAM

2-1(P).   Given an actual aircraft engine or mockup, complete an operational check of a fuel selector valve and record your findings. [Level 3]

2-2(P).   Given an actual aircraft engine or mockup, inspect an engine fuel filter assembly for leaks and record your findings. [Level 3]

2-3(P).   Given an actual aircraft engine or mockup, inspect a repair to an engine fuel system and record your findings. [Level 3]

2-4(P).   Given an actual aircraft engine or mockup, complete an operational check of a fuel boost pump and record your findings. [Level 3]

2-5(P).   Given an actual aircraft engine or mockup, appropriate publications, and tooling, repair a fuel selector valve and record maintenance. [Level 3]

2-6(P).   Given an actual aircraft engine or mockup, inspect a main fuel filter assembly for leaks and record your findings. [Level 3]

2-7(P).   Given an actual aircraft engine or mockup, complete an operational check of a remotely located fuel valve and record your findings. [Level 3]

2-8(P).   Given an actual aircraft engine or mockup, locate and identify a turbine engine fuel heater. [Level 2]

2-9(P).   Given an actual aircraft engine or mockup, appropriate publications, equipment, and materials service an engine fuel strainer and record maintenance. [Level 3]

2-10(P). Given an actual aircraft engine or mockup, inspect an engine driven fuel pump for leaks and security and record your findings. [Level 3]

2-11(P). Given an actual aircraft engine or mockup and appropriate publication, complete an operational check of the engine fuel pressure and record your findings. [Level 3]

2-12(P). Given an actual aircraft engine or mockup, appropriate publications, equipment and tooling repair an engine fuel system. [Level 3]

2-13(P). Given an actual aircraft engine or mockup, appropriate publications, equipment and tooling repair an engine fuel system component. [Level 3]

2-14(P). Given an actual aircraft engine or mockup, appropriate publications, appropriate testing equipment, if necessary and an unknown discrepancy, troubleshoot a fuel pressure system and record your findings. [Level 3]

2-15(P). Given an actual aircraft engine or mockup, appropriate publications, equipment and tooling remove and install the accelerating pump in a float-type carburetor and record maintenance. [Level 3]

2-16(P). Given an actual aircraft engine or mockup, appropriate publications, equipment and tooling remove and install the accelerating pump in a float-type carburetor and record maintenance. [Level 3]

2-17(P). Given an actual aircraft engine or mockup, appropriate publications, equipment and tooling check and adjust the float level of a float-type carburetor and record maintenance. [Level 3]

PRACTICAL EXAM

2-18(P).   Given an actual aircraft engine or mockup, appropriate publications, equipment and tooling check the needle and seat in a float-type carburetor for proper operation and record your findings. [Level 2]

2-19(P).   Given an actual aircraft engine or mockup, appropriate publications, equipment and tooling check a fuel injection nozzle for proper spray pattern and record your findings. [Level 2]

2-20(P).   Given an actual aircraft engine or mockup, appropriate publications, equipment and tooling install a fuel injector nozzle and record maintenance. [Level 3]

2-21(P).   Given an actual aircraft engine or mockup, appropriate publications, equipment and tooling check and adjust the idle mixture and record maintenance. [Level 3]

2-22(P).   Given an actual aircraft engine or mockup, appropriate publications, equipment and tooling install a turbine engine fuel nozzle and record maintenance. [Level 3]

2-23(P).   Given an actual aircraft engine or mockup, locate and identify various fuel metering system components. [Level 2]

2-24(P).   Given an actual aircraft engine or mockup, appropriate publications, equipment, and tooling service a carburetor fuel screen and record maintenance. [Level 3]

PAGE LEFT BLANK INTENTIONALLY

INDUCTION AND EXHAUST SYSTEMS

Carburetor Induction Systems, Turbine Engine Inlet Systems,
Reciprocating Engine Exhaust Systems, and Exhaust Vectoring

QUESTIONS

3-1 AM.III.D.K4
Where on a reciprocating engine is manifold
pressure measured?
  A. As the air/fuel mixture flows past the throttle plate.
  B. As the airflow mixture enters one or more cylinders.
  C. At a pre-calibrated point within a manifold tube.

3-4 AM.III.J.K1
The action of a carburetor air scoop is to supply air to the
carburetor, but it may also
  A. cool the engine.
  B. keep fuel lines cool and prevent vapor lock.
  C. increase the pressure of the incoming air by ram effect.

3-2 AM.III.J.K7
One source commonly used for carburetor air heat is
  A. turbocharger heated air.
  B. alternate air heat.
  C. warm ducted air from around the exhaust system.

3-5 AM.III.J.K7
During engine operation, if carburetor heat is applied, it will
  A. increase air to fuel ratio.
  B. increase engine RPM.
  C. decrease air density to the carburetor.

3-3 AM.III.J.K7
On an airplane equipped with an alternate air door in the
carburetor air box, when the main air duct air filter becomes
blocked or clogged, the
  A. system will automatically allow warm, unfiltered air
     to be drawn into the engine through a spring loaded
     alternate air valve.
  B. the carburetor heat door will automatically open to
     supply the engine.
  C. alternate air must be selected in the cockpit to continue
     induction into the engine.

3-6 AM.III.E.K1
In the event of an engine fire during start-up, what type of fire
extinguisher is most effective to put out the fire?
  A. Dry Powder
  B. Carbon Dioxide
  C. Water

INDUCTION AND EXHAUST SYSTEMS

ANSWERS

3-1 Answer A
Filtered air enters the fuel metering device (carburetor or fuel injector) where the throttle plate controls the amount of air flowing into the engine. The air coming out of the throttle is referred to as manifold pressure which is the primary control of engine output power.
Ref: Powerplant Handbook H-8083-32B-ATB Chapter 3 Page 1

3-2 Answer C
The carburetor heat valve admits air from the outside air scoop for normal operation and it admits warm air from the engine compartment for operation during icing conditions. The carburetor heat is operated by a push-pull control in the cockpit. When selected, warm ducted air from around the exhaust system is directed into the carburetor. This raises the intake air temperature.
Ref: Powerplant Handbook H-8083-32B-ATB Chapter 3 Page 1

3-3 Answer A
On a basic carburetor induction system found on a light aircraft with reciprocating engine, an induction air box allows air to be drawn from a scoop mounted in the nose cowling or, when selected, from inside the cowling for the purpose of warming the carburetor by ducting air past the exhaust system. However, an alternate air door can be opened by engine suction if the normal route of airflow should be blocked by something. The valve is spring loaded closed and is sucked open by the engine if needed.
Ref: Powerplant Handbook H-8083-32B-ATB Chapter 3 Page 2

3-4 Answer C
The carburetor air filter is installed in the air scoop in front of the carburetor air duct. The air duct provides passage for outside air to the carburetor. Air enters the duct through the scoop. The intake opening is located in the slipstream so air is forced into the induction system giving ram air effect to the incoming airflow (raises pressure).
Ref: Powerplant Handbook H-8083-32B-ATB Chapter 3 Page 3, 4

3-5 Answer C
Improper or careless use of carburetor heat can be just as dangerous as the most advanced stage of induction system ice. Increasing the temperature of the air causes it to expand and decrease in density. This action reduces the weight of the charge delivered to the cylinder and causes a noticeable loss in power because of decreased volumetric efficiency.
Ref: Powerplant Handbook H-8083-32B-ATB Chapter 3 Page 3

3-6 Answer C
Carbon Dioxide (CO_2) is the most effective agent against fires involving liquids, such as gasoline. Because burning liquids will float on top of water, water extinguishers should not be used with fuel based fires. Dry powder may also be effective, but causes corrosion and so is not often used with aircraft. Halon extinguishers may also be effective.
Ref: Powerplant Handbook H-8083-32B-ATB Chapter 3 Page 5

3-7 AM.III.A.K9
When starting a piston engine equipped with a carburetor air heater, in what position should the carburetor heat control be placed?
   A. Always in its hot position.
   B. Always in its cold position.
   C. Adjusted for ambient temperature and humidity.

3-10 AM.III.J.K3
What concern is common among all internally driven reciprocating supercharger systems
   A. overheated fuel air mixture.
   B. difficulty of cooling the supercharger mechanism.
   C. difficulty of inspection and maintenance.

3-8 AM.III.J.K3
Ground boosted engine manifold pressure is generally considered to be any manifold pressure above
   A. 14.7 inches Hg.
   B. 50 inches Hg.
   C. 30 inches Hg.

3-11 AM.III.J.K4
What directly regulates the speed of a turbocharger?
   A. Turbine
   B. Waste Gate
   C. Throttle

3-9 AM.III.J.K3
What is used to drive a supercharger on a radial engine?
   A. Exhaust gases.
   B. Gear train from the crankshaft.
   C. Belt drive through a pulley arrangement.

3-12 AM.III.J.K4
If the turbocharger waste gate is completely closed,
   A. none of the exhaust gases are directed through the turbine.
   B. the turbocharger is in the OFF position.
   C. all the exhaust gases are directed through the turbine.

INDUCTION AND EXHAUST SYSTEMS

ANSWERS

3-7 Answer B
When there is no danger of icing, the carburetor heat control is normally kept in the COLD position. To prevent damage to the heater valve in the case of backfire, carburetor heat should not be used while starting the engine. Also during ground operation, only enough carburetor heat should be used to give smooth engine performance.
Ref: Powerplant Handbook H-8083-32B-ATB Chapter 3 Page 4

3-8 Answer C
A true supercharged engine, called a ground boosted engine, can boost the manifold pressure above 30 inches Hg. In other words, a true supercharger boosts manifold pressure above ambient pressure which is 29.92 inches Hg. So in general, boost manifold pressure or "boost pressure" when discussing manifold pressure is manifold pressure above 30 inches Hg.
Ref: Powerplant Handbook H-8083-32B-ATB Chapter 3 Page 5

3-9 Answer B
A fuel distribution impeller is connected directly to the crankshaft to aid in even fuel distribution. Since it operates at the same speed as the crankshaft, this is accomplished without materially increasing boost or increasing the pressure on the fuel/air mixture flowing into the cylinders. A supercharger, or blower impeller, is designed to increase the pressure on the charge delivered to the cylinders. It is driven through a gear train from the crankshaft so that it can rotate at a higher speed than the crankshaft to compress the charge.
Ref: Powerplant Handbook H-8083-32B-ATB Chapter 3 Page 6

3-10 Answer A
An internally mounted supercharger system compresses the air at a point in between the carburetor and intake ports. This compression causes the air to be heated resulting in lost efficiency and detonation. An externally driven supercharger (turbocharger) compresses air before entering the carburetor, giving more time and distance for it to cool.
Ref: Powerplant Handbook H-8083-32B-ATB Chapter 3 Page 6

3-11 Answer B
The turbine wheel, driven by exhaust gases, drives the compressor impeller. The turbocharger housing collects and directs the exhaust gases onto the turbine wheel. The waste gate regulates the amount of exhaust gases directed to the turbine. As such, it regulates the speed of the rotor (the turbine and impeller on the common shaft). By regulating the speed of the turbocharger rotor, the amount of compression applied to the engine induction air is controlled.
Ref: Powerplant Handbook H-8083-32B-ATB Chapter 3 Page 9

3-12 Answer C
If the waste gate is completely closed, all the exhaust gases are "backed up" and forced through the turbine wheel. If the waste gate is partially closed, a corresponding amount of exhaust gas is directed to the turbine. When the waste gate is fully open, nearly all of the exhaust gases pass overboard providing little or no boost.
Ref: Powerplant Handbook H-8083-32B-ATB Chapter 3 Page 9

3-13 AM.III.J.K4
What is the purpose of a normalized turbocharger system used on a small reciprocating aircraft engine?
   A. Compresses the air to hold the cabin pressure constant after the aircraft has reached its critical altitude.
   B. Maintains constant air velocity in the intake manifold.
   C. Compresses air to maintain manifold pressure constant from sea level to the critical altitude of the engine.

3-14 AM.III.J.K4
What are the three basic regulating components of a sea level boosted turbocharger system?
   1. Exhaust Bypass Assembly
   2. Compressor Assembly
   3. Pump And Bearing Casing
   4. Density Controller
   5. Differential Pressure Controller
   A. 2, 3, and 4
   B. 1, 4, and 5
   C. 1, 2, and 3

3-15 AM.III.J.K4
To what altitude will a turbocharger maintain sea level pressure?
   A. Critical Altitude
   B. Service Ceiling
   C. Pressure Altitude

3-16 AM.III.J.K4
What is the purpose of the density controller in a turbocharger system?
   A. Limits the maximum manifold pressure that can be produced at other than full throttle conditions.
   B. Limits the maximum manifold pressure that can be produced at full throttle.
   C. Maintains constant air velocity at the carburetor inlet.

3-17 AM.III.J.K4
What is the purpose of an after-cooler on a turbocharged reciprocating engine?
   A. To cool the exhaust gases before entering the turbodrive.
   B. To cool the turbocharger bearings.
   C. To cool turbocharged air entering the induction system.

3-18 AM.III.K.K2
The purpose of the engine inlet on a turbine engine is to
   A. provide a well-mixed volume of air to the inlet of the compressor.
   B. provide a uniform and steady airflow to avoid compressor stall.
   C. reduce the speed of the incoming air and direct it at the correct angle toward the compressor blades.

INDUCTION AND EXHAUST SYSTEMS

ANSWERS

3-13 Answer C
A normalizing turbocharger system found on a small aircraft engine compensates for the power lost due to pressure drop resulting from increased altitude. It is designed to operate only above the altitude at which the engine can no longer develop full power. As such, it is not a true "supercharger" because it does not provide a pressure boost of the induction air above 30 inches Hg.
Ref: Powerplant Handbook H-8083-32B-ATB Chapter 3 Page 9

3-14 Answer B
A sea level boosted turbocharger system is regulated by the position of the oil controlled exhaust bypass assembly. The density controller which is designed to limit the manifold pressure below the turbocharger's critical altitude, repositions the oil bleed valve that sends the controlling oil to exhaust gas bypass assembly. The differential pressure controller functions during all positions of the exhaust bypass valve except the fully open position. It compares pressure on both sides of the throttle valve and adjusts oil bleed return to the crankcase which affects the position of the exhaust bypass valve.
Ref: Powerplant Handbook H-8083-32B-ATB Chapter 3 Page 10

3-15 Answer A
When the waste gate of a turbocharger system is fully closed, the maximum volume of exhaust gases flow into the turbocharger turbine. This provides the maximum pressurization of the induction air. Critical altitude is the altitude above which, even with the waste gate fully closed, maximum power (manifold pressure) cannot be maintained. Since air is most dense at sea level, power developed at sea level is the same as that developed at the critical altitude. Above critical altitude, only power less than that which can be developed at sea level can be achieved.
Ref: Powerplant Handbook H-8083-32B-ATB Chapter 3 Page 12

3-16 Answer B
The density controller is designed to limit the manifold pressure below the turbocharger's critical altitude. A nitrogen-filled bellows reacts to temperature and density changes. It repositions the oil bleed valve which changes the pressure sent to the exhaust vent valve to move it to the correct position at full throttle. In this way, the density controller prevents over-boost of the engine.
Ref: Powerplant Handbook H-8083-32B-ATB Chapter 3 Page 13

3-17 Answer C
When the turbocharger compresses air for induction, the temperature of the air increases. If the air is too hot, it can exceed maximum throttle inlet temperature which can lead to detonation of the fuel air charge in the combustion chamber. The after-cooler cools the compressed air from the turbocharger compressor which increases the charge air density resulting in better engine performance.
Ref: Powerplant Handbook H-8083-32B-ATB Chapter 3 Page 14

3-18 Answer B
The engine inlet of a turbine engine is designed to provide a relatively distortion-free flow of air in the required quantity to the inlet of the compressor. Many engines use inlet guide vanes to help straighten the airflow and direct it into the first stages of the compressor. A uniform steady airflow is necessary to avoid compressor stall and excessive internal temperatures in the turbine section.
Ref: Powerplant Handbook H-8083-32B-ATB Chapter 3 Page 16

3-19 AM.III.K.K6
Ram recovery refers to
- A. increasing pressure and airflow to make up for thrust loss at high speeds.
- B. conversion of drag to useful air velocity.
- C. the use of inlet air doors to guide the air into the inlet.

3-22 AM.III.K.K8
Which statement is true concerning inlet icing of turbine engines?
- A. Turboprops rely on propeller anti-icing to keep the inlet(s) free from ice.
- B. Most turbofan inlets use AC powered electric anti-icing.
- C. Most turboprop engines rely on electrical anti-icing.

3-20 AM.III.K.K6
A divided-entrance inlet air duct on a turbine powered aircraft
- A. is found on newer designs because it reduces the frontal area of the inlet duct.
- B. has better flow characteristics than a single opening.
- C. presents difficulty to designers due to the amount of drag produced.

3-23 AM.III.K.K8
Turbofan engine inlets
- A. divert air away from the center of the fan blades.
- B. contain sound reducing materials.
- C. have unconventional air inlets to eliminate Foreign Object Damage (FOD).

3-21 AM.III.K.K2
The purpose of a bellmouth compressor inlet is to
- A. provide an increase in ram air effect at low airspeeds.
- B. maximize aerodynamic efficiency of the inlet.
- C. provide an increased pressure drop in the inlet.

3-24 AM.III.L.K1
Which is an advantage of a collector type exhaust system of a reciprocating engine?
- A. Superior noise reduction.
- B. Most efficient in minimizing power loss.
- C. Simplest for inspection and maintenance.

INDUCTION AND EXHAUST SYSTEMS

ANSWERS

3-19 Answer A

As aircraft speed increases, thrust tends to decrease somewhat. As the aircraft speed reaches a certain point, ram recovery compensates for the losses caused by the increases in speed. The inlet must be able to recover as much of the total pressure of the free airstream as possible. As air molecules are trapped and begin to be compressed in the inlet, much of the pressure loss is recovered. This added pressure at the inlet of the engine increases the pressure and airflow to the engine. This is known as ram recovery or total pressure recovery.
Ref: Powerplant Handbook H-8083-32B-ATB Chapter 3 Page 17

3-20 Answer C

The divided air duct can be either a wing-root inlet or a scoop at each side of the fuselage. The inlet scoops are generally placed as far forward as possible to permit a gradual bend toward the compressor inlet for smoother air flow. Two entrances present more problems to the aircraft designer than a single-entrance duct because of the difficulty of obtaining sufficient air scoop area without imposing prohibitive amounts of drag. The divided-entrance turbine engine inlet duct is found primarily on military aircraft.
Ref: Powerplant Handbook H-8083-32B-ATB Chapter 3 Page 17

3-21 Answer B

A bellmouth inlet is usually installed on a turbine engine undergoing testing in a test cell. The bellmouth is designed with the single objective of obtaining very high aerodynamic efficiency. Essentially, the inlet is a bell-shaped funnel having carefully rounded shoulders which offer practically no air resistance. Duct loss is so slight that it is considered to be zero.
Ref: Powerplant Handbook H-8083-32B-ATB Chapter 3 Page 19

3-22 Answer C

The inlet for many types of turboprop engines are anti-iced by using electrical elements in the lip opening of the air intake area. Deflector doors are sometimes used to deflect ice or dirt away from the intake as well. Warm bleed air is drawn from the compressor and circulated on the inside of the inlet lip for anti-icing on turbofan engines.
Ref: Powerplant Handbook H-8083-32B-ATB Chapter 3 Page 20

3-23 Answer B

Inside the inlet of a turbofan engine, sound reducing materials lower the noise generated by the large diameter fan. The fan permits the use of a conventional air inlet duct, resulting in low inlet duct loss. The fan also reduces engine damage from the ingestion of foreign material because much of any material that may be ingested is thrown radially outward and passes through the fan discharge rather than through the core of the engine.
Ref: Powerplant Handbook H-8083-32B-ATB Chapter 3 Page 20

3-24 Answer A

Either short stack or collector type exhaust systems are found on reciprocating aircraft engines. Short stack is the simplest method, but only suitable on small engines when noise reduction is not a major factor.
Ref: Powerplant Handbook H-8083-32B-ATB Chapter 3 Page 21

3-25 AM.III.L.K1
Gray streaks found on an exhaust system is most often the result of
- A. a crack in the exhaust pipes or fittings.
- B. misalignment of exhaust system components.
- C. carbon monoxide leakage.

3-28 AM.III.L.K1
Reciprocating engine exhaust systems that have repairs or sloppy weld beads which protrude internally are unacceptable because they cause
- A. base metal fatigue.
- B. localized cracks.
- C. local hot spots.

3-26 AM.III.L.K1
How may reciprocating engine exhaust leaks be detected?
- A. An exhaust trail of the tailpipe on the airplane exterior.
- B. Fluctuating manifold pressure indication.
- C. Signs of exhaust soot inside the cowling and on adjacent components.

3-29 AM.III.L.K2
The exhaust section of a turbine engine is designed to
- A. impart a high exit velocity to the exhaust gases.
- B. increase temperature, therefore increase velocity.
- C. decrease temperature, therefore decreasing the pressure.

3-27 AM.III.L.K1
When an exhaust system on a turbocharged engine is operated at high altitude, it is more susceptible to damage and failure; mostly because of
- A. increased power demands.
- B. lower ambient cooling.
- C. lower external pressure.

3-30 AM.III.L.K2
In a convergent exhaust nozzle, the diameter of the outlet
- A. doesn't affect exhaust gas velocity.
- B. must not be too large or energy will be wasted.
- C. is as small as possible without stalling the engine.

INDUCTION AND EXHAUST SYSTEMS

ANSWERS

3-25 Answer B
An exhaust leak is indicated by a flat gray or sooty black streaks on the pipes in the area of the leak and is usually the result of poor alignment of two mated exhaust system members.
Ref: Powerplant Handbook H-8083-32B-ATB Chapter 3 Page 23

3-26 Answer C
An exhaust leak is indicated by a flat gray or a sooty black streak on the pipes, on the cowling in the area of the leak, or on adjacent components.
Ref: Powerplant Handbook H-8083-32B-ATB Chapter 3 Page 23

3-27 Answer C
During high pressure altitude operation on a turbocharged aircraft, the exhaust system pressure is maintained by the engine at near sea level conditions. However the opposing ambient pressure is less. Because of these pressure differentials, any leaks in the system will be accentuated and thus hot air escaping gases can expand those leaks or cracks and cause damage to nearby components.
Ref: Powerplant Handbook H-8083-32B-ATB Chapter 3 Page 24

3-28 Answer C
When welded repairs are necessary, the original contours should be retained. The exhaust system alignment must not be warped or otherwise affected. Repairs or sloppy weld beads that protrude internally are not acceptable as they cause local hot spots and may restrict exhaust gas flow.
Ref: Powerplant Handbook H-8083-32B-ATB Chapter 3 Page 24

3-29 Answer A
On turbine engines, through the use of a convergent exhaust nozzle, the exhaust gases increase in velocity before they are discharged from the exhaust nozzle. Increasing the velocity of the gases increases their momentum and increases the thrust produced (15-20 percent of total engine thrust is typical on a turbofan engine). The exception to this is the turboshaft engine in which all possible energy produced by the engine is designated for rotating the shaft and a divergent duct may be used.
Ref: Powerplant Handbook H-8083-32B-ATB Chapter 3 Page 25

3-30 Answer B
The restriction of the opening of the outlet of the exhaust nozzle is limited by two factors. If the nozzle opening is too big, thrust is being wasted. If it is too little, the flow is choked in the other components of the engine. In other words, the exhaust nozzle acts as an orifice the size of which determines the density and velocity of the gases as they emerge from the engine. This is critical to thrust performance.
Ref: Powerplant Handbook H-8083-32B-ATB Chapter 3 Page 26

3-31 AM.III.L.K4
Engines using cold stream or cold and hot stream
reversing include
  A. high bypass turbofan engines.
  B. turbojets.
  C. turbojets with afterburners.

3-32 AM.III.L.K4
The purpose of cascade vanes in a thrust reversing system
is to
  A. form a solid blocking door in the jet exhaust path.
  B. turn the exhaust gases forward just after exiting the
     exhaust nozzle.
  C. turn the fan airstream in a forward direction.

3-33 AM.III.L.K4
Turbojet and turbofan thrust reverser systems are generally
powered by
  A. electricity or exhaust gases.
  B. hydraulics or pneumatics.
  C. hydraulics only.

3-34 AM.III.L.K3
Noise suppressors on turbine engines work by
  A. Converting low frequency noise into high
     frequency noise.
  B. Converting high frequency noise into low
     frequency noise.
  C. Converting noise energy into heat.

3-35 AM.III.L.K2
Turbine engine emissions
  A. are caused by high combustion temperatures.
  B. are caused by low combustion temperatures.
  C. account for so little of all emissions into the atmosphere
     that they are of little concern.

3-36 AM.III.L.K2
What device will allow an automatic speed and output of the
turbocharger requiring no pilot action up to critical altitude?
  A. Absolute pressure controller.
  B. Differential pressure controller.
  C. Atmospheric pressure controller.

INDUCTION AND EXHAUST SYSTEMS

ANSWERS

3-31 Answer A
Mechanical blockage thrust reversing is accomplished by placing a removable obstruction in the exhaust gas stream rear of the exhaust nozzle. This type is generally used with ducted turbofan engines where the fan and core flow mix in a common nozzle before exiting the engine. In the aerodynamic blockage type of thrust reverser, used mainly with unducted turbofan engines, only fan air is used to slow the aircraft. Therefore, turbofan engines may use cold stream or cold and hot stream obstruction for thrust reversing. Note: turbojets do not have cold stream airflow. All air passes through the core of the engine (hot stream).
Ref: Powerplant Handbook H-8083-32B-ATB Chapter 3 Page 27

3-32 Answer C
In the aerodynamic blockage type of thrust reverser, used mainly with unducted turbofan engines, only fan air is used to slow the aircraft. A modern aerodynamic thrust reverser system consists of a translating cowl, blocker doors, and cascade vanes that redirect the fan airflow to slow the aircraft. If the thrust levers are at idle position and the aircraft has weight on wheels, moving the thrust levers aft activates the translating cowl to open. This closes the blocker doors and stops the fan airflow from going aft. It redirects the air through the cascade vanes which direct airflow forward to slow the aircraft.
Ref: Powerplant Handbook H-8083-32B-ATB Chapter 3 Page 27

3-33 Answer B
A thrust reverser systems consist of several components that move either the clam shell doors or the blocker doors and translating cowl. Actuating power is generally pneumatic or hydraulic and uses gearboxes, flex-drives, jackscrews, control valves, and air or hydraulic motors to deploy or stow the thrust reverser systems.
Ref: Powerplant Handbook H-8083-32B-ATB Chapter 3 Page 27

3-34 Answer A
Low frequency sounds travel the furthest from their point of generation and are thus of the greatest concern. By breaking up the single stream of exhaust flow into several smaller streams, the frequency of the noise is increased as will be its rate of dissipation.
Ref: Powerplant Handbook H-8083-32B-ATB Chapter 3 Page 29

3-35 Answer A
Lowering exhaust emission from gas turbine engines, especially oxides of nitrogen (NOx), continues to require improvement. Most advanced designs rely on a method of premixing the fuel/air before it enters the combustion burner area. High energy swirlers adjacent to the fuel nozzles create a more thorough and leaner mix of fuel which burns at lower temperatures than in previous gas turbine engines. The NOx levels are higher if the burning fuel/air mixture stays at high temperatures for a longer time.
Ref: Powerplant Handbook H-8083-32B-ATB Chapter 3 Page 31

3-36 Answer A
One device used to control the speed and output of the turbocharger, but controls the system only at maximum output, is the absolute pressure controller. The absolute pressure controller contains an aneroid bellows that is referenced to upper deck pressure. It operates the wastegate, which diverts, more or less, exhaust gas over the turbine. As an absolute pressure setting is reached, it bypasses oil, and relieves the pressure on the waste gate actuator. This allows the absolute pressure controller to control the maximum turbocharger compressor discharge pressure. The turbocharger is completely automatic, requiring no pilot action up to the critical altitude.
Ref: Powerplant Handbook H-8083-32B-ATB Chapter 3 Page 14

3-37 AM.III.J.K7
A method commonly used to prevent carburetor icing is to
A. preheat the intake air.
B. mix alcohol with the fuel.
C. electrically heat the throttle valve.

3-38 AM.III.J.K4
Which of the following is a function of the differential pressure controller?
A. It limits the maximum manifold pressure that can be produced by the turbocharger at full throttle conditions.
B. It controls all positions of the waste gate except at fully open position.
C. It controls the position of the waste gate after the aircraft has reached its critical altitude.

3-39 AM.III.J.K4
The pressure between the turbocharger and the throttle valve is called
A. turbocharger boost pressure.
B. induction manifold pressure.
C. upper deck pressure.

3-40 AM.III.L.K1
Dislodged internal muffler baffles on a small reciprocating aircraft engine may cause
A. excessive exhaust back pressure.
B. an engine overspeed problem.
C. high oil consumption.

3-41 AM.III.L.K4
The rearward thrust capability of an engine with an aerodynamic blockage type thrust reverser system deployed is
A. less than its forward capability.
B. greater than its forward capability.
C. equal to its forward capability.

3-42 AM.III.L.K2
Which of the following techniques has the effect of lowering the volume of Nitrogen Oxides and other environmentally damaging emissions from a turbine engine?
A. Swirling the fuel/air mixture entering the combustion camber.
B. Straightening the fuel/air mixture entering the combustion chamber.
C. Depressurizing the fuel/air mixture entering the combustion chamber.

INDUCTION AND EXHAUST SYSTEMS

ANSWERS

3-37 Answer A
Induction system icing can be prevented or eliminated by raising the temperature of the air that passes through the system. For this purpose a carburetor heat system is located upstream of the induction system inlet and well ahead of the dangerous icing zones.
Ref: Powerplant Handbook H-8083-32B-ATB Chapter 3 Page 3

3-40 Answer A
Internal muffler failures of the baffles or diffusers can cause partial or complete power loss by restricting the flow of the exhaust gases. In addition, local hot spots caused by uneven exhaust gas flow can result in burning, bulging or a rupture of the outer muffler wall.
Ref: Powerplant Handbook H-8083-32B-ATB Chapter 3 Page 23

3-38 Answer B
One side of the diaphragm in the differential pressure controller senses air pressure upstream of the throttle. The other side samples pressure on the cylinder side of the throttle valve. Thus the differential pressure controller functions during all positions of the waste gate other than the fully open position which is controlled by the density controller.
Ref: Powerplant Handbook H-8083-32B-ATB Chapter 3 Page 12

3-41 Answer A
An aerodynamic thrust reverser is powered by the engine's fan which typically produces about 80% of the engine's thrust. Thus an engine with its thrust reverser's deployed produces less thrust than when ii is in its forward thrust mode.
Ref: Powerplant Handbook H-8083-32B-ATB Chapter 3 Page 27

3-39 Answer C
In a turbocharger system, several types of controllers restrict or allow oil flow back to the engine. The more this flow is restricted, the more pressure is applied to close the waste gate. This causes more exhaust gases to pass through the turbine, increasing the speed of the compressor and so raising the inlet pressure. This pressure from the outlet of the compressor to the throttle is referred to as upper deck pressure.
Ref: Powerplant Handbook H-8083-32B-ATB Chapter 3 Page 10

3-42 Answer A
Most noxious emissions are formed by a reaction of oxygen and nitrogen burning at high temperatures. Swirling the air as it enters the combustion chamber creates a more thorough and leaner mix of fuel and air which then burns at a lower temperature, thus reducing emissions.
Ref: Powerplant Handbook H-8083-32B-ATB Chapter 3 Page 31

ORAL EXAM

3-1(O). What are some indications of a leak in the induction system?

3-2(O). What are some inspection procedures for ice control systems?

3-3(O). Describe the automatic and manual operation of the alternate air valve.

3-4(O). What can be done to troubleshoot ice control systems?

3-5(O). Explain how a carburetor heat system operates and the procedure to verify proper operation.

3-6(O). What is the cause and effect of one kind of induction system ice?

3-7(O). Explain the function and operation of one type of supercharging.

3-8(O). Name some indicators of an exhaust leak or methods of detecting exhaust leaks.

3-9(O). Explain thrust reverser system operation and some of the main components.

3-10(O). Explain the differences between a cascade and a mechanical blockage door thrust reverser.

3-11(O). What are the hazards of exhaust system failure?

3-12(O). What are the effects of using improper materials to mark on exhaust system components?

3-13(O). What is the function and operation of a turbine engine exhaust nozzle?

INDUCTION AND EXHAUST SYSTEMS

ANSWERS

ORAL EXAM

3-1(O).   Leaks in the induction system can cause an engine to idle improperly, run rough, or overheat. In severe cases, the engine may not start or may cut out. It also could fail to develop full power. A visual inspection for cracks and leaks should occur during all regularly scheduled engine inspections including ensuring the security of mounting of all components.
Ref: Powerplant Handbook H-8083-32B-ATB Chapter 3 and Chapter 10

3-2(O).   Controlling ice in the induction system of a reciprocating aircraft engine is primarily accomplished by raising the temperature of the induction air. This is done with what is known as carburetor heat. The air intake ducting is equipped with a valve controlled from the flight deck. When opened, warm air that has been circulated around the exhaust system is diverted into carburetor. Carburetor heat should only be used when needed. An excessively hot fuel air charge can result in a loss of power, detonation, and engine failure. Therefore, inspection procedures for this ice control system must include the integrity and free motion of this valve and its control cable. It must fully open and fully close to ensure safe operation. Follow the manufacturer's instruction for lubricating the cable and valve hinge.
Ref: Powerplant Handbook H-8083-32B-ATB Chapter 3

3-3(O).   An engine may be fitted with an alternate induction system air inlet that incorporates a dust filter. This type of air filter system normally consists of a filter element and a door that is electrically operated from the flight deck. The pilot opens the door manually with the electric actuator when operating in dusty conditions. Some installations have a spring loaded filter door that automatically opens when the filter is excessively restricted. This prevents the air from being cut off when the filter is clogged with dirt or ice.
Ref: Powerplant Handbook H-8083-32B-ATB Chapter 3

3-4(O).   An ice control system like carburetor heat is very simple and relatively trouble free. Regular inspection of the ducting, valve, and operating mechanism should reveal any operational problems. When the carburetor heat valve is fully opened, it should only be a matter of a few minutes until the ice is cleared. If this is reported as not being the case, then, if application of the heat was timely, it is likely that the valve is not opening all the way. Check the cable and the valve itself for unrestricted movement and full travel. Any report of low power could be the result of the carburetor heat valve not closing fully. Again, inspect the cable and the valve for proper operation.
Ref: Powerplant Handbook H-8083-32B-ATB Chapter 3

3-5(O).   Eliminating ice in the induction system of a reciprocating engine is primarily accomplished by raising the temperature of the induction air. This is done with a carburetor heat system. The air intake ducting is equipped with a valve controlled from the flight deck. When opened, warm air that has been circulated around the exhaust system is diverted into the carburetor. This carburetor heat should only be used when needed. An excessively hot fuel air charge can result in a loss of power, detonation, and engine failure. Therefore inspection procedure for this ice control system must include the integrity and free motion of this valve and its control cable. It must fully open and fully close to ensure safe operation. Follow the manufacturer's instruction for lubricating the cable and valve hinge. If running up the engine on the ground, application of full carburetor heat should be accompanied by a reduction in manifold pressure because the intake air becomes less dense.
Ref: Powerplant Handbook H-8083-32B-ATB Chapter 3

3-6(O).   Fuel evaporation ice is formed because of the decrease in temperature resulting from the evaporation of fuel when it is introduced into the intake airstream at the fuel discharge nozzle. The temperature of the air and components around the evaporating fuel reduces to below freezing and any moisture present becomes ice that settles on the discharge nozzle and nearby structure. This ice builds up and can interfere with fuel flow, affect mixture distribution and lower manifold pressure.
Ref: Powerplant Handbook H-8083-32B-ATB Chapter 3

ORAL EXAM

3-7(O).   A turbosupercharger or turbocharger system functions to increase manifold pressure on a reciprocating engine. It is an externally driven supercharger that compresses the intake air before it is delivered to the fuel metering device. Engine exhaust gases are directed against a turbine that drives an independent impeller mounted on the same shaft. The impeller compresses the intake air and sends it to the fuel metering device. A controller modulates a wastegate valve in the exhaust stream. The amount of gases directed against the turbine is varied by the position of the wastegate. Thus, the amount of intake air compression is controlled which directly affects the power output of the engine.
Ref: Powerplant Handbook H-8083-32B-ATB Chapter 3

3-8(O).   An exhaust leak is indicated by a flat gray or sooty black streak on the pipes near the leak. Misaligned exhaust system pipes or components are an indicator that a leak may exist.
Ref: Powerplant Handbook H-8083-32B-ATB Chapter 3

3-9(O).   Without any adverse effect of the engine, a thrust reverser system prevents continued forward thrust of the engine by not allowing the engine fan and/or exhaust airflow to flow aft. Typically, a mechanical blockage or redirection of the air occurs through the use of hydraulic or pneumatic power. When the thrust lever on the flight deck is moved aft of idle, and the aircraft has weight on wheels, a control valve diverts the power to a motor. Through the use of jackscrews, flex-drives, and gear boxes, the reverser mechanism unlocks and deploys to change the direction of the engine outflow. When the aircraft has slowed, the power lever is moved forward and the thrust reverser mechanism stows.
Ref: Powerplant Handbook H-8083-32B-ATB Chapter 3

3-10(O).   The two types of thrust reverser systems are the mechanical blockage and the aerodynamic blockage systems. The mechanical blockage system places a removable obstruction in the exhaust gas stream. This is usually done rear of the exhaust nozzle. The exhaust gases therefore are mechanically blocked and diverted at a suitable angle in the reverse direction. The obstruction can be cone-shaped, clamshell-like in appearance or a half-sphere. Since it is directly in the path of the hot exhaust gases, the mechanical blockage type thrust reverser must be able to withstand high temperatures. The aerodynamic blockage type of thrust reverser is used on turbofan engines. Since 80 percent of the forward thrust comes from the fan of a turbofan engine, the aerodynamic thrust reverser redirects the fan air to slow the aircraft. Typically, a translating cowl slides aft and as it does so, blocking panels are deployed into the fan airstream. These redirect the air through cascade vanes that further direct the air forward to slow the aircraft. Since the aerodynamic thrust reverser system deflects fan air, it does not have to be particularly resistant to heat.
Ref: Powerplant Handbook H-0083-32B ATB Chapter 3

3-11(O).   Any exhaust system failure should be regarded as a severe hazard. Depending on the location and type of failure, it can result in carbon monoxide poisoning of crew and passengers, partial or complete loss of engine power, or an aircraft fire.
Ref: Powerplant Handbook H-8083-32B-ATB Chapter 3

3-12(O).   Exhaust systems marked with a lead pencils as well as the use of galvanized or zinc-plated tools must be avoided. The lead, zinc, or galvanized mark is absorbed by the metal of the exhaust system when heated. This creates a distinct change in the molecular structure of the metal. This change softens the metal in the area of the mark causing cracks and eventual failure.
Ref: Powerplant Handbook H-8083-32B-ATB Chapter 3

INDUCTION AND EXHAUST SYSTEMS

ORAL EXAM

3-13(O).   A turbine engine exhaust nozzle directs the exhaust gases. While doing so, it aids in the extraction of power from the engine. A converging nozzle will speed up the gases and extract more thrust. A divergent nozzle will slow the gases and reduce thrust. A nozzle can also help straighten the gases when they exit the turbine or reduce turbulence. A turboprop or turboshaft engine extracts most of the energy for rotating a propeller, rotor blades, or driving accessories such as in an APU. The exhaust nozzle on these engines does little more than direct the gases clear of the aircraft structure since no directional thrust is required. They typically use divergent nozzles or tailpipes. Turbofan engines gain 15 to 20 percent of thrust from the exhaust gases. Therefore convergent exhaust nozzles are common on turbofan engines. Unducted turbofans use two nozzles – one for the fan air and one for the engine core exhaust gases. The fan air exhaust nozzle and the engine core cowling combine to direct fan air aft with as little disturbance as possible using a convergent nozzle shape. The engine core exhaust gases also use a convergent nozzle to extract as much thrust from these gases as possible. Note that the length and opening size of an exhaust nozzle are calculated to ensure the correct gas volume, velocity, and pressure at the rear of the engine.
Ref: Powerplant Handbook H-8083-32B-ATB Chapter 3

PRACTICAL EXAM

3-1(P). Given an actual aircraft engine or mockup, inspect an engine ice control system and record your findings. [Level 3]

3-2(P). Given an actual aircraft engine or mockup, inspect the induction manifolds and record your findings. [Level 3]

3-3(P). Given an actual aircraft engine or mockup, appropriate publications, and tooling, repair a defective condition in a carburetor heat box and record maintenance. [Level 3]

3-4(P). Given an actual aircraft engine or mockup, complete an operational check of an engine anti-ice system and record your findings. [Level 3]

3-5(P). Given an actual aircraft engine or mockup, appropriate publications, and tooling, rig a carburetor heat box and record maintenance. [Level 3]

3-6(P). Given an actual aircraft engine or mockup, inspect an induction system and record your findings. [Level 3]

3-7(P). Given an actual aircraft engine or mockup, appropriate publications, and tooling, replace an induction system manifold gasket and record maintenance. [Level 3]

3-8(P). Given an actual aircraft engine or mockup, appropriate publications, and tooling, replace an induction tube and record maintenance. [Level 3]

3-9(P). Given an actual aircraft engine or mockup, appropriate publications, equipment, and supplies service an induction system air filter and record maintenance. [Level 3]

3-10(P). Given an actual aircraft engine or mockup, appropriate publications, required tooling, equipment, and an unknown discrepancy troubleshoot an engine malfunction resulting from a defective induction system and record your findings. [Level 3]

3-11(P). Given an actual aircraft engine or mockup, appropriate publications, required tooling, equipment, and an unknown discrepancy troubleshoot an engine malfunction resulting from a supercharging system and record your findings. [Level 3]

3-12(P). Given an actual aircraft engine or mockup, inspect an exhaust system and record your findings. [Level 3]

3-13(P). Given an actual aircraft engine or mockup, inspect a turbocharger system and record your findings. [Level 3]

3-14(P). Given an actual aircraft engine or mockup, determine if components of the exhaust system are serviceable and record your findings. [Level 2]

3-15(P). Given an actual aircraft engine or mockup and the appropriate publications demonstrate the procedures to accomplish a pressurization check of an exhaust system. [Level 2]

INDUCTION AND EXHAUST SYSTEMS

QUESTIONS

PRACTICAL EXAM

3-16(P). Given an actual aircraft engine or mockup, appropriate publications, and tooling, repair an exhaust system component and record maintenance. [Level 3]

3-17(P). Given an actual aircraft engine or mockup, complete an operational check of an engine exhaust system and record your findings. [Level 3]

3-18(P). Given an actual aircraft engine or mockup, appropriate publications, and tooling, replace an exhaust gasket and record maintenance. [Level 3]

3-19(P). Given an actual aircraft engine or mockup, appropriate publications, and tooling, install an engine exhaust and record maintenance. [Level 3]

3-20(P). Given an actual aircraft engine or mockup, complete an operational check of a turbocharger and waste gate system and record your findings. [Level 3]

3-21(P). Given an actual aircraft engine or mockup, appropriate publications, appropriate testing equipment, if necessary and an unknown discrepancy, troubleshoot a turbine engine thrust reverser system and record your findings. [Level 3]

3-22(P). Given an actual aircraft engine or mockup, appropriate publications, appropriate testing equipment, if necessary and an unknown discrepancy, troubleshoot a turbine engine thrust reverser component and record your findings. [Level 3]

3-23(P). Given an actual aircraft engine or mockup, appropriate publications, and tooling, repair a turbine engine thrust reverser and record maintenance. [Level 3]

3-24(P). Given an actual aircraft engine or mockup, appropriate publications, and tooling, repair a turbine engine thrust reverser component and record maintenance. [Level 3]

ENGINE IGNITION AND ELECTRICAL SYSTEMS

CHAPTER 4

Magneto-ignition Systems, FADEC Systems, Spark Plugs, Timing Devices,
Powerplant Electrical Systems, and Cable Stripping

QUESTIONS

4-1 AM.III.H.K1
In a four-stroke aircraft engine, when does the ignition event take place?
  A. Before the piston reaches TDC on the compression stroke.
  B. At the moment the piston reaches TDC on the compression stroke.
  C. After the piston reaches TDC on the compression stroke.

4-2 AM.III.H.K4
Which of the following are distinct circuits of a high tension magneto?
  A. Magnetic, primary, and secondary
  B. Magnetic, E-gap, and P lead
  C. Primary, P lead, and secondary

4-3 AM.III.H.K8
Which components make up the magnetic system of a magneto?
  A. Pole shoes, the pole shoe extensions, and the primary coil.
  B. Primary and Secondary coils.
  C. Rotating magnet, the pole shoes, the pole shoe extensions, and the coil core.

4-4 AM.III.H.K8
What is the radial location of the two North poles of a four-pole rotating magnet in a high tension magneto? (Figure 4-3)
  A. 180° Apart
  B. 270° Apart
  C. 90° Apart

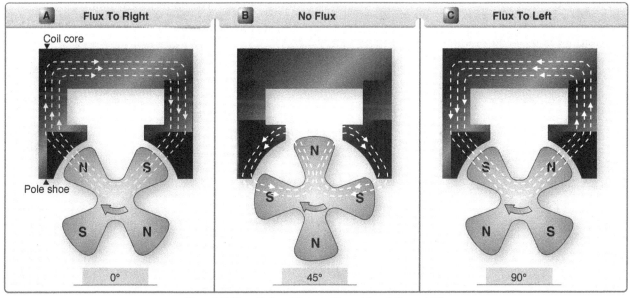

Figure 4-3. Magnetic flux at three positions of the rotating magnet.

ENGINE IGNITION AND ELECTRICAL SYSTEMS

ANSWERS

4-1 Answer A
All ignition systems must deliver a high-tension spark across the electrodes of each spark plug in each cylinder of the engine in the correct firing order. The piston in the No. 1 cylinder must be in a position a prescribed number of degrees before top dead center on the compression stroke.
Ref: Powerplant Handbook H-8083-32B-ATB Chapter 4 Page 1

4-2 Answer A
The high-tension magneto system can be divided for purposes of discussion into three distinct circuits: magnetic, primary electrical, and secondary electrical circuits. The magnetic circuit consists of a permanent multi-pole rotating magnet, a soft iron core, and pole shoes. The primary electrical circuit consists of a set of breaker contact points, a condenser, and the primary windings of the coil. The secondary circuit contains the secondary windings of the coil, distributor rotor, distributor cap or block, ignition leads and spark plugs.
Ref: Powerplant Handbook H-8083-32B-ATB Chapter 4 Page 2

4-3 Answer C
The magnetic circuit consists of a permanent multi-pole rotating magnet, a soft iron core which is called the coil core, and pole shoes which are shaped with extension that protrude to the area when the rotating magnet passes. The primary and secondary coils are separate systems of the magneto which make the other answers incorrect.
Ref: Powerplant Handbook H-8083-32B-ATB Chapter 4 Page 2, Figure 4-3

4-4 Answer A
The poles of the magnet are arranged in alternate polarity so the flux can pass out of the north pole through the coil core and back to the south pole of the magnet. On a 4-pole magnet, this results in the north poles being opposite each other, and the south poles being opposite each other, or radially 180° apart. (See Figure 4-3)
Ref: Powerplant Handbook H-8083-32B-ATB Chapter 4 Page 2

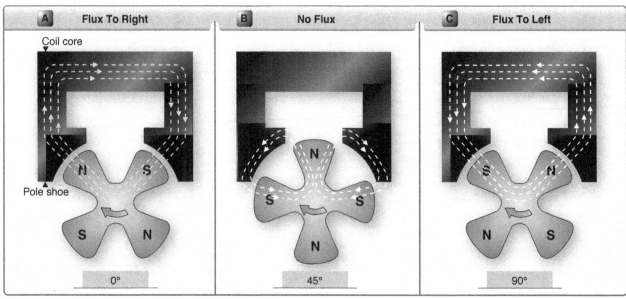

Figure 4-3. Magnetic flux at three positions of the rotating magnet.

4-5 AM.III.H.K8

The greatest density of flux lines in the magnetic circuit of a rotating magnet-type magneto occurs when the magnet is in what position?

A. Full alignment with the field shoe faces.

B. A certain angular displacement beyond the neutral position referred to as E-gap angle or position.

C. The position where the contact points are open.

4-6 AM.III.H.K8

What is the electrical location of the primary capacitor in a high tension magneto? (Figure 4-5)

A. In parallel with the breaker points.

B. In series with the breaker points.

C. In series with the primary and secondary windings.

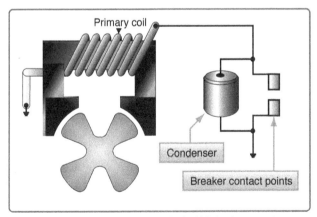

Figure 4-5. Primary electrical circuit of a high-tension magneto.

4-7 AM.III.H.K8

What is the approximate position of the rotating magnet in a high-tension magneto when the points first close?

A. Full register.

B. Neutral.

C. A few degrees after neutral.

4-8 AM.III.H.K8

The E-gap angle is usually defined as the number of degrees be tween the neutral position of the rotating magnet and position

A. where the contact points close.

B. where the contact points open.

C. of greatest magneto flux density.

4-9 AM.III.H.K8

At what point must magneto breaker points be timed to open?

A. When the rotating magnet is a few degrees before neutral.

B. When the greatest magnetic field stress exists in the circuit.

C. When the rotating magnet is in the full register position.

ENGINE IGNITION AND ELECTRICAL SYSTEMS

ANSWERS

4-5 Answer A

When the north pole is aligned with one of the coil core pole shoes and the south pole is aligned with the other coil core pole shoe, the number of magnetic lines of flux through the coil is maximum because the two magnetically opposite poles are perfectly aligned with the pole shoes. This position of the magnet is called the full register position. When the magnet is moved away from the full register position, the amount of flux passing through the coil core begins to decrease because some lines of flux take a shorter route from pole to pole through the pole shoe extensions.
Ref: Powerplant Handbook H-8083-32B-ATB Chapter 4 Page 2, 3

4-6 Answer A

The primary electrical circuit consists of a set of breaker contact points, a condenser (capacitor), and an insulated coil. The capacitor is wired in parallel with the breaker points. The capacitor prevents arcing at the points when the circuit is opened and hastens the collapse of the magnetic field about the primary coil. (Figure 4-5)
Ref: Powerplant Handbook H-8083-32B-ATB Chapter 4 Page 3, Figure 4-5

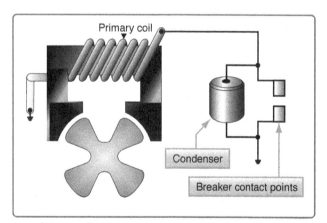

Figure 4-5. Primary electrical circuit of a high-tension magneto.

4-7 Answer A

The primary breaker points close at approximately full register position. When the breaker points are closed, the primary electrical circuit is completed and the rotating magnet induces current flow in the primary circuit. This current flow generates its own magnetic field which is in a direction that opposes any change in the magnetic flux of the permanent magnet's circuit.
Ref: Powerplant Handbook H-8083-32B-ATB Chapter 4 Page 3

4-8 Answer B

The current flowing in the primary circuit holds the flux in the core at a high value in one direction until the rotating magnet has time to rotate through the neutral position to a point a few degrees beyond neutral. This position is called the E-gap position (E stands for efficiency). A very high rate of flux change can be obtained by opening the primary breaker points in this position.
Ref: Powerplant Handbook H-8083-32B-ATB Chapter 4 Page 3

4-9 Answer B

Without current flowing through the primary coil, the flux in the coil core gradually decreases to zero as the magnet rotor turns to neutral and flux starts to increase in the opposite direction. However, it is the rate of change of the flux lines that controls the magnitude of the current flow induced in the coil(s). When the primary coil is added to the magnet and coil core, the electromagnetic action of the primary coil prevents the gradual change in flux in the coil core. It temporarily holds the field in place even though the magnet has rotated past the pole shoe. The breaker points are timed to open when the magnetic field stress is the greatest because it causes the flux field to rapidly collapse thus inducing the greatest amount of voltage in the coils.
Ref: Powerplant Handbook H-8083-32B-ATB Chapter 4 Page 4

4-10 AM.III.H.K4
To which two points are the secondary coil windings of an ignition system connected?
A. Primary coil and distributor cap.
B. Primary coil and distributor rotor.
C. Primary coil and breaker assembly.

4-11 AM.III.H.K1
What is the relationship between the distributor and crankshaft speed of an aircraft reciprocating engines?
A. The distributor turns at one-half crankshaft speed.
B. The distributor turns at one and one half crankshaft speed.
C. The crankshaft turns at one-half distributor speed.

4-12 AM.III.H.K8
The secondary coil of a magneto is grounded through the
A. ignition switch.
B. primary coil.
C. ground side of the breaker points.

4-13 AM.III.H.K1
What is a result of "flash-over" in a distributor?
A. Intense voltage at the spark.
B. Reversal of current flow.
C. Conductive carbon trail.

4-14 AM.III.H.K8
Aircraft magneto housings are usually ventilated in order to
A. prevent the entrance of outside air which may contain moisture.
B. allow heated air from the accessory compartment to keep the internal parts of the magneto dry.
C. provide cooling and remove corrosive gases produced by normal arcing.

4-15 AM.III.H.K2
Shielding is used on spark plug and ignition wires to
A. protect the wires from short circuits as a result of chafing and rubbing.
B. prevent outside electromagnetic emissions from disrupting the operation of the ignition system.
C. prevent interference with radio reception.

ENGINE IGNITION AND ELECTRICAL SYSTEMS

ANSWERS

4-10 Answer B
The secondary circuit consists of turns of fine insulated wire. One end of this wire is electrically grounded to the primary coil or coil core. The other is connected to the distributor rotor. This electrical force then moves to the distributor rotor which is then sent to each point on the cap and onto the appropriate cylinder.
Ref: Powerplant Handbook H-8083-32B-ATB Chapter 4 Page 6

4-11 Answer A
It is the function of the distributor to send a spark to each cylinder in the engine. Therefore it contains the same number of contacts as there are cylinders in the engine. The engine crankshaft, however, must rotate twice to have all of the cylinders travel to TDC on the compression stroke in order to combust the fuel air mixture. Therefore, the distributor rotates at one-half of the crankshaft speed so that each cylinder receives a spark in one revolution of the distributor during two revolutions of the crankshaft.
Ref: Powerplant Handbook H-8083-32B-ATB Chapter 4 Page 6

4-12 Answer B
The secondary circuit contains the secondary windings of the coil, distributor rotor, cap, ignition lead and spark plug. It is made up of windings of fine insulated wire, one end of which is electrically grounded to the primary coil and the other end connected to the distributor.
Ref: Powerplant Handbook H-8083-32B-ATB Chapter 4 Page 5

4-13 Answer C
The high-voltage current that normally arcs across the air gaps of the distributor can flash across a wet insulating surface to ground, or the high-voltage current can be misdirected to some spark plug other than the one that should be fired. This condition is known as flash-over and usually results in cylinder misfiring. Flash-over can lead to carbon tracking. The carbon trail results from the electric spark burning dirt particles that contain hydrocarbon materials. The water in the hydrocarbon material is evaporated during flash-over leaving carbon to form a conductive path for current.
Ref: Powerplant Handbook H-8083-32B-ATB Chapter 4 Page 7

4-14 Answer C
Magnetos cannot be hermetically sealed to prevent moisture from entering a unit because the magneto is subject to pressure and temperature changes in altitude. Adequate drains and proper ventilation reduce the tendency of flash-over and carbon tracking. Good magneto circulation also ensures that corrosive gases produced by normal arcing across the distributor gap, such as ozone, are carried away.
Ref: Powerplant Handbook H-8083-32B-ATB Chapter 4 Page 7

4-15 Answer C
The ignition harness leads serve a dual purpose. It provides the conductor path for the high-tension voltage to the spark plug. It also serves as a shield for stray magnetic fields that surround the wires as they momentarily carry high-voltage current. By conducting these magnetic lines of force to ground, the ignition harness cuts down electrical interference with the aircraft radio and other electrically sensitive equipment.
Ref: Powerplant Handbook H-8083-32B-ATB Chapter 4 Page 7

4-16 AM.III.H.K1

How does the high tension ignition shielding tend to reduce radio interference?

A. Prevents ignition flash-over at high altitudes.

B. Reduces voltage drop in the transmission of high-tension current.

C. Receives and grounds high frequency waves coming from the magneto and high-tension ignition leads.

4-17 AM.III.H.K1

To which two points are an ignition switch connected?

A. Primary electrical circuit and ground.

B. Secondary electrical circuit and ground.

C. Secondary electrical circuit and the condenser.

4-18 AM.III.H.K8

What component of a dual magneto is shared by both ignition systems?

A. High-Tension Coil

B. Rotating Magnet

C. Capacitor

4-19 AM.III.H.K3

When a "shower of sparks" ignition system is activated at an engine start, a spark plug fires

A. as soon as the advance breaker point opens.

B. while both the retard and advance breaker points are closed.

C. while both the retard and advance breaker points are open.

4-20 AM.III.F.K5

What is the primary consideration when selecting the voltage output (14 or 28 volts) of a DC generator?

A. The power requirements of the aircraft.

B. The number of electrical devices on the aircraft.

C. The voltage of the battery installed on the aircraft.

4-21 AM.III.H.K6

Which statement is true regarding the coil packs of a FADEC Powerlink ignition system?

A. Low voltage coils are mounted above the Electronic Control Unit (ECU).

B. High voltage units are triggered from the crankshaft position.

C. An individual coil for each spark plug is located on each cylinder head.

ENGINE IGNITION AND ELECTRICAL SYSTEMS

ANSWERS

4-16 Answer C
A magneto is a high frequency radiation emanating (radio wave) device during its operation. If the magneto and ignition leads are not shielded, they would form antennas and transmit the random frequencies from the ignition system. By conducting the magnetic lines of flux associated with the high frequencies to ground, ignition harness and magneto radio interference are reduced.
Ref: Powerplant Handbook H-8083-32B-ATB Chapter 4 Page 7

4-17 Answer A
The type of ignition switch used varies with the number of engines on the aircraft and the type of magnetos used. All switches, however, turn the system ON and OFF in much the same manner. The ignition switch is different in at least one respect from all other type of switches: when the ignition switch is in the OFF position, a circuit is completed through the switch to ground. In other switches, the OFF position normally breaks or opens the circuit.
Ref: Powerplant Handbook H-8083-32B-ATB Chapter 4 Page 9

4-18 Answer B
High-tension system magnetos used on aircraft engines are either single or dual type magnetos. The dual magneto incorporates two magnetos contained in a single housing. One rotating magnet and a cam are common to two sets of breaker points and coils. Two distributor units are mounted in the magneto.
Ref: Powerplant Handbook H-8083-32B-ATB Chapter 4 Page 10

4-19 Answer C
The action of an electrically operated vibrator rapidly opening and closing causes the current flowing through the primary coil to interrupt several times per second, in turn causing the magnetic field surrounding the primary coil to build and collapse at the same rate. This succession of voltages induced into the secondary coil produces a "shower of sparks" across a selected spark plug when both breaker points are open.
Ref: Powerplant Handbook H-8083-32B-ATB Chapter 4 Pages 17

4-20 Answer C
The aircraft's generator voltage depends on which battery is selected for that aircraft. Batteries are either 12 or 24 volts when fully charged. The generator selected must have a voltage output slightly higher than the battery voltage; thus 14 or 28 volts.
Ref: Powerplant Handbook H-8083-32B-ATB Chapter 4 Page 13

4-21 Answer B
The PowerLink ignition system of a reciprocating engine FADEC unit consists of the high voltage coils atop of the ECU, the high voltage harness, and spark plugs. One end of each ignition lead on the high voltage harness attaches to a spark plug and the other end of the lead wire attaches to the spark plug towers on each ECU. Each coil pack generates a high-voltage pulse for two spark plug towers. The ignition spark is timed to the engine's crankshaft position. The timing is variable throughout the engine's operating range.
Ref: Powerplant Handbook H-8083-32B-ATB Chapter 4 Page 14

4-22 AM.III.H.K1

A booster coil on a radial engine
- A. uses battery power to boost the magnet in the magneto during starting.
- B. uses three coils windings to achieve a hotter spark for starting than the magneto.
- C. operates off of battery power and a trailing finger in the distributor.

4-23 AM.III.H.K3

What is the purpose of an impulse coupling with a magneto?
- A. To absorb impulse vibrations between the magneto and the engine.
- B. To compensate for backlash in the magneto and the engine gears.
- C. To produce a momentary high rotational speed of the magneto.

4-24 AM.III.H.K3

In a light reciprocating engine aircraft a retard breaker magneto eliminates the need for a(n) _____ when starting.
- A. condenser
- B. impulse coupling
- C. vibrator

4-25 AM.III.D.K8

An EICAS system contains an upper and lower display screen. For which of these functions, would you consult the lower screen?
- A. Exhaust gas temperature
- B. Fuel temperature
- C. Operating advisories

4-26 AM.III.H.K2

A spark plug's heat range is the result of
- A. the area of the plug exposed to the cooling airstream.
- B. its ability to transfer heat from the firing end of the spark plug to the cylinder head.
- C. the heat intensity of the spark.

4-27 AM.III.H.K2

The term reach as applied to spark plug design and/or type indicates the (Figure 4-35)
- A. linear distance from the shell gasket seat to the end of the threads on the shell skirt.
- B. length of the center electrode exposed to the flame of combustion.
- C. length of the shielded barrel.

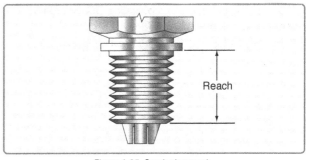

Figure 4-35. Spark plug reach.

ENGINE IGNITION AND ELECTRICAL SYSTEMS

ANSWERS

4-22 Answer C
The booster coil is separate from the magneto and can generate a series of sparks on its own. During the start cycle, these sparks are routed to the trailing finger on the distributor rotor and then to the appropriate cylinder ignition lead. The primary winding has one end grounded at the internal grounding strip and its other end connected to the moving contact point. The stationary contact is fitted with a terminal to which battery voltage is applied when the magneto switch is placed in the start position, or automatically applied when the starter is engaged.
Ref: Powerplant Handbook H-8083-32B-ATB Chapter 4 Page 18

4-23 Answer C
Many opposed engines are equipped with an impulse coupling as the auxiliary starting system. An impulse coupling gives one of the magnetos attached to the engine, generally the left, a brief acceleration that produces a more intense spark for engine starting. Without an impulse coupling or other starting aid, the intensity of magneto spark magneto sparks produced during start is low because of the slow rotation speed of the engine and, therefore, the magneto.
Ref: Powerplant Handbook H-8083-32B-ATB Chapter 4 Page 17

4-24 Answer B
During the start cycle, the spark must be both strong and occur earlier as the piston just reaches top dead center (retarded). This is basically the function of an impulse coupling. A high tension retard breaker vibrator serves this need without the inherent problems of an impulse coupling by providing multiple sparks during this cycle by changing the DC from the battery into a pulsating DC through a vibrator coil to the primary coil.
Ref: Powerplant Handbook H-8083-32B-ATB Chapter 4 Page 21

4-25 Answer B
EICAS provides full time primary engine parameters (EPR, N1, EGT) on the top, primary monitor. Advisories and warnings are also shown there. Secondary engine parameters and non-engine system status are displayed on the bottom screen. The lower screen is also used for maintenance diagnosis when the aircraft is on the ground.
Ref: Powerplant Handbook H-8083-32B-ATB Chapter 4 Page 17

4-26 Answer B
The heat range of a spark plug is a measure of its ability to transfer the heat of combustion to the cylinder head. The length of the nose core is the principle factor in establishing the plug's heat range. Hot plugs have a long insulator nose that creates a long heat transfer path; cold plugs have a relatively short insulator to provide a rapid transfer of heat to the cylinder head.
Ref: Powerplant Handbook H-8083-32B-ATB Chapter 4 Page 24

4-27 Answer A
A spark plug with the proper reach ensures that the electrode end inside the cylinder is in the best position to achieve ignition. The spark plug reach is the length of the threaded portion that is inserted in the spark plug bushing of the cylinder. (Figure 4-35)
Ref: Powerplant Handbook H-8083-32B-ATB Chapter 4 Page 25, Figure 4-36

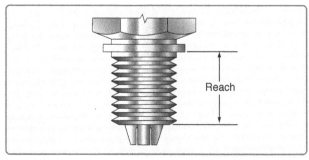

Figure 4-35. Spark plug reach.

4-28 AM.III.H.K8
When installing a magneto on an engine, the
- A. piston in the No. 1 cylinder must be a prescribed number of degrees before top center on the compression stroke.
- B. magneto breaker points must be just closing.
- C. piston in the No. 1 cylinder must be a prescribed number of degrees after top center on the intake stroke.

4-29 AM.III.H.K1
What tool is generally used to measure the crankshaft rotation in degrees?
- A. Dial Indicator
- B. Timing Disk
- C. Prop Protractor

4-30 AM.III.H.K8
When internally timing a magneto, the breaker points begin to open when
- A. the piston has just past TDC at the end of the compression stroke.
- B. the magnet poles are a few degrees beyond the neutral position.
- C. the magnet poles are fully aligned with the pole shoes.

4-31 AM.III.H.K8
In what position should the ignition switch be placed when attempting to use a timing light to time the magneto to the engine?
- A. OFF
- B. Left
- C. Both

4-32 AM.III.H.K8
If the ignition switch is moved from BOTH to either LEFT or RIGHT during an engine ground check, normal operation is usually indicated by a
- A. large drop in RPM.
- B. momentary interruption of both ignition systems.
- C. slight drop in RPM.

4-33 AM.III.H.K8
When a magneto is operating, what is the probable cause for a shift in internal timing?
- A. The rotating magnet loses its magnetism.
- B. The distributor gear teeth are wearing on the rotor gear teeth.
- C. The cam follower wear and/or the breaker points wear or pitting.

ENGINE IGNITION AND ELECTRICAL SYSTEMS

ANSWERS

4-28 Answer A
The ignition timing requires precise adjustment and painstaking care so that the following four conditions occur at the same instant: 1. The piston in the No. 1 cylinder must be in a position a prescribed number of degrees before top dead center on the compression stroke. 2. The rotating magnet of the magneto must be in the E-gap position. 3. The beaker points must be just opening on the No. 1 cam lobe, and, 4. The distributor finger must be aligned with the electrode serving the No. 1 cylinder.
Ref: Powerplant Handbook H-8083-32B-ATB Chapter 4 Page 26

4-29 Answer B
Most timing disk devices are mounted to the crankshaft flange and use a timing plate. The markings vary according to the specifications of the engine. This plate is temporarily installed on the crankshaft flange with a scale numbered in crankshaft degrees and the pointer attached to the timing disk.
Ref: Powerplant Handbook H-8083-32B-ATB Chapter 4 Page 27

4-30 Answer B
When replacing or preparing a magneto for installation, the first concern is with the internal timing of the magneto. For each magneto model, the manufacturer determines how many degrees beyond the neutral position a pole of the rotor magnet should be to obtain the strongest spark at the instant of breaker point separation. This angular displacement from the neutral position, known as the E-gap angle, varies with different magneto models.
Ref: Powerplant Handbook H-8083-32B-ATB Chapter 4 Page 29

4-31 Answer C
When using a timing light to check a magneto in a complete ignition system installed on the aircraft, the ignition switch for the engine must be turned to BOTH. Otherwise, the lights do not indicate when the breaker points will open. In the OFF position, the primary circuit will be grounded so current will flow to ground not through the points or to the timing light. In the LEFT or RIGHT position of the ignition switch, one or the other of the left or right breaker points will be grounded so only one light will illuminate when the breaker points open.
Ref: Powerplant Handbook H-8083-32B-ATB Chapter 4 Page 28

4-32 Answer C
The ignition system has checks performed on it during the aircraft engine run-up before flight. At a manufacturer specified RPM, the ignition switch is moved from the BOTH position to the LEFT position. The drop in RPM is noted and the switch is returned to the BOTH position. After the engine RPM stabilizes, the switch is moved to the RIGHT position and the RPM drop is noted. The magneto drop should be even for both magnetos and is generally slight, in the area of 25-75 RPM for each magneto. This RPM drop is because operation on one magneto is not as efficient as it is with two magnetos providing sparks in the cylinder.
Ref: Powerplant Handbook H-8083-32B-ATB Chapter 4 Page 31

4-33 Answer C
Buildup results from the transfer of contact material by means of the arc as the point separate. This condition may result from excessive breaker point spring tension that retards the opening of the points.
Ref: Powerplant Handbook H-8083-32B-ATB Chapter 4 Page 29

ENGINE IGNITION AND ELECTRICAL SYSTEMS

QUESTIONS

4-34 AM.III.H.K2
A spark plug is fouled when
   A. its spark grounds by jumping electrodes.
   B. it causes preignition.
   C. its spark grounds without jumping electrodes.

4-35 AM.III.H.K2
Upon inspection of the spark plugs in an aircraft engine, the plugs were found caked with a heavy black soot. This indicates
   A. worn oil seal rings.
   B. a rich mixture.
   C. a lean mixture.

4-36 AM.III.H.K2
Spark plug fouling caused by lead deposits occurs most often
   A. during cruise with rich mixtures.
   B. when cylinder head temperatures are relatively low.
   C. when cylinder head temperature are relatively high.

4-37 AM.III.H.K2
What will be the effect of a spark plug that is gapped too wide?
   A. Insulation Failure
   B. Hard Starting
   C. Lead Damage

4-38 AM.III.H.K2
Which is the likely cause if when removing a spark plug a high amount of torque is required to remove it from a cylinder?
   A. Warpage may have occurred to overly hot operations.
   B. Corrosion may have formed within the spark plug threads.
   C. Excess carbon may have resulted by overly rich operation.

4-39 AM.III.H.K2
To obtain the correct gap setting on a spark plug before it is installed in an aircraft engine
   A. a feeler gauge must be used.
   B. a wire thickness gauge should be used.
   C. a sight gauge is recommended.

ENGINE IGNITION AND ELECTRICAL SYSTEMS

ANSWERS

4-34 Answer C
Spark plug operation can often be a major source of engine malfunctions. Many spark plug failures can be minimized by good operational and maintenance practices. A spark plug is considered to be "fouled" if it has stopped allowing the spark to bridge the electrode gap either completely or intermittently.
Ref: Powerplant Handbook H-8083-32B-ATB Chapter 4 Page 33

4-35 Answer B
A rich fuel/air mixture is detected by soot or black smoke coming from the exhaust and by an increase in RPM when idling fuel/air mixture is leaned to best power. The soot that forms as a result of overly rich idle fuel/air mixture settles on the inside of the combustion chamber because the heat of the engine and turbulence in the combustion chamber are slight. The heavy black soot on the spark plug is known as carbon fouling.
Ref: Powerplant Handbook H-8083-32B-ATB Chapter 4 Page 33

4-36 Answer B
Lead fouling may occur at any power setting but perhaps the power setting most conducive to lead fouling is cruising with lean mixtures. At this power, the cylinder head temperature is relatively low and there is more oxygen than needed to consume all the fuel in the fuel air mixture. When all of the fuel is consumed, some of the excess oxygen unites with some of the lead in the fuel and forms lead/oxygen compounds that solidify and build up in layers as they contact the relatively cool cylinder walls and the spark plugs.
Ref: Powerplant Handbook H-8083-32B-ATB Chapter 4 Page 34

4-37 Answer B
As the air gap of a spark plug increases, the resistance that the spark plug must overcome in jumping the gap also increases. This means that the magneto must produce a higher voltage to overcome the higher resistance. Wide spark plug gap settings raise the coming in speed of the magneto and therefore cause hard starting.
Ref: Powerplant Handbook H-8083-32B-ATB Chapter 4 Page 35

4-38 Answer C
If excess carbon deposits have occurred as byproducts of an overly rich combustion, some of those deposits may have worked their way into the threads of the cylinder head and spark plug, and so requiring excess torque for its removal. This is typically not a problem for the spark plug so long as the wrench is held straight and torque evenly applied.
Ref: Powerplant Handbook H-8083-32B-ATB Chapter 4 Page 35

4-39 Answer B
Spark plug electrode gap setting should be checked with a round wire-thickness gauge. A flat type gauge gives an incorrect clearance indication because the massive ground electrodes are contoured to the shape of the round center electrode. When using a wire-thickness gauge, insert the gauge in each gap parallel to the centerline of the center electrode. If the gauge is tilted slightly, the indication is incorrect. Do not install a plug that does not have an air gap within the specified clearance range.
Ref: Powerplant Handbook H-8083-32B-ATB Chapter 4 Page 38

4-40 AM.III.H.K2

Aircraft engine spark plugs should be installed
A. in the exact same position as they were in the engine when removed.
B. finger tight and torqued with a torque wrench.
C. be installed finger tight and then 1/4 rotation farther to crush the copper shoulder gasket for a gas tight fit.

4-43 AM.III.H.K8

What is commonly used to clean accessible condensers and coil cases in a magneto?
A. Acetone
B. MEK
C. Mineral Spirits

4-41 AM.III.H.K8

What would be the result if a magneto breaker point mainspring did not have sufficient tension?
A. The points will stick.
B. The points will not open to the specified gap.
C. The points will float or bounce.

4-44 AM.III.H.K9

Which statement is correct regarding the ignition system of a turbine engine?
A. The system is normally de-energized as soon as the engine starts.
B. It is energized during starting and warm-up periods only.
C. The system generally includes a polar inductor-type magneto.

4-42 AM.III.H.K1

Which of the following breaker points characteristics is associated with a faulty capacitor?
A. Crowned
B. Fine Grained
C. Coarse Grained

4-45 AM.III.H.K9

The capacitor type ignition system is used almost universally on turbine engines primarily because of its high voltage and
A. low amperage.
B. long life.
C. high heat intensity spark.

ENGINE IGNITION AND ELECTRICAL SYSTEMS

ANSWERS

4-40 Answer B
To install a spark plug, start it into the cylinder without using a wrench of any kind and turn it until the spark plug is seated on the gasket. If high torque is needed to install the plug, dirty or damaged threads on either the plug or plug bushing is indicated. This should be remedied before installing the plug. After a spark plug has been seated with the fingers, use a torque wrench and tighten to the specified torque.
Ref: Powerplant Handbook H-8083-32B-ATB Chapter 4 Page 38

4-41 Answer C
If the breaker contact points are spread wider than recommended, the mainspring (the spring carrying the movable contact point) is likely to take a permanent set. If the mainspring takes a permanent set, the movable contact point loses some of its closing tension and the points then either bounce or float, preventing the normal induction buildup of the magneto.
Ref: Powerplant Handbook H-8083-32B-ATB Chapter 4 Page 39

4-42 Answer C
The condition caused by a faulty capacitor or an opened circuit capacitor is easily recognized by the coarse, crystalline surface and the black "sooty" appearance of the sides of the points. The lack of effective condenser action results in an arc of intense heat being formed each time the points open. This, together with the oxygen in the air, rapidly oxidizes and erodes the platinum surface of the points, producing a coarse, crystalline, or frosted appearance.
Ref: Powerplant Handbook H-8083-32B-ATB Chapter 4 Page 40

4-43 Answer A
A phase of magneto inspection is the dielectric inspection. This inspection is a visual check for cleanliness and cracks. If the inspection reveals that the coil cases, condensers, distributor rotor, or blocks are oily or dirty or have any trace of carbon tracking, they require cleaning and possibly waxing to restore their dielectric qualities. Clean all accessible condensers and coil cases by wiping them with a lint-free cloth moistened with acetone. Do not dip, submerge, or saturate the parts in any solution because the solution used may seep inside the condenser and short out the plates.
Ref: Powerplant Handbook H-8083-32B-ATB Chapter 4 Page 38

4-44 Answer A
Since turbine engine ignition systems are operated mostly for a brief period during the engine starting cycle, they are, as a rule, more trouble free than the typical reciprocating engine ignition system. The turbine engine ignition system does not need to be timed to spark during an exact point in the operational cycle. It is used to ignite the fuel in the combustor and then it is switched off.
Ref: Powerplant Handbook H-8083-32B-ATB Chapter 4 Page 43

4-45 Answer C
The fuel in turbine engines can be ignited readily in ideal atmospheric conditions but, since they often operate in the low temperature of high altitudes, it is imperative that the system be capable of supplying a high heat intensity spark.
Ref: Powerplant Handbook H-8083-32B-ATB Chapter 4 Page 44

4-46 AM.III.H.K9

The type of ignition system used on most turbine aircraft engines is
- A. high resistance.
- B. low tension.
- C. capacitor discharge.

4-47 AM.III.H.K9

Why are turbine engine igniter's less susceptible to fouling than reciprocating engine spark plugs?
- A. The high intensity spark cleans the igniter.
- B. The frequency of the spark is less for igniter's.
- C. Turbine igniter's operate at cooler temperatures.

4-48 AM.III.H.K9

Which of the following are included in a turbine engine exciter unit?
1. Two Igniter Plugs
2. Two Transformers
3. Two Storage Capacitors
- A. 1, 2, and 3
- B. 2, and 3 only
- C. 3, only

4-49 AM.III.H.K7

For safety purposes, to eliminate the possibility of the technician receiving a lethal shock; when removing a turbine engine igniter plug, what is done in addition to turning off the ignition switch?
- A. The ignition switch is disconnected from the power circuit.
- B. Disconnect the low voltage lead from the exciter, then wait 1 minute before disconnecting the high voltage lead.
- C. Disconnect the high voltage lead from the exciter, then wait 1 minute before removing the igniter.

4-50 AM.III.F.K7

Which electrical wire size gauge number offers the least amount of heat produced with a given voltage per length of conductor?
- A. #1 gauge wire.
- B. #00 gauge wire.
- C. #40 gauge wire.

4-51 AM.III.F.K7

In which circumstance would aluminum be a preferred conductor in an aircraft environment?
- A. When the intensity of corona is a concern.
- B. When the wire will be subject to increased vibration.
- C. When soldered connections are used.

ENGINE IGNITION AND ELECTRICAL SYSTEMS

ANSWERS

4-46 Answer C
Most gas turbine engines are equipped with a high energy, capacitor-type ignition system and are cooled by fan airflow. Some gas turbine engines may be equipped with an electronic-type ignition system, which is a variation of the simpler capacitor type system.
Ref: Powerplant Handbook H-8083-32B-ATB Chapter 4 Page 44

4-47 Answer A
The employment of a high-frequency triggering transformer, with a low-reactance secondary winding, holds the time duration of the discharge for the igniter spark to a minimum. The concentration of maximum energy in minimum time achieves an optimum spark across the igniter electrodes capable of blasting carbon deposits. The spark is of great heat intensity which burns away any foreign deposits on the electrodes. Thus, electrode fouling is minimized by the heat of the high intensity spark.
Ref: Powerplant Handbook H-8083-32B-ATB Chapter 4 Page 45

4-48 Answer B
Typical turbine engine ignition systems vary in construction but most include a dual ignition exciter unit which prepares electricity for the igniter plug. The energy is stored in the capacitors inside the unit. Each discharge circuit incorporates two storage capacitors. The voltage across the capacitors is stepped up by transformer units. The exciter is a dual unit that produces sparks at each of the two igniter plugs. The igniter plugs are located in the combustion section of the engine.
Ref: Powerplant Handbook H-8083-32B-ATB Chapter 4 Page 44

4-49 Answer B
First disconnect the low voltage lead. With it disconnected, energy stored in the ignitor will dissipate in about 1 minute. It is then safe to handle the high voltage components of the igniter.
Ref: Powerplant Handbook H-8083-32B-ATB Chapter 4 Page 46

4-50 Answer B
Wire gauge numbers range from #0000 being the largest to #40 being the smallest. The greater diameter the conductor, the least electrical resistance it offers and so the least amount of heat produced and so the least amount of voltage drop in a comparable length.
Ref: Powerplant Handbook H-8083-32B-ATB Chapter 4 Page 48

4-51 Answer A
Comparing aluminum to copper wiring; aluminum reduces corona for a given degree of conductivity, has greater discharge to a given gauge, is lighter, and cheaper. Copper offers greater conductivity, is more ductile, has a higher tensile strength and is more easily soldered.
Ref: Powerplant Handbook H-8083-32B-ATB Chapter 4 Page 50

ENGINE IGNITION AND ELECTRICAL SYSTEMS

QUESTIONS

4-52 AM.III.F.K10
In general, the two most common materials for conductors in aircraft applications are
  A. copper and silver.
  B. nickel and aluminum.
  C. copper and aluminum.

4-54 AM.III.F.K10
In a 28 volt system, what is the maximum continuous current that can be carried by a single No. 10 copper wire 25 feet long, routed in free air? Refer to the graph Figure 4-79.
  A. 20 Amperes
  B. 30 Amperes
  C. 40 Amperes

4-53 AM.III.F.K10
The resistance of the current return path through the aircraft is always considered negligible, provided the
  A. voltage drop across the circuit is checked.
  B. generator is properly grounded.
  C. structure is adequately bonded.

4-55 AM.III.F.K7
What is primarily signified by the codes printed on wires?
  A. Its schematic identification number.
  B. The manufacturer and its wire type.
  C. Its maximum allowable voltage.

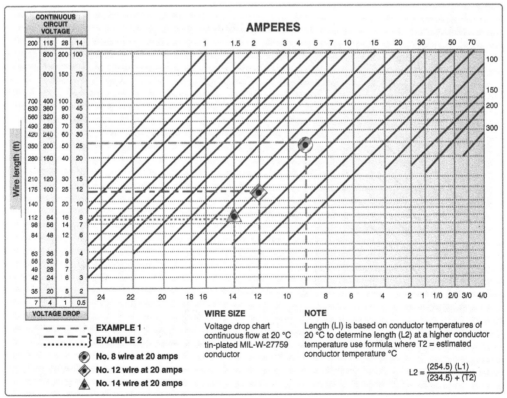

Figure 4-79. Conductor graph—continuous flow.

ENGINE IGNITION AND ELECTRICAL SYSTEMS

ANSWERS

4-52 Answer C

Although silver is the best conductor, its cost limits its use to special circuits where a substance with high conductivity is required. The two most generally used conductors are copper and aluminum. Each has advantages and disadvantages. Copper has higher conductivity per cross sectional area, is more ductile, can be drawn out, has relatively high tensile strength, can be easily soldered, and has fewer issues with corrosion. However, it is more expensive than aluminum. Pound for pound, aluminum is a better conductor and its use can save weight on an aircraft. larger diameters used to match conductivity also reduce corona. However, aluminum is prone to high resistance connections due to its natural tendency to form a protective oxide coating which requires more attention to details when crimping or bonding.
Ref: Powerplant Handbook H-8083-32B-ATB Chapter 4 Page 50

4-53 Answer C

The resistance of the current path through the aircraft may not be negligible if the aircraft is not properly bonded. A resistance measurement of 1.5 ohms from ground point of the generator or battery to ground terminal of any electrical device is considered acceptable.
Ref: Powerplant Handbook H-8083-32B-ATB Chapter 4 Page 50

4-54 Answer B

In the table on the left side of the illustration, find the column that represents 28 volts. This becomes the vertical scale for the graph on the right side of the illustration. The vertical scale is the length of the wire to be used so locate 25 on the vertical scale and follow that across the graph until it intersects with the vertical line drawn upward from wire size No. 10 found on the horizontal scale of the graph. The two intersect on a diagonal red line which represents the amount of amps able to be carried with a 1 volt drop (30 amps). Note: be sure you are referencing the correct chart for continuous versus intermittent current flow when making calculations using this kind of graph. (Figure 4-79)
Ref: Powerplant Handbook H-8083-32B-ATB Chapter 4 Page 56, Figure 4-79

4-55 Answer A

In order to identify a complete single wire, identification numbers are typically printed near its ends and then every 15 inches along its length. These letters and numbers provide easy identification of a wire relative to others within its bundle or as it needs to be attached to a connector.
Ref: Powerplant Handbook H-8083-32B-ATB Chapter 4 Page 53

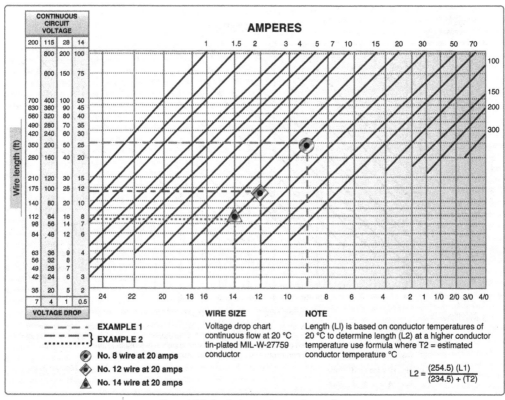

Figure 4-79. Conductor graph—continuous flow.

4-56 AM.III.F.K7

What is the purpose of installing a rubber grommet when passing a wire bundle through a bulkhead?

- A. Provide electrical insulation.
- B. Protection from chafing.
- C. Facilitate directional changes.

4-59 AM.III.F.K10

Splicing of individual aircraft electrical wires (Figure 4-86)

- A. must be staggered so that the bundle does not become excessively large.
- B. is allowed but the splice must be located within 12" of the wire end.
- C. is not allowed.

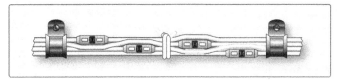

Figure 4-86. Staggered splices in wire bundle.

4-57 AM.III.F.K10

When installing electrical wiring parallel to a fuel line, the wiring should be

- A. in metal conduit.
- B. in a non-conductive fire-resistant sleeve.
- C. above the fuel line.

4-60 AM.III.F.K10

When using hand crimped wire terminals,

- A. copper is preferred and should be used on aluminum or copper wires.
- B. only aluminum terminals should be used on aluminum wire.
- C. aluminum is preferred and should be used on aluminum or copper wires.

4-58 AM.III.F.K10

Aircraft wire groups or bundles should be tied where supports are more than 12 inches apart using

- A. nylon tie-wraps.
- B. Teflon® tie-wraps.
- C. waxed cotton cord, nylon cord, or fiberglass cord.

4-61 AM.III.F.K10

A damaged aluminum wire

- A. must be fully replaced.
- B. may be temporarily repaired with a crimped splice.
- C. may be temporarily repaired by soldering.

ENGINE IGNITION AND ELECTRICAL SYSTEMS

ANSWERS

4-56 Answer B
Wires and wire groups should be installed so they are protected against chafing or abrasion in locations where contact with sharp objects are possible. When passing through a bulkhead, if wires come closer than 1/4" to the edge of the hole, a suitable grommet is used in the hole.
Ref: Powerplant Handbook H-8083-32B-ATB Chapter 4 Page 53

4-57 Answer C
When wiring must be routed parallel to combustible fluid or oxygen lines for short distances, as much separation as possible should be maintained. The wires should be on a level with or above the plumbing lines. Clamps should be spaced so that, if a wire is broke at a clamp, it will not contact the fluid line.
Ref: Powerplant Handbook H-8083-32B-ATB Chapter 4 Page 57

4-58 Answer C
All wire groups or bundles should be tied where supports are more than 12 inches apart. Ties are made using waxed cotton cord, nylon cord, or fiberglass cord. Some manufacturers permit the use of pressure-sensitive vinyl electrical tape. When permitted, the tape should be wrapped around the bundle and the ends heat sealed to prevent unwinding of the tape. Whether lacing or tying, bundles should be secured tightly enough to prevent slipping but not so tightly that the cord cuts into or deforms the insulation.
Ref: Powerplant Handbook H-8083-32B-ATB Chapter 4 Page 59

4-59 Answer A
Splicing of aircraft cable should be kept to a minimum and avoided entirely in locations subject to extreme vibrations. Individual wires in a group or bundle can usually be spliced if the completed splice is where it can be inspected periodically. The splices should be staggered so that the bundle does not become excessively large. (Figure 4-86)
Ref: Powerplant Handbook H-8083-32B-ATB Chapter 4 Page 54, Figure 4-86

4-60 Answer B
Aluminum wire is being used increasingly in aircraft systems because of its weight advantage over copper. However, bending aluminum causes work hardening of the metal making it brittle. Only aluminum terminals should be used on aluminum wire. To counter the formation of aluminum oxide, aluminum terminal lugs are filled with petrolatum-zinc dust compound. This removes the oxide film from the aluminum by a grinding process during the crimping operation.
Ref: Powerplant Handbook H-8083-32B-ATB Chapter 4 Page 62

4-61 Answer A
Broken copper wires can be temporarily repaired by means of a crimped splices or by soldering. However, this repair should be considered as temporary only and should be replaced with a permanent repair as soon as possible. Damaged aluminum wires may never be temporarily spliced. However, always check the manufacturer's instructions, as some manufacturers prohibit splicing in all circumstances.
Ref: Powerplant Handbook H-8083-32B-ATB Chapter 4 Page 63

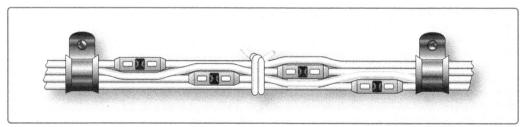

Figure 4-86. Staggered splices in wire bundle.

4-62 AM.III.F.K10

Terminal lugs

  A. are too small to be torqued with a torque wrench and must be finger tight plus 1/4 turn.

  B. cannot be aluminum if used with on a copper terminal block.

  C. should be installed so they are locked against movement in the direction of loosening.

4-63 AM.III.F.K10

Bonding jumpers should be designed and installed in such a manner that they

  A. are not subject to flexing by relative motion of airframe or engine components.

  B. provide a low electrical resistance in the ground circuit.

  C. prevent build-up of a static electrical charge between the airframe and the surrounding atmosphere.

4-64 AM.III.F.K10

In order to reduce the possibility of ground shorting the circuits when the connectors are separated for maintenance, the AN and MA electrical connectors should be installed with the

  A. socket section on the ground side of the electrical circuit.

  B. pin section on the ground side of the electrical circuit.

  C. pin section on the positive side of the electrical circuit.

4-65 AM.III.F.K8

When more than one generator is used in parallel, the total rated output

  A. can be 100% of a single generator.

  B. must be 80% of both generator outputs combined.

  C. is the combined output of both generators.

4-66 AM.III.F.K10

Automatic reset circuit breakers

  A. reduce the load on the pilot.

  B. reset themselves periodically and should not be used on aircraft.

  C. reset after the initial surge of current has passed.

4-67 AM.III.F.K10

When installing a conventional aircraft electrical switch, for which application should a switch which is derated from its nominal current rating?

  A. DC motor circuits.

  B. Capacitive circuits

  C. Conductive circuits.

ENGINE IGNITION AND ELECTRICAL SYSTEMS

ANSWERS

4-62 Answer C
Terminal lugs should be installed on terminal blocks in such a manner that they are locked against movement in the direction of loosening. Aluminum and copper lugs can be used on the same block as long as washers of the specified material are installed between each. As a general rule, use a torque wrench to tighten nuts to ensure sufficient contact pressure. Manufacturer's instructions provide installation torques for all types of terminals.
Ref: Powerplant Handbook H-8083-32B-ATB Chapter 4 Page 64

4-63 Answer B
Bonding is the electrical connecting of two or more conducting objects not otherwise connected adequately. Bonding jumpers should be made as short as practicable and installed so that the resistance of each connection does not exceed 1.3 ohm. The jumper should not interfere with the operation of movable aircraft elements, such as surface controls; normal movement of these elements should not result in damage to the bonding jumper.
Ref: Powerplant Handbook H-8083-32B-ATB Chapter 4 Page 65

4-64 Answer B
Connectors (plugs and receptacles) facilitate maintenance when frequent disconnection is required. When replacing connector assemblies, the socket-type insert should be used on the half of the connector that is "live" or "hot" which means that the pin section of the connector should be on the ground side of the circuit. Thus, after the connector is disconnected, unintentional grounding will not occur if an exposed pin of the connector touches a conductive surface.
Ref: Powerplant Handbook H-8083-32B-ATB Chapter 4 Page 69

4-65 Answer C
When more than one generator is used in parallel, the total rated output is the combined output of the installed generators. The results in the requirement for quickly coping with sudden overloads which could be caused by a generator failure when the total connected system load exceeds the rated output of one generator. A quick load-reduction system can be employed or a specified procedure must be followed for reducing the total load to a quantity that is less than the rated output of the remaining functional generators.
Ref: Powerplant Handbook H-8083-32B-ATB Chapter 4 Page 70

4-66 Answer B
All resettable circuit breakers should open the circuit in which they are installed when an overload or circuit fault exists. This should occur regardless of the position of the operating control. This is known as a "trip-free" circuit breaker. This means one cannot hold the control switch in the ON position and obtain current flow if there is something wrong in the circuit. Automatic reset circuit breakers automatically reset themselves periodically. They should not be used as circuit protection devices in aircraft.
Ref: Powerplant Handbook H-8083-32B-ATB Chapter 4 Page 70

4-67 Answer C
The nominal current rating of the conventional aircraft switch is usually stamped on the switch housing. This rating represents the continuous current rating with the contacts closed. Switches should be derated from their nominal current rating for high rush-in circuits such as incandescent lamp circuits. Inductive circuits, which release magnetic energy when the switch is opened, should employ derated switches as should DC motor circuits. Motors draw several times their rated current during starting. Magnetic energy stored in the armature and field coils is released when the control switch is opened.
Ref: Powerplant Handbook H-8083-32B-ATB Chapter 4 Page 71

ORAL EXAM

4-1(O).   If the ignition switch is place in the OFF position but the aircraft engine continues to run, what is the probable cause of the problem?

4-2(O).   During an engine run-up magneto check, what is the range of RPM drop considered to be normal when the mag switch is placed in the LEFT or RIGHT position?

4-3(O).   A reciprocating engine either fails to start, fails to idle properly, or has low power and runs unevenly. All of these conditions could be caused by what common defective ignition system part(s)?

4-4(O).   What can be done to verify if a turbine engine igniter is firing?

4-5(O).   What precautions need to be taken when removing an igniter plug from an engine?

4-6(O).   What is the purpose of checking the "P" lead for a proper ground?

4-7(O).   What are two types of spark plug fouling and what causes each?

4-8(O).   What are the components in the primary electrical circuit of a magneto?

4-9(O).   What is "E" gap?

4-10(O).   How is the p-lead circuit related to the production of a spark in a magneto?

4-11(O).   What is the difference between a low-tension and a high-tension ignition system?

4-12(O).   What is the procedure for locating the correct electrical cable/wire size needed to fabricate a replacement cable/wire?

4-13(O).   What are some installation practices for wires running close to exhaust stacks or heating ducts?

4-14(O).   What procedures must be adhered to when operating electrical system components.

ENGINE IGNITION AND ELECTRICAL SYSTEMS

ANSWERS

ORAL EXAM

4-1(O). The "P" lead is not grounded.
Ref: Powerplant Handbook H-8083-32B-ATB Chapter 4

4-2(O). 25-75 RPM.
Ref: Powerplant Handbook H-8083-32B-ATB Chapter 4

4-3(O). Defective or improperly gapped spark plugs.
Ref: Powerplant Handbook H-8083-32B-ATB Chapter 4

4-4(O). The igniter can be heard snapping while rotating the engine or the igniter can be removed from the engine and the spark can be observed while activating the start cycle.
Ref: Powerplant Handbook H-8083-32B-ATB Chapter 4

4-5(O). The low voltage lead to the exciter box should be disconnected and wait one minute (minimum) before removing the ignition lead from the plug.
Ref: Powerplant Handbook H-8083-32B-ATB Chapter 4

4-6(O). A grounded "P" lead disables the ignition and the magneto will not fire. An ungrounded "P" lead results in the ignition being "hot" and movement of the propeller could cause the engine to start.
Ref: Powerplant Handbook H-8083-32B-ATB Chapter 4

4-7(O). Carbon fouling – fuel/air mixtures too rich to burn or extremely lean.
Oil fouling – oil past the rings and valve guides into the cylinder.
Lead fouling – when using leaded fuel, lead oxide forms during combustion when cylinder temperature is low.
Graphite fouling – excessive application of anti-seize compound on spark plug threads.
Ref: Powerplant Handbook H-8083-32B-ATB Chapter 4

4-8(O). The breaker contact points, a condenser, and an insulated coil.
Ref: Powerplant Handbook H-8083-32B-ATB Chapter 4

4-9(O). The rotational position of a permanent magnet a few degrees past the neutral position where the breaker points are opened.
Ref: Powerplant Handbook H-8083-32B-ATB Chapter 4

4-10(O). Current is induced in the p-lead circuit by a rotating magnet. This creates a magnetic field. When the breaker points open the p-lead circuit, the field collapses across the secondary coil windings. This produces a high-voltage current that is directed to the spark plug to jump the electrode gap.
Ref: Powerplant Handbook H-8083-32B-ATB Chapter 4

4-11(O). The low-tension ignition system creates a low-voltage that is distributed to a transformer coil near each spark plug where it is changed to high voltage to fire the plug. A high-tension ignition system uses a secondary coil inside the magneto to create the high voltage which is distributed to every spark plug.
Ref: Powerplant Handbook H-8083-32B-ATB Chapter 4

4-12(O). Wire size considerations take into account allowable power loss, permissible voltage drop, and the current carrying capability of the conductor. Allowance must also be made for the influence of external heating on the wire. Replacement wire can be the same wire as the original wire. Wire can be measured with a wire gauge. It can also be found by consulting a table produced by the American Wire Gauge if the circuit load information is known. Additionally, wires often contain identification markings. Consulting the manufacturer's data can reveal exactly which wire is required by deciphering the markings which are typically coded.
Ref: Powerplant Handbook H-8083-32B-ATB Chapter 4

ORAL EXAM

4-13(O). If possible, wires should be kept separate from high-temperature equipment. When wires must be run through hot areas, the wires must be insulated with high-temperature rated material such as asbestos, fiberglass or Teflon®. Running coaxial cables through hot area should be avoided. To guard against abrasion, asbestos wires should be in a conduit lined with a high temperature rubber liner or they can be individually enclosed in high temperature plastic tubes before being installed in the conduit.
Ref: Powerplant Handbook H-8083-32B-ATB Chapter 4

4-14(O). The maximum load from the operation of electrical equipment should not exceed the rated limits of the wiring or protection devices. If loads can exceed the output limits of the alternator or generator, the load should be reduced so that an overload does not occur. If a battery is part of the electrical power system, it should be continuously charged in flight except for momentary intermittent heavy loads such as the operation of a landing gear motor or flaps, etc. Placards should be used to alert flight crews concerning operations that may cause an overload. The total continuous load should be held to 80% of the rated generator or alternator output when assurance is needed that the battery power source is being charged in flight. When two generators are in use, a specified procedure for quick load-reduction should be employed if, for whatever reason, only one generator is functioning and the load must be reduced to that which the single generator can handle without overload.
Ref: Powerplant Handbook H-8083-32B-ATB Chapter 4

ENGINE IGNITION AND ELECTRICAL SYSTEMS

PRACTICAL EXAM

4-1(P).   Given an actual aircraft engine or mockup, appropriate publications, and tooling, flash a generator field. [Level 3]

4-2(P).   Given an actual aircraft engine or mockup, appropriate publications, and tooling install an engine driven generator or alternator and record maintenance. [Level 3]

4-3(P).   Given an engine electrical wiring schematic and an unknown discrepancy, explain the schematic's layout and symbols and demonstrate how it can be used to troubleshoot for the cause of the discrepancy. [Level 2]

4-4(P).   Given an actual aircraft engine or mockup, appropriate publications, and tooling install a tachometer generator and record maintenance. [Level 3]

4-5(P).   Given an actual aircraft engine or mockup, appropriate publications, materials, and tooling fabricate an electrical system cable. [Level 3]

4-6(P).   Given an actual aircraft engine or mockup, appropriate publications, materials, and tooling repair damaged engine electrical system wire and record maintenance. [Level 3]

4-7(P).   Given an actual aircraft engine or mockup, appropriate publications, materials, and tooling replace and check a current limiter and record maintenance. [Level 3]

4-8(P).   Given an actual aircraft engine or mockup, appropriate publications, materials, and tooling complete a functional or operational check of one or more specified engine electrical system components and record maintenance. [Level 3]

4-9(P).   Given an actual aircraft engine or mockup, appropriate publications, materials, and tooling service one or more specified engine electrical system components and record maintenance. [Level 3]

4-10(P).   Given an actual aircraft engine or mockup, appropriate publications, materials, and tooling complete an adjustment on one or more specified engine electrical system components and record maintenance. [Level 3]

4-11(P).   Given an actual aircraft engine or mockup, appropriate publications, required tooling, equipment, and an unknown discrepancy troubleshoot an engine electrical system component and record your findings. [Level 3]

4-12(P).   Given an actual aircraft engine or mockup, appropriate publications, and tooling inspect a turbine engine ignition system for proper installation and record your findings. [Level 3]

4-13(P).   Given an actual aircraft engine or mockup, appropriate publications, and tooling inspect a starter/generator for proper installation and record your findings. [Level 3]

4-14(P).   Given an actual aircraft engine or mockup, appropriate publications, and tooling inspect magneto points and record your findings. [Level 3]

PRACTICAL EXAM

4-15(P). Given an actual aircraft engine or mockup, appropriate publications, and tooling perform a functional check of the engine timing and record maintenance. [Level 3]

4-16(P). Given an actual aircraft engine or mockup, appropriate publications, and tooling perform an operational check of a magneto switch and record maintenance. [Level 3]

4-17(P). Given an actual aircraft engine or mockup, appropriate publications, and tooling install a magneto, set the timing and record maintenance. [Level 3]

4-18(P). Given an actual aircraft engine or mockup, appropriate publications, materials, and tooling, repair an engine starter system and record maintenance. [Level 3]

4-19(P). Given an actual aircraft engine or mockup, appropriate publications, materials, and tooling, repair an engine ignition system and record maintenance. [Level 3]

4-20(P). Given an actual aircraft engine or mockup, appropriate publications, materials, and tooling, complete the following: remove and inspect turbine engine igniter plugs and record findings, install turbine engine igniter plugs, perform a functional check of the igniter system, and record maintenance. [Level 3]

4-21(P). Given an actual aircraft engine or mockup, appropriate publications, materials, and tooling, inspect generator or starter-generator brushes and record findings. [Level 3]

4-22(P). Given an actual aircraft engine or mockup, appropriate publications, and tooling install brushes in a starter or starter-generator and record maintenance. [Level 3]

4-23(P). Given an actual aircraft engine or mockup, appropriate publications, and tooling install breaker points in a magneto, internally time the magneto, and record maintenance. [Level 3]

4-24(P). Given an actual aircraft engine or mockup, appropriate publications, materials, and tooling, repair an engine direct drive electric starter and record maintenance. [Level 3]

4-25(P). Given an ignition harness with a high-tension lead tester, appropriate publications, materials, equipment, and tooling, inspect and test the harness and record your findings. [Level 3]

4-26(P). Given an aircraft spark plug(s), appropriate publications, materials, equipment, and tooling, inspect them and record your findings. [Level 3]

4-27(P). Given an aircraft spark plug(s), appropriate publications, materials, equipment, and tooling, service and install them and record maintenance. [Level 3]

4-28(P). Given an ignition system component, appropriate publications, materials, and tooling, bench test the component and record your findings. [Level 2]

PAGE LEFT BLANK INTENTIONALLY

QUESTIONS

5-1 AM.III.H.K7
In older reciprocating aircraft inertia starting systems, energy for cranking the engine is stored in the
A. flywheel.
B. battery.
C. generator.

5-4 AM.III.H.K7
What assists the starter jaw in retracting after the starter motor is disengaged on a typical direct cranking reciprocating engine starter?
A. Centrifugal Force
B. Return Spring
C. Oil Pressure

5-2 AM.III.H.K7
What type of electric motor is used with a direct-cranking engine starter?
A. Direct current shunt-wound motor.
B. Direct current series-wound motor.
C. Synchronous motor.

5-5 AM.III.H.K7
Reciprocating engine starters
A. are capable of continuous cranking for up to five minutes.
B. have starting limits which restrict continuous cranking to one minute.
C. use a two minute ON, two minute OFF cranking cycle.

5-3 AM.III.H.K7
The starter gear section on the typical direct cranking starter used for starting a large reciprocating aircraft engine
A. converts the low starter motor speed into low torque to crank the engine.
B. uses oil pressure to engage and disengage with the flywheel.
C. uses a sun and planetary gear reduction system to transfer the energy of the starter motor to the engine flywheel.

5-6 AM.III.H.K7
In automatic starting systems on small reciprocating engine aircraft,
A. a starter solenoid is energized to allow current to flow to the starter motor.
B. current flows through the ignition switch directly to the starter.
C. starter current passes through the induction vibrator to ensure a hot spark is available before cranking.

ENGINE STARTING SYSTEMS

ANSWERS

5-1 Answer A
In the inertia starter, energy is stored slowly during an energizing process by a manual hand crank or electrically with a small motor. During the energizing of the starter, all movable parts within it, including the flywheel, are set in motion. When the starter is engaged, or meshed, flywheel energy is transferred to the engine through sets of reduction gears and a torque overload release clutch.
Ref: Powerplant Handbook H-8083-32B-ATB Chapter 5 Page 1

5-2 Answer B
The most widely used starting system on all types of reciprocating engines utilizes the direct cranking electric starter. The direct cranking electric starter consists of an electric motor, reduction gears, and an automatic engaging and disengaging mechanism. The typical starter motor is a 12 or 24-volt, series-wound motor that develops high starting torque.
Ref: Powerplant Handbook H-8083-32B-ATB Chapter 5 Page 2, 3

5-3 Answer C
The starter gear section consists of an external housing with an integral mounting flange, planetary gear reduction, a sun and integral gear assembly, a torque-limiting clutch, and a jaw and cone assembly. The torque developed in the starter motor is transmitted to the starter jaw through the reduction gear train and clutch. The starter gear train converts the high speed low torque of the motor to the low speed high torque required to crank the engine. A sun gear drives three planetary gears which transmit torque to the starter jaw.
Ref: Powerplant Handbook H-8083-32B-ATB Chapter 5 Page 3, 4

5-4 Answer B
When the engine starts, the rapidly moving engine jaw teeth (of the starter ring gear), striking the slower moving starter jaw teeth hold the starter jaw disengaged. As soon as the starter comes to rest, the engaging force is removed and the small return spring throws the starter jaw into its fully retracted position where it remains until the next start.
Ref: Powerplant Handbook H-8083-32B-ATB Chapter 5 Page 5

5-5 Answer B
All starting systems have operating time limits because of the high energy used during cranking or rotating the engine. These limits are referred to as starting limits and must be observed or overheating and damage to the starter occurs. After energizing the starter for 1 minute, it should be allowed to cool for at least one minute. After a second or subsequent cranking period of one minute, it should cool for five minutes.
Ref: Powerplant Handbook H-8083-32B-ATB Chapter 5 Page 6

5-6 Answer A
A small aircraft automatic starting systems, or remote solenoid engaged starting system, employs an electric starter mounted on an engine adapter. A starter solenoid is activated by either a push- button or by turning the ignition key on the instrument panel. When the solenoid is activated, its contacts close and electrical energy energizes the starter motor. Initial rotation of the starter motor engages the starter to the engine via the starter adapter and reduction gears.
Ref: Powerplant Handbook H-8083-32B-ATB Chapter 5 Page 6

5-7 AM.III.H.K7

If a starter commutator on a reciprocating engine is found with a glazed surface
   A. the contacting surface should be cleaned with sandpaper.
   B. the contacting surfaces should be cleaned with an approved solvent.
   C. the commutator should be replaced.

5-8 AM.III.H.K7

What is used to polish commutators or slip rings?
   A. Very fine sandpaper.
   B. Crocus cloth or fine oilstone.
   C. Aluminum oxide or garnet paper.

5-9 AM.III.H.K9

What is the purpose of the second set of windings in a turbine engine starter-generator?
   A. As a backup for the primary winding.
   B. One winding is for starting, the second is for generator applications.
   C. To add additional torque for starting.

5-10 AM.III.H.K3

The purpose of the undercurrent relay in a starter-generator system is to
   A. provide back-up for the starter relay.
   B. disconnect power from the starter-generator and ignition when sufficient engine speed is reached.
   C. keep current flow to the starter-generator under the circuit capacity maximum.

5-11 AM.III.F.K3

In a turbine engine starter-generator system, in which circumstance may it be necessary to use the stop/start switch?
   A. Hung Start
   B. Hot Start
   C. Defective Undercurrent Relay

5-12 AM.III.H.K7

At which point does the drive coupling of a turbine engine air starter stop turning?
   A. When the sprag clutch disengages.
   B. When the starter reaches its overrun speed.
   C. When the engine is shut down.

ENGINE STARTING SYSTEMS

ANSWERS

5-7 Answer A
A glazed or dirty starter commutator can be cleaned with a strip of double-0 sandpaper or a brush seating stone. Do not use Emery cloth or a carbon based sandpaper, as this could cause electrical shorting.
Ref: Powerplant Handbook H-8083-32B-ATB Chapter 5 Page 6, 7

5-8 Answer A
A glazed or dirty starter commutator can be cleaned by holding a strip of double 0 sandpaper or a brush seating stone against the commutators as it is turned. The sandpaper or stone should be moved back and forth across the commutators to avoid wearing a groove. Emery paper and carborundum should never be used for this purpose because of their possible shorting action.
Ref: Powerplant Handbook H-8083-32B-ATB Chapter 5 Page 7

5-9 Answer B
The starter-generator is a shunt generator with an additional C field winding. During normal generation, a shunt winding, compensating wing and commutating windings are used. For starting a C field winding is engaged and the shunt winding disengaged as it serves no practical use.
Ref: Powerplant Handbook H-8083-32B-ATB Chapter 5 Page 10

5-10 Answer B
In a starter-generator system, as the starter motor builds up speed, the current draw of the starter decreases. As it decreases to less than 200 amps, the undercurrent relay opens. This action breaks the circuit from the positive bus to the coils of the motor, ignition and battery cutout relays. The de-energizing of these relay coils halts the start operation.
Ref: Powerplant Handbook H-8083-32B-ATB Chapter 5 Page 11

5-11 Answer A
On a normal start on an engine with a starter-generator system, once the starter speed reaches a speed due to the engine having started, the undercurrent relay opens and the starter (and ignition) is taken off line. The engine should be operating efficiently and ignition should be self sustaining. If the engine fails to reach sufficient speed to halt starter operation (hung start), the start-stop switch can be used to break the circuit from the positive battery bus to the main circuit of the undercurrent relay.
Ref: Powerplant Handbook H-8083-32B-ATB Chapter 5 Page 12

5-12 Answer C
When an air starter reaches its overrun speed, the sprag clutch allows the gear train to coast to a halt. However, the output shaft and drive coupling continue to turn for as long as the engine is running.
Ref: Powerplant Handbook H-8083-32B-ATB Chapter 5 Page 12, 14

5-13 AM.III.H.K1

(Refer to Figure 5-1) With power applied to the bus bar, what wire supplies standby power to the starter relay contact?

A. 4
B. 7
C. 8

5-14 AM.III.H.K1

(Refer to Figure 5-1) When an external power source is connected to the aircraft,

A. the battery can not be connected to the bus.
B. both battery and external power are available to the bus.
C. the starter relay has a path to ground.

5-15 M.III.H.K7

Airflow to the pneumatic starter from a ground unit is normally prevented from causing starter over speed during engine start by

A. stator nozzle design which stabilizes the turbine wheel speed.
B. a rotor actuator switch.
C. a preset times cutout of the airflow at the source.

5-16 AM.III.H.K7

Air turbine starters are generally designed so that reduction gear distress or damage may be detected by

A. characteristic sounds from the starter assembly during start.
B. breakage of a shear section on the starter drive.
C. inspection of a magnetic chip detector.

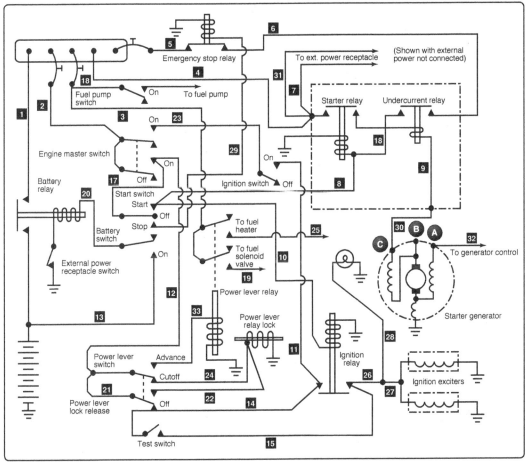

Figure 5-1. Starter-generator circuit.

ENGINE STARTING SYSTEMS

ANSWERS

5-13 Answer A
The powered bus bar is connected to the contactor of the starter relay with wire #4 and so allowing current to flow through the relay when it is activated.
Ref: Powerplant Handbook H-8083-32B-ATB Chapter 5 Page 10

5-15 Answer B
When the starter reaches overrun speed, a rotor actuator switch mounted in the turbine rotor opens the turbine switch. Opening the turbine switch closes the start valve and shuts the air supply to the starter hub.
Ref: Powerplant Handbook H-8083-32B-ATB Chapter 5 Page 13

5-14 Answer A
The system shown can not be operated by both battery power or external power at the same time. To prevent both sources from supplying power simultaneously, an external power switch is placed just past the battery solenoid coil which cuts off power from the battery solenoid and battery power from the bus when the external power is plugged in.
Ref: Powerplant Handbook H-8083-32B-ATB Chapter 5 Page 10

5-16 Answer C
Normal maintenance for air turbine starters includes checking the oil level, inspecting the magnetic chip detector for metal particles and checking for leaks.
Ref: Powerplant Handbook H-8083-32B-ATB Chapter 5 Page 13

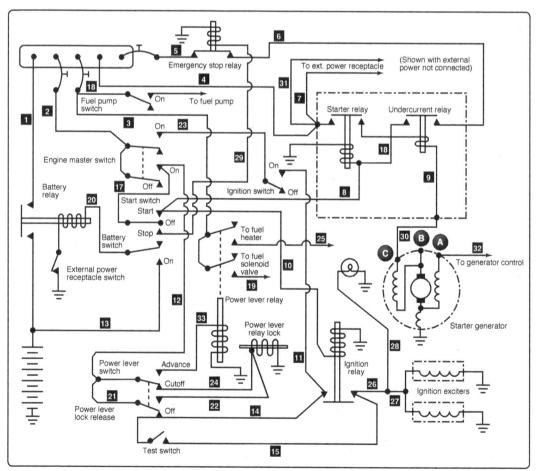

Figure 5-1. Starter-generator circuit.

5-17 AM.III.H.K7
Which is the basic component of pneumatic starter?
A. An axial flow turbine.
B. A centrifugal flow compressor.
C. Dual rotor turbine.

5-19 AM.III.H.K7
Inspection of pneumatic starters by maintenance technicians usually includes checking the
A. oil level and magnetic drain plug condition.
B. stator and rotor blades for FOD.
C. rotor alignment.

5-18 AM.III.H.K7
Pneumatic starters contain a turbine which is driven by air and rotates the reduction gear train through a sprag clutch. The clutch is
A. manually engaged and automatically disengaged.
B. automatically engaged and manually disengaged.
C. automatically engaged and automatically disengaged.

5-20 AM.III.H.K7
On many turbine powered aircraft, the start valve works in conjunction with what other valve to supply the correct flow of air to the pneumatic starter?
A. Starter outflow valve.
B. Bleed air backflow regulator valve.
C. Pressure-regulating and shutoff valve.

ENGINE STARTING SYSTEMS

ANSWERS

5-17 Answer A
The typical air turbine starter consists of an axial flow turbine that turns a drive coupling through a reduction gear train and a starter clutch mechanism. The air to operate the starter is supplied from either a ground source or an onboard source (i.e., APU, bleed air from another engine). Only one source of 30-50 psi air is used at a time to start the engine. The starter is operated by introducing air into the starter inlet. The air passes into the starter turbine housing where it is directed against the axial flow turbine blades causing the starter to rotate.
Ref: Powerplant Handbook H-8083-32B-ATB Chapter 5 Page 12

5-19 Answer A
Normal maintenance for air turbine starters includes checking the oil level, inspecting the magnetic chip detector, and checking for leaks. The starter housing incorporates a sight gauge that is used to check the oil quantity. A magnetic drain plug in the transmission drain opening attracts any ferrous particles that may be in the oil. The starter uses turbine oil, the same as the engine, but starter oil does not circulate through the engine.
Ref: Powerplant Handbook H-8083-32B-ATB Chapter 5 Page 13

5-18 Answer C
As the rotor of a pneumatic clutch turns, it drives the reduction gears and carrier, sprag clutch assembly, output shaft assembly, and drive coupling. The sprag clutch assembly engages automatically as soon as the rotor starts to turn but disengages as soon as the drive coupling turns more rapidly than the rotor side of the starter. When the starter reaches this overrun speed, the action of the sprag clutch allows the gear train to coast to a halt.
Ref: Powerplant Handbook H-8083-32B-ATB Chapter 5 Page 12

5-20 Answer C
The starting air path is directed through a combination Pressure-Regulating and Shutoff Valve (PRSOV) that controls all duct pressure flowing to the starter inlet ducting. This valve regulates the pressure of the starter operating air and shuts off the supply of operating air when required. Downstream of the PRSOV, the start valve, usually mounted at the inlet to the starter, opens and closes to control the airflow into the starter.
Ref: Powerplant Handbook H-8083-32B-ATB Chapter 5 Page 14

ORAL EXAM

5-1(O).   Name two possible causes of a starter motor that drags.

5-2(O).   Name two starter maintenance procedures to keep a starter in proper operational condition.

5-3(O).   What is the purpose for the undercurrent relay in a starter-generator circuit?

5-4(O).   What are the sources of air for a pneumatic starter as used on a gas turbine engine?

5-5(O).   Why is an air turbine starter cut out after engine self-accelerating speed?

5-6(O).   Explain the inspection and replacement criterion for brushes on a starter-generator.

5-7(O).   Explain the operation of a turbine engine starter-generator.

ENGINE STARTING SYSTEMS

ANSWERS

ORAL EXAM

5-1(O). Low battery, starter switch or relay controls burned or dirty, defective starter, and inadequate brush spring tension.
Ref: Powerplant Handbook H-8083-32B-ATB Chapter 5

5-2(O). Replacing brushes and brush springs, surfacing or turning down the commutator, checking the security of the mounting bolts, ensuring the drive gear and the flywheel ring gear are in good condition, and checking the electrical connection for security and corrosion.
Ref: Powerplant Handbook H-8083-32B-ATB Chapter 5

5-3(O). To open the circuit causing current flow to the motor for its use as a starter so that it can be used as a generator.
Ref: Powerplant Handbook H-8083-32B-ATB Chapter 5

5-4(O). A ground operated cart, an APU, or cross-bleed from a running engine on the aircraft.
Ref: Powerplant Handbook H-8083-32B-ATB Chapter 5

5-5(O). To prevent overspeed since the engine turns at a higher RPM.
Ref: Powerplant Handbook H-8083-32B-ATB Chapter 5

5-6(O). Inspection of starter-generator bushes and brush springs is standard starting system maintenance. Typically, brushes are replaced when worn to approximately one-half the original length. Brush spring tension should be sufficient to give brushes a good, firm contact with the commutator. The brush leads should also be inspected to ensure that they are unbroken and that the lead terminal connection is tight.
Ref: Powerplant Handbook H-8083-32B-ATB Chapter 5

5-7(O). A starter-generator is a shunt generator with an additional heavy series winding. This series winding is electrically connected to produce a strong field and results in high torque for starting. The starter-generator is engaged with the engine at all times. The two-in-one configuration saves both space and weight. To engage the starter, the master switch must first be closed. Then, closing the battery and start switch energizes the starter portion of the unit through an undercurrent relay. As the motor builds up speed, the current draw or the motor begins to decrease. As it decreases to less than 200 amps, the undercurrent relay opens and thus the circuit from the positive bus to the series winding of the starter motor is interrupted. This halts the start operation and the shut generator comes on line.
Ref: Powerplant Handbook H-8083-32B-ATB Chapter 5

PRACTICAL EXAM

5-1(P).   Given an actual aircraft engine or mockup, appropriate publications, and tooling inspect a starter for proper installation and record findings. [Level 3]

5-2(P).   Given an actual aircraft engine or mockup, appropriate publications, materials, and tooling, repair an engine starter system and record maintenance. [Level 3]

5-3(P).   Given an actual aircraft engine or mockup, appropriate publications, and tooling inspect a starter-generator and record findings. [Level 3]

5-4(P).   Given an actual aircraft engine or mockup, appropriate publications, and tooling install brushes in a starter and record maintenance. [Level 3]

5-5(P).   Given an actual aircraft engine or mockup, appropriate publications, and tooling install brushes in a starter-generator and record maintenance. [Level 3]

5-6(P).   Given an actual aircraft engine or mockup, appropriate publications, materials, and tooling, repair an engine direct drive electric starter and record maintenance. [Level 3]

PAGE LEFT BLANK INTENTIONALLY

LUBRICATING AND COOLING

Reciprocating Engine Lubrication Systems, Lubrication System Maintenance,
Changing Oil and Turbine Engine Lubricants

CHAPTER 6

QUESTIONS

6-1 AM.III.G.K1
To be most useful as a preservative oil for long term storage,
which should be one characteristic of that oil?
  A. Low Viscosity
  B. High Viscosity
  C. High Pour Point

6-4 AM.III.G.K1
If the flash point of an aviation oil is too low, during
operations at elevated temperatures, it will
  A. produce flammable vapors.
  B. ignite.
  C. lose its minimum viscosity.

6-2 AM.III.G.K2
What is the source of most of the heat that is absorbed by
the lubricating oil in a reciprocating engine?
  A. Crankshaft and main bearings
  B. Exhaust valves
  C. Pistons and cylinder walls

6-5 AM.III.G.K1
Which of the following factors helps determine the proper
grade of oil to use in a particular engine?
  A. Adequate lubrication in various attitudes of flight.
  B. Positive introduction of oil to the bearings.
  C. Operating speeds of bearings.

6-3 AM.III.G.K1
The viscosity of a liquid is a measure of its
  A. resistance to flow.
  B. rate of change of internal friction with change
     in temperature.
  C. weight, or density.

6-6 AM.III.G.K1
Upon what quality or characteristic of a lubricating oil is its
viscosity index based?
  A. Its resistance to flow at a standard temperature
     as compared to high grade paraffin-base oil at the
     same temperature.
  B. Its rate of change in viscosity with temperature change.
  C. Its rate of flow through an orifice at a standard temperature.

LUBRICATING AND COOLING

ANSWERS

6-1 Answer B
Oil prevents corrosion in the interior of an engine by leaving a coating of oil on the engine parts when it is shut down. An oil with a high viscosity will flow off those surfaces slower and so provide and increased time it can hold off corrosion.
Ref: Powerplant Handbook H-8083-32B-ATB Chapter 6 Page 2

6-2 Answer C
As oil circulates through the engine, it absorbs heat from the pistons and cylinder walls. In reciprocating engines, these components are especially dependent on the oil for cooling. Crankshafts and main bearings are not exposed to the high temperature of the combustion chamber. Exhaust valves have no significant contact with the oil in a reciprocating engine.
Ref: Powerplant Handbook H-8083-32B-ATB Chapter 6 Page 1

6-3 Answer A
While there are several important properties that satisfactory reciprocating engine oil must possess, its viscosity is most important in engine operation. The resistance of an oil to flow is known as viscosity. Oil that flows slowly is viscous or has high viscosity; if it flows freely, the oil has low viscosity.
Ref: Powerplant Handbook H-8083-32B-ATB Chapter 6 Page 2

6-4 Answer A
At its flash point, the oil begins to emit ignitable vapors. Those vapors are then capable of flashing and supporting a fire.
Ref: Powerplant Handbook H-8083-32B-ATB Chapter 6 Page 3

6-5 Answer C
Several factors must be considered in determining the proper grade of oil to use in a particular engine, the most important of which are the operating load, rotational speeds, and operating temperatures. The grade of the lubricating oil to be used is determined by the operating conditions to be met in the various types of engines.
Ref: Powerplant Handbook H-8083-32B-ATB Chapter 6 Page 2

6-6 Answer B
The viscosity index is a number that indicates the effect of temperature changes on the viscosity of the oil. When oil has a low viscosity index, it signifies a relatively large change of viscosity across temperature variations. The oil becomes thin at high temperatures and thick at low temperatures. Oils with a high viscosity index have small changes in viscosity over a wide temperature index. The best oil for most purposes is one that maintains a constant viscosity throughout temperature changes (high viscosity index).
Ref: Powerplant Handbook H-8083-32B-ATB Chapter 6 Page 2

6-7 AM.III.G.K1
Specific gravity is a comparison of the weight of a substance to the weight of an equal volume of
  A. oil at a specific temperature.
  B. distilled water at a specific temperature.
  C. mercury at a specific temperature.

6-8 AM.III.G.K1
What type of oil do most engine manufacturers recommend for new reciprocating engine break-in?
  A. Ashless-dispersant oil.
  B. Straight mineral oil.
  C. Semi-synthetic oil.

6-9 AM.III.G.K1
What type of oil do most engine manufacturers recommend after new reciprocating engine break-in?
  A. Metallic ash detergent oil.
  B. Ashless-dispersant oil.
  C. Straight mineral oil.

6-10 AM.III.G.K2
If an oil filter element becomes completely clogged, the
  A. oil flow to the engine will be restricted.
  B. oil will be bypassed back to the oil tank.
  C. the oil pump will supply unfiltered oil.

6-11 AM.III.G.K2
An oil tank having a capacity of 5 gallons, must have an expansion space of
  A. 2 quarts.
  B. 4 quarts.
  C. 5 quarts.

6-12 AM.III.G.K2
In order to maintain a constant oil pressure as the clearances between the moving parts of an engine increase through normal wear, the supply pump output
  A. increases as the resistance offered to the flow of oil increases with more oil being returned to the pump inlet by the relief valve.
  B. remains relatively constant at a given rpm with less oil being returned to the pump inlet by the relief valve.
  C. remains relatively constant at a given rpm with more oil being returned to the pump inlet by the relief valve.

LUBRICATING AND COOLING

ANSWERS

6-7 Answer B
Specific gravity is a comparison of the weight of a substance to the weight of an equal volume of distilled water at a specified temperature. As an example, water weighs approximately 8 pounds to the gallon. Oil with a specific gravity of .9 would weigh 7.2 pounds to the gallon (8 × .9 = 7.2).
Ref: Powerplant Handbook H-8083-32B-ATB Chapter 6 Page 3

6-8 Answer B
Oil grades 65, 80, and 120 are straight mineral oils blended from select high viscosity index base oil. These oils do not contain any additives except for very small amounts of pour point depressant, which helps improve fluidity at very low temperatures and an antioxidant. This type of oil is used during the break-in period of a new aviation piston engine or those recently overhauled. The additives in some of the ashless dispersant oils may retard the break in of the piston rings and cylinder walls causing high oil consumption. This condition can be avoided by the use of mineral oil until normal oil consumption is obtained, then change to ashless dispersant oil.
Ref: Powerplant Handbook H-8083-32B-ATB Chapter 6 Page 4

6-9 Answer B
The ashless-dispersant grades of oil are recommended for aircraft engines subject to wide variations of ambient temperature, particularly the turbocharged series engines that require oil to activate the various turbo controllers. The ashless dispersant grades contain additives which extend operating temperature range and improve cold weather starting. They permit flight through wider ranges of climactic changes without the necessity of changing oil.
Ref: Powerplant Handbook H-8083-32B-ATB Chapter 6 Page 3

6-10 Answer C
Dirty oil is better than no oil at all. Thus, a relief valve is used in case the oil filter becomes clogged. It will open in the event of an obstruction in flow to allow oil to bypass the filter and so prevent the engine components from oil starvation.
Ref: Powerplant Handbook H-8083-32B-ATB Chapter 6 Page 7

6-11 Answer A
Each oil tank used with a reciprocating engine must have expansion space of not less than the greater of 10 percent of the tank capacity or .5 gallons. A 5 gallon tank has a 20 quart capacity. 10 percent of 20 quarts is 2 quarts (.1 × 20 = 2). Since this is the same as .5 gallons, neither is larger, so the required expansion space is 2 quarts.
Ref: Powerplant Handbook H-8083-32B-ATB Chapter 6 Page 4

6-12 Answer B
The output of the oil pump is somewhat higher than what is required under any given RPM. Therefore, in order to maintain constant pressure as parts incur normal wear, a regulating valve (relief valve) opens to direct oil back to the pump inlet to relieve that excess pressure which could result in damage or leakage of the oil system.
Ref: Powerplant Handbook H-8083-32B-ATB Chapter 6 Page 8

6-13 AM.III.G.K4

Why is an aircraft reciprocating engine oil tank on a dry sump lubricating system equipped with a vent line?
- A. To prevent pressure buildup in the reciprocating engine crankcase.
- B. To eliminate foaming in the oil tank.
- C. To prevent pressure buildup in the oil tank.

6-14 AM.III.G.K4

What is the primary purpose of the hopper located in the oil supply tank of some dry sump engine installations?
- A. To reduce the time required to warm the oil to operating temperature.
- B. To reduce surface aeration of the hot oil and thus reduce oxidation and the formation of sludge and varnish.
- C. To impart a centrifugal motion to the oil entering the tank so that the foreign particles in the oil will separate more readily.

6-15 AM.III.G.K2

In what location (flow sequence) on a reciprocating engine is the main oil filter located?
- A. Just after the scavenge pump.
- B. Just before entering the oil pressure pump.
- C. Just after exiting the oil pressure pump.

6-16 AM.III.G.K2

On a gear type oil pump consisting of a drive gear and an idler gear
- A. both gears turn clockwise.
- B. both gears turn counter clockwise.
- C. one gear turns clockwise, and the other turns counter clockwise.

6-17 AM.III.G.K2

A Bourdon tube type oil pressure gauges measures the difference in oil pressure between a location
- A. after the oil pump and the atmosphere.
- B. before and after the oil pump.
- C. after the oil pump and that of a factory preset value.

6-18 AM.III.G.K4

Where is the oil temperature bulb located on a dry sump reciprocating engine?
- A. Oil inlet line
- B. Oil cooler
- C. Oil cooler outlet line

LUBRICATING AND COOLING

ANSWERS

6-13 Answer C
Oil tank vent lines are provided to ensure proper tank ventilation in all altitude of flight. These lines are usually connected to the engine crankcase to prevent the loss of oil through the vents. This indirectly vents the tanks to the atmosphere through the crankcase breather.
Ref: Powerplant Handbook H-8083-32B-ATB Chapter 6 Page 5

6-14 Answer A
To help with engine warm up, some oil tanks have a built-in hopper or temperature accelerating unit. This well extends from the oil return fitting on top of the oil tank to the outlet fitting in the sump in the bottom of the tank. By separating the circulating oil from the surrounding oil in the tank, less oil is circulated. This hastens the warming of the oil when the engine is started. Very few of these tanks are still in use and most are associated with radial engines installations.
Ref: Powerplant Handbook H-8083-32B-ATB Chapter 6 Page 5, 6

6-15 Answer C
Full flow oil filters are the most widely used oil filters on aircraft reciprocating engines. The filter is positioned between the oil pump and the engine bearings which filters the oil of any contaminants before they pass through the engine bearing surfaces.
Ref: Powerplant Handbook H-8083-32B-ATB Chapter 6 Page 6

6-16 Answer C
Both the drive and the idler gear turn in opposite directions allowing oil to flow under pressure in the space wear the gears mesh in between them. While is is typical for the driven gear to turn counter clockwise, it will work either way, as long as both turn in the center in the direction of the oil flow.
Ref: Powerplant Handbook H-8083-32B-ATB Chapter 6 Page 6

6-17 Answer A
A Bourdon tube gauge measures the difference between the oil pressure in the system and cabin or atmospheric pressure. The oil system location is measured in line after being boosted by the oil pump. The gauge is similar to all other Bourdon tube devices except for the small size of the oil opening to prevent pressure surges from the pump from damaging the gauge.
Ref: Powerplant Handbook H-8083-32B-ATB Chapter 6 Page 8

6-18 Answer A
In dry sump lubricating systems, the oil temperature bulb may be anywhere in the oil inlet line between the supply tank and the engine. The bulb is located so that it measures the temperature of the oil before it enters the hot sections of the engine.
Ref: Powerplant Handbook H-8083-32B-ATB Chapter 6 Page 9

6-19 AM.III.G.K2
In order to relieve excess pump pressure in an engine's internal oil system, most engines are equipped with a
A. vent.
B. bypass valve.
C. relief valve.

6-22 AM.III.G.K2
Cylinder walls are usually lubricated by
A. splashed or sprayed oil.
B. a direct pressure system fed through the crankshaft, connecting rods, and piston pins to the oil control ring groove in the piston.
C. oil that is picked up by the oil control ring when the piston is at bottom center.

6-20 AM.III.G.K2
If the oil in the oil cooler core and annular jacket becomes congealed, what unit prevents damage to the cooler?
A. Oil pressure relief valve
B. Airflow control valve
C. Surge protection valve

6-23 AM.III.G.K4
The oil temperature regulator is usually located between which of the following on a dry sump reciprocating engine?
A. the engine oil supply pump and the internal lubrication system
B. the scavenge pump outlet and the oil storage tank
C. the oil storage tank and the engine oil supply pump

6-21 AM.III.G.K2
A floating control thermostat is used on some reciprocating aircraft engines. How does this device help to regulate oil temperature?
A. It controls oil flow through the oil cooler.
B. It controls valves which recirculates hot oil back through the sump.
C. It controls air flow through the oil cooler.

6-24 AM.III.G.K4
The pumping capacity of the scavenger pump in a dry sump aircraft engine's lubrication system
A. is greater than the capacity of the oil pressure pump.
B. is less than the capacity of the oil supply pump.
C. is usually equal to the capacity of the oil supply pump in order to maintain constant oiling conditions.

LUBRICATING AND COOLING

ANSWERS

6-19 Answer C
An oil pressure regulating valve limits oil pressure to a predetermined value, depending on the installation. This valve is sometimes called a relief valve but its real function is to regulate the oil pressure at a preset pressure level.
Ref: Powerplant Handbook H-8083-32B-ATB Chapter 6 Page 7, Figure 6-6

6-22 Answer A
The engine cylinder surfaces receives oil sprayed from the crankshaft and also from the crankpin bearings. Since oil seeps slowly through the small crankpin clearances before it is sprayed on the cylinder walls, considerable time is required for enough oil to reach the cylinder walls, especially on a cold day when oil flow is more sluggish.
Ref: Powerplant Handbook H-8083-32B-ATB Chapter 6 Page 12

6-20 Answer C
When oil in the system is congealed, the scavenger pump may build up a very high pressure in the oil return line. To prevent this high pressure from bursting the oil cooler or blowing off the hose connections, some aircraft have surge protection valves in the engine lubricating systems. One type of surge valve is incorporated in the oil cooler flow control valve; another type is a separate unit in the oil return line.
Ref: Powerplant Handbook H-8083-32B-ATB Chapter 6 Page 10, 11

6-23 Answer B
Oil collected in the sump is picked up by the scavenge pump as quickly as it accumulates On dry sump engines, this oil leaves the engine, passes through the oil cooler and returns to the supply tank.
Ref: Powerplant Handbook H-8083-32B-ATB Chapter 6 Page 12

6-21 Answer C
One of the most widely used automatic oil temperature control devices is a floating control thermostat that provides manual and automatic control of the engine oil inlet temperatures. With this type of control, the oil cooler air exit door is opened and closed. This regulates the amount of air flowing through the cooler and thus the temperature of the oil that passes through the cooler on its way to the engine.
Ref: Powerplant Handbook H-8083-32B-ATB Chapter 6 Page 11

6-24 Answer A
Oil collected in the sump is picked up by the scavenge pump as quickly as it accumulates. These pumps have a greater capacity than the pressure pump. This is needed because the volume of the oil has generally increased due to foaming (mixing with air).
Ref: Powerplant Handbook H-8083-32B-ATB Chapter 6 Page 13

6-25 AM.III.G.K1
What is the primary purpose of changing aircraft engine lubricating oils at predetermined periods?
   A. The oil becomes diluted with gasoline washing past the pistons into the crankcase.
   B. The oil becomes contaminated with moistures, acids, and finely divided suspended solid particles.
   C. Exposure to heat and oxygen causes a decreased ability to maintain a film under load.

6-26 AM.III.G.K2
When does the oil cooler bypass valve open?
   A. When the oil pressure exceeds a specified amount.
   B. When oil temperature exceeds a specified amount.
   C. When oil temperature falls below a specified amount.

6-27 AM.III.G.K1
Compared to reciprocating engine oils, the types of oils used in turbine engines
   A. are required to carry and disperse a higher level of combustion by-products.
   B. may permit a somewhat higher level of carbon formation in the engine.
   C. have less tendency to produce lacquer or coke.

6-28 AM.III.K.K3
From what source is secondary cooling air acquired in a turbine engine in order to provide additional cooling of the turbine bearings?
   A. bypass air
   B. ram inlet air
   C. compressor bleed air

6-29 AM.III.G.K2
Which of the following prevents oil from entering the main accessory case of a turbine engine when the engine is not running?
   A. pressure valve
   B. hydraulic fuse
   C. check valve

6-30 AM.III.G.K2
Oil picks up the most heat from which of the following turbine engine components?
   A. rotor coupling
   B. exhaust turbine bearing
   C. compressor bearing

LUBRICATING AND COOLING

ANSWERS

6-25 Answer B
Oil in service is constantly exposed to many harmful substances that reduce its ability to protect moving parts. The main contaminants are: gasoline, moisture, acids, dirt, carbon, and metallic particles. Because of the accumulation of these harmful substances, common practice is to drain the entire lubrication system at regular intervals and refill with new oil.
Ref: Powerplant Handbook H-8083-32B-ATB Chapter 6 Page 17

6-26 Answer C
With the engine operating and an oil temperature below 150°F, the oil cooler bypass valves opens, allowing the oil to bypass the core of the cooler. The valve begins to close when the oil temperature reaches approximately 150°F and completely closes at 185°F, sending all oil through the cooler to employ its maximum cooling capability.
Ref: Powerplant Handbook H-8083-32B-ATB Chapter 6 Page 14

6-27 Answer C
The many requirements for lubricating oils are met in the synthetic oils developed specifically for turbine engines. Synthetic oil has principle advantages over petroleum oil. It has a lower tendency to deposit lacquer and coke (solids left after solvents from the oil have been evaporated) because it does not evaporate the solvents from the oil at high temperature.
Ref: Powerplant Handbook H-8083-32B-ATB Chapter 6 Page 18

6-28 Answer C
In some engines, air cooling is used in addition to oil cooling for the main bearings. Air cooling, referred to as secondary air flow, is cooling air provided by bleed air from the early stages of the compressor. This internal flow has many uses on the inside of the engine, including cooling of turbine disk, vanes, and blades.
Ref: Powerplant Handbook H-8083-32B-ATB Chapter 6 Page 21

6-29 Answer C
Check valves are sometimes installed in oil supply lines of dry-sump turbine oil systems to prevent reservoir oil from seeping (by gravity) through the oil pump elements and high pressure lines into the engine after shutdown. By stopping flow in an opposite direction, check valves prevent accumulations of oil in the accessory gearbox, compressor, and combustion chamber.
Ref: Powerplant Handbook H-8083-32B-ATB Chapter 6 Page 26

6-30 Answer B
The exhaust turbine bearing is the most critical lubricating point in a gas turbine engine because of the high temperature normally present. In some engines, air cooling is used in addition to oil cooling of the turbine bearings.
Ref: Powerplant Handbook H-8083-32B-ATB Chapter 6 Page 20

6-31 AM.III.G.K2
Which of the following is a function of the fuel oil heat exchanger on a turbojet engine?
  A. Aerates the fuel.
  B. Emulsifies the oil.
  C. Increases fuel temperature.

6-32 AM.III.G.K2
What is the purpose of the relief valve installed in the venting system of a turbine engine oil tank?
  A. Prevent oil pump cavitations by maintaining positive pressure on its inlet.
  B. Maintain tank pressure at ambient atmospheric levels.
  C. Maintain tank pressure upon engine shutdown to prevent oil pump cavitations on start-up.

6-33 AM.III.G.K2
The type of oil pump most commonly used on turbine powered engines are classified as
  A. positive displacement.
  B. variable displacement.
  C. constant speed.

6-34 AM.III.G.K2
What is the purpose of a last chance oil filter?
  A. to prevent damage to the oil pump gears
  B. to prevent clogging of the oil spray nozzles that spray the main bearings
  C. to assure a clean supply of oil to the lubrication system

6-35 AM.III.G.K2
What is the primary purpose of the oil breather pressurization system that is used on turbine engines?
  A. Prevents foaming of the oil.
  B. Allows aeration of the oil for better lubrication because of the air/oil mist.
  C. Provides a proper oil spray pattern from the main bearing oil jets.

6-36 AM.III.G.K2
Which type of valve prevents oil from entering the main accessory case when the engine is not running?
  A. bypass
  B. relief
  C. check

LUBRICATING AND COOLING

ANSWERS

6-31 Answer C
When an oil cooler is required on a gas turbine engine, a greater quantity of oil is required to provide for circulation between the cooler and the engine. To ensure proper temperature, oil is routed through either an air-cooled or fuel-cooled oil cooler. The fuel-cooled system is also used to heat (regulate) the fuel to prevent ice in the fuel.
Ref: Powerplant Handbook H-8083-32B-ATB Chapter 6 Page 21

6-32 Answer A
In most oil tanks, a pressure buildup is desired within the tank to ensure a positive flow of oil to the oil pump inlet. The pressure buildup is made possible by running the vent line through an adjustable check relief valve. The check relief valve is usually set to relieve at about 4 psi, keeping positive pressure on the oil pump inlet.
Ref: Powerplant Handbook H-8083-32B-ATB Chapter 6 Page 21

6-33 Answer A
Turbine engine oil pumps may be one of several types, each having certain advantages and limitations. The two most common oil pumps are the gear and gerotor, with the gear-type being the most commonly used. Both gear and gerotor pumps are constant displacement pumps since they deliver a fixed volume of oil with each rotation of the gears.
Ref: Powerplant Handbook H-8083-32B-ATB Chapter 6 Page 22

6-34 Answer B
Main oil filters strain the oil as it leaves the pump before being piped to the various points of lubrication in the engine. In addition to main oil filters, there are also secondary filters. Fine-mesh screens called last chance filters are used to strain the oil just before it passes from spray nozzles onto the main bearing surfaces. These filters are located at each bearing and help screen out contaminants that could plug the oil spray nozzles.
Ref: Powerplant Handbook H-8083-32B-ATB Chapter 6 Page 24, 25

6-35 Answer C
Breather subsystems are used to remove excess air from the bearing cavities and return the air to the oil tank where it is separated from any oil mixed in the vapor of air and oil by the deaerator. Then, the air is vented overboard. This allows air free oil to be pumped to engine lubrication points to provide the required lubrication.
Ref: Powerplant Handbook H-8083-32B-ATB Chapter 6 Page 25

6-36 Answer C
Check valves are sometimes used in the oil supply lines of dry-sump oil systems to prevent reservoir oil from seeping (by gravity) through the oil pump elements and high pressure lines into the engine after shutdown. Check valves, by stopping flow in an opposite direction, prevent accumulations of undue amounts of oil in the accessory gearbox, compressor rear housing, and the combustion chamber.
Ref: Powerplant Handbook H-8083-32B-ATB Chapter 6 Page 26

6-37 AM.III.G.K5
What is used on most turbine engines to monitor engine wear possibly providing notification in advance of an internal engine problem?
   A. sight gauges at the bearings and accessory housing
   B. magnetic chip detectors at key oil scavenge locations
   C. oil conductivity transmitters in the sump or oil reservoirs

6-38 AM.III.G.K4
What does oil pressure depend on in most modern turbofan engines?
   A. The FADEC controller
   B. engine RPM
   C. restrictor and relief valves

6-39 AM.III.J.K1
The greatest portion of heat generated by combustion in a typical aircraft reciprocating engine is
   A. converted into useful power.
   B. carried out with the exhaust gases.
   C. dissipated through the cylinder walls and heads.

6-40 AM.III.J.K1
What is the function of a blast tube as used on aircraft reciprocating engines?
   A. a means of cooling the engine by utilizing the propeller backwash
   B. a tube used to load a cartridge starter
   C. a device to cool an engine accessory

6-41 AM.III.J.K9
The primary purpose of baffles and deflectors installed around cylinders of air-cooled aircraft engines is to
   A. create a low pressure area aft of the cylinders.
   B. force cooling air into close contact with all parts of the cylinders.
   C. increase the volume of air used to cool the engine.

6-42 AM.III.J.K8
During climb, cowl flaps are left
   A. fully open.
   B. partially open.
   C. fully closed.

LUBRICATING AND COOLING

ANSWERS

6-37 Answer B
Magnetic chip detectors are used in the oil system to detect and catch ferrous (magnetic) particles present in the oil. Chip detectors are placed in several locations but generally are in the scavenge lines for each scavenge pump, oil tank, and in the oil sumps. If metal is found on a chip detector, an investigation should be made to find the source of the metal on the detector.
Ref: Powerplant Handbook H-8083-32B-ATB Chapter 6 Page 28

6-38 Answer B
Most large turbofan engine pressure systems are variable pressure systems in which the pump output pressure (oil pressure) depends on the engine RPM. In other words, the pump output pressure is proportional to engine's speed.
Ref: Powerplant Handbook H-8083-32B-ATB Chapter 6 Page 29

6-39 Answer B
About one-fourth of the heat released by combustion in a reciprocating aircraft engine is converted into useful power. The remainder of the heat must be dissipated so that it is not destructive to the engine. In a typical powerplant, half of the heat goes out with the exhaust and the remainder is absorbed by the engine to be redistributed by the oil or the cooling air.
Ref: Powerplant Handbook H-8083-32B-ATB Chapter 6 Page 32

6-40 Answer C
Blast tubes are built into the engine compartment baffles to direct jets of cooling air onto engine accessories to prevent overheating. Most often the tubes route air to areas with heat sensitive components that may not receive adequate cooling air. Rear spark plug elbows are often the focus of blast tube air as are alternators.
Ref: Powerplant Handbook H-8083-32B-ATB Chapter 6 Page 32

6-41 Answer B
Cowling and baffles are designed to force air over the cylinder cooling fins. The baffles direct the air close around cylinders and prevent air from forming hot pools of stagnant air while the main streams rush by unused. The air baffle blocks the flow of air and forces it to circulate between the cylinder and the deflector.
Ref: Powerplant Handbook H-8083-32B-ATB Chapter 6 Page 32

6-42 Answer B
The function of cowl flaps is to regulate (increase) cooling. However, they incur a penalty of increased drag on the airframe. In flight, during high powered climb, cowl flaps are opened just enough to keep the engine below red line temperatures.
Ref: Powerplant Handbook H-8083-32B-ATB Chapter 6 Page 33

6-43 AM.III.J.K5
1. Some exhaust systems include an augmenter system to draw additional air over the engine for cooling.
2. Augmenter systems are used to create a low pressure area at the lower rear of the aircraft engine cowling.

Regarding the above statements,
   A. Only No. 1 is true.
   B. Both No. 1 and No. 2 are true.
   C. Only No. 2 is true.

6-44 AM.III.J.K8
Where are cooling fins located on the outside of air-cooled engines?
   A. crankcase and oil sump
   B. cylinder heads and cylinder barrels
   C. cylinder barrels and engine cowl baffles

6-45 AM.III.J.K8
Which of the following defects would likely cause a hot spot on a reciprocating engine cylinder?
   A. too much cooling fin area broken off
   B. a cracked cylinder baffle
   C. cowling air seal leak

6-46 AM.III.J.K1
A bent cooling fin on an aluminum cylinder head should be
   A. sawed off and filed smooth.
   B. left alone if no crack has formed.
   C. straightened out as much as possible without breaking.

6-47 AM.III.K.K3
How are combustion liner walls cooled in a gas turbine engine?
   A. by secondary air flowing through the combustion chamber
   B. by the pattern of holes and louvers cut in the diffuser section
   C. by bleed air vented from the engine air inlet

6-48 AM.III.K.K2
What air is used to cool the exterior and nacelle of a turbofan engine?
   A. compressor bleed air
   B. conditioned air from the air cycle machine
   C. fan air

LUBRICATING AND COOLING

ANSWERS

6-43 Answer B
Some aircraft use augmenters to provide additional cooling airflow. The exhaust gas mixes with air that has passed over the engine and heats it to form a high temperature, low pressure, jet like exhaust. The low pressure area in the augmenters draws additional cooling air over the engine.
Ref: Powerplant Handbook H-8083-32B-ATB Chapter 6 Page 33

6-44 Answer B
The cylinder fins radiate heat from the cylinder walls and heads. As the air passes over the fins, it absorbs this heat, carries it away from the cylinder, and is exhausted overboard through the bottom rear of the cowl.
Ref: Powerplant Handbook H-8083-32B-ATB Chapter 6 Page 34

6-45 Answer A
If total fins broken on any cylinder head exceed a certain number of square inches of area, the cylinder is removed and replaced. The reason for removal is that missing fin area of a large size would cause a hot spot on the cylinder since very little heat transfer would occur. Applicable manufacturer's instructions should be consulted when determining allowable fin area missing or damaged.
Ref: Powerplant Handbook H-8083-32B-ATB Chapter 6 Page 36

6-46 Answer B
As the cooling of an aluminum cylinder head depends mostly on the total area of the cooling fins, a bent fin should have little effect and may be left alone. Consequently, any attempt to bend the fin back into position could result in its cracking which would then cause a more serious problem.
Ref: Powerplant Handbook H-8083-32B-ATB Chapter 6 Page 36

6-47 Answer A
The secondary air passing through the engine cools the combustion chamber liners. The liners are constructed to induce a thin, fast-moving film of air over both the inner and outer surfaces of the liner.
Ref: Powerplant Handbook H-8083-32B-ATB Chapter 6 Page 38

6-48 Answer C
Internal bleed air from the engine compressor section is vented to the bearings and other parts of the engine for cooling. The engine exterior and the engine nacelle are cooled by passing fan air around the engine and the nacelle.
Ref: Powerplant Handbook H-8083-32B-ATB Chapter 6 Page 38

ORAL EXAM

6-1(O). Name two items to be inspected to ensure adequate cooling of a reciprocating aircraft engine.

6-2(O). In what position should cowl flaps be placed for ground operation and why?

6-3(O). How is the combustion section of a turbine engine cooled?

6-4(O). What cools the bearings on a turbine engine?

6-5(O). What would be the effect of removing the engine baffles and seals from around a reciprocating air-cooled aircraft engine and why?

6-6(O). What are the two common types of heat exchangers used to cool engine oil on turbine engine aircraft?

6-7(O). What is the function and operation of an augmenter cooling system?

6-8(O). What is the difference between straight mineral oil, ashless-dispersant oil, and synthetic oil?

6-9(O). What types of oils are used for different climates?

6-10(O). What are the functions of engine oil?

6-11(O). How can the technician identify and select the proper lubricants?

6-12(O). Name two maintenance actions that are part of servicing an aircraft engine lubrication system.

6-13(O). What is the reason for changing engine oil at specified intervals?

6-14(O). What are two reasons for excessive oil consumption on a reciprocating engine that shows no signs of oil leakage?

LUBRICATING AND COOLING

ANSWERS

ORAL EXAM

6-1(O).   Cowling, cowling seals, cowl flaps, cylinder fins, cylinder baffles, and deflector system.
Ref: Powerplant Handbook H-8083-32B-ATB Chapter 6

6-2(O).   Fully OPEN because in this position they provide for the greatest amount of airflow over the engine and thus the greatest amount of cooling.
Ref: Powerplant Handbook H-8083-32B-ATB Chapter 6

6-3(O).   Using air that has been drawn through the compressor which is routed through combustion chamber liners that provide a thin, fast-moving film of air that carries the heat away. Air is also routed to join with the burned gases aft of the burners to cool the hot gases before they enter the turbines.
Ref: Powerplant Handbook H-8083-32B-ATB Chapter 6

6-4(O).   Air that is bled from the compressor section of the engine and sometimes air that is drawn from outside the engine for cooling purposes is routed to the bearings. Heat is also transferred to the oil that lubricates the bearings.
Ref: Powerplant Handbook H-8083-32B-ATB Chapter 6

6-5(O).   The engine would overheat because the baffles and seals are designed to route cooling air close by and past the engine cylinders and thus draw away heat from the engine.
Ref: Powerplant Handbook H-8083-32B-ATB Chapter 6

6-6(O).   Fuel oil heat exchangers and air oil heat exchangers.
Ref: Powerplant Handbook H-8083-32B-ATB Chapter 6

6-7(O).   The function is to draw ambient air through the engine compartment for better cooling. It is accomplished with augmenter tubes or ejector tubes into which the exhaust gas is directed. This causes a low pressure and increases the flow of ambient air through augmenter and, thus, through the nacelle.
Ref: Powerplant Handbook H-8083-32B-ATB Chapter 6

6-8(O).   Straight mineral oil is blended from specifically selected petroleum based stocks. It has no additives except small amounts of pour point depressant and an antioxidant. It is used during the break-in period of a new or recently overhauled engine. Ashless dispersant oil is straight mineral oil with non-metallic, non-ash forming polymeric additives such as viscosity stabilizers. It extends operating temperature range and improves cold engine starting and lubrication during warm-up. It permits flight through a wide range of climactic changes without having to change oils. Synthetic oil is specially formulated and is used in turbine engines. It is more viscous than ashless or straight mineral oil and has a lower tendency to deposit lacquer and coke. It also resists oxidation and has superior load carrying ability. It provides long service life and prevents seal wear.
Ref: Powerplant Handbook H-8083-32B-ATB Chapter 6

6-9(O).   Ashless dispersant grades of oil are recommended for aircraft engines subject to wide variations of ambient temperatures. However, below 20°F, preheating the engine and oil supply tank is normally required regardless of the type of oil used. In all cases, refer to the manufacturer's specifications.
Ref: Powerplant Handbook H-8083-32B-ATB Chapter 6

6-10(O).   Engine oil acts as a cushion between metal parts and reduces friction. It cools the engine, seals, cleans, and reduces abrasive wear. Oil also prevents corrosion on the inside of the engine.
Ref: Powerplant Handbook H-8083-32B-ATB Chapter 6

ORAL EXAM

6-11(O). Aircraft oils are classified by a numbering system that is an approximation of their viscosity. There are different systems in use such as SAE and MIL-spec. Letters, such as a W, are also used to describe the oil or its characteristics. Many factors are considered when determining the proper oil for a particular engine including operating load, rotational speeds, and operating temperatures. In all cases, refer to the engine manufacturer's information when oil type or time in service is being considered.
Ref: Powerplant Handbook H-8083-32B-ATB Chapter 6

6-12(O). Periodic oil changes, oil filter change, inspection of oil filter contents, inspection and cleaning of oil screen(s), checking and adjustment of oil pressure relief valve, cleaning oil cooler of obstructions.
Ref: Powerplant Handbook H-8083-32B-ATB Chapter 6

6-13(O). Oil in service accumulates contaminants such as gas, moisture, acids, dirt, carbon, and metallic particles which reduce the ability of the oil to protect moving parts. Replacing the oil periodically ensure the oil can do what it is designed to do.
Ref: Powerplant Handbook H-8083-32B-ATB Chapter 6

6-14(O). Low grade oil or improper oil such as ashless-dispersant oil used in a new or overhauled engine, failing or failed crankshaft bearing(s).
Ref: Powerplant Handbook H-8083-32B-ATB Chapter 6

LUBRICATING AND COOLING

PRACTICAL EXAM

6-1(P).   Given an actual aircraft engine or mockup, appropriate publications, and tooling inspect an engine lubrication system to ensure continued operation and record your findings. [Level 3]

6-2(P).   Given an actual aircraft engine or mockup, appropriate publications, and tooling inspect oil lines and filter/screen for leaks and record your findings. [Level 3]

6-3(P).   Given an actual aircraft engine or mockup, appropriate publications, and tooling replace a defective oil cooler and record maintenance. [Level 3]

6-4(P).   Given an actual aircraft engine or mockup, appropriate publications, and tooling replace a defective oil cooler component and record maintenance. [Level 3]

6-5(P).   Given an actual aircraft engine or mockup, appropriate publications, and tooling replace a gasket in the oil system, accomplish a leak check, and record maintenance. [Level 3]

6-6(P).   Given an actual aircraft engine or mockup, appropriate publications, and tooling replace a seal in the oil system, accomplish a leak check, and record maintenance. [Level 3]

6-7(P).   Given an actual aircraft engine or mockup, appropriate publications, and tooling adjust the oil pressure and record maintenance. [Level 3]

6-8(P).   Given an actual aircraft engine or mockup, appropriate publications, equipment, tooling and supplies complete the following: change engine oil, inspect screen(s) and/or filter, leak check the engine, and record maintenance. [Level 3]

6-9(P).   Given an actual aircraft engine or mockup, and appropriate publications, pre-oil an engine. [Level 2]

6-10(P).   Given an actual aircraft engine or mockup, appropriate publications, and tooling inspect an engine cooling system and record your findings. [Level 3]

6-11(P).   Given an actual aircraft engine or mockup, appropriate publications, and tooling check cowl flap operation, inspect rigging and record maintenance. [Level 3]

6-12(P).   Given an actual aircraft engine or mockup, appropriate publications, materials, and tooling, repair one or more cylinder cooling fins and record maintenance. [Level 3]

6-13(P).   Given an actual aircraft engine or mockup, appropriate publications, materials, and tooling, repair an engine pressure baffle plate and record maintenance. [Level 3]

6-14(P).   Given an actual aircraft engine or mockup, appropriate publications, and tooling inspect a heat exchanger and record your findings. [Level 3]

6-15(P).   Given an actual aircraft engine or mockup, appropriate publications, tooling, equipment and an unknown discrepancy troubleshoot an engine cooling system and record your findings. [Level 3]

6-16(P).   Given an actual rotorcraft engine or mockup, locate and identify specified rotorcraft cooling system components. [Level 3]

PROPELLERS

Propeller Aerodynamics, Propeller Placement, Types of Propellers, Propeller Governors, Vibration and Balancing, Servicing and Overhaul

7-1 AM.III.M.K1
The angle of attack of a propeller blade is the difference between its
  A. chord line and the relative wind.
  B. relative wind and the longitudinal axis of the aircraft.
  C. chord line and pitch angle.

7-4 AM.III.M.K1
The actual distance a propeller moves forward through the air during one revolution is known as the
  A. effective pitch.
  B. geometric pitch
  C. slip.

7-2 AM.III.M.K1
A propeller typically produces its greatest amount of thrust at which pitch angle?
  A. 85°
  B. 12°
  C. 30°

7-5 AM.III.M.K1
Blade angle is an angle formed by a line perpendicular to the crankshaft and a line formed by the
  A. relative wind.
  B. chord of the blade.
  C. blade face.

7-3 AM.III.M.K1
Geometric pitch of a propeller is defined as
  A. effective pitch minus slippage.
  B. effective pitch plus slippage.
  C. angle between the blade chord and the plane of rotation.

7-6 AM.III.M.K2
Propeller blade station numbers increase from
  A. hub center line to tip.
  B. tip to hub center line.
  C. blade shank butt to tip.

PROPELLERS

ANSWERS

7-1 Answer A
The angle of attack is the difference between the chord line and the relative wind. This measurement changes as the aircraft pitches up or down or as the propeller blade moves from fine to course pitch. Pitch angle compares the chord line to the longitudinal axis.
Ref: Powerplant Handbook H-8083-32B-ATB Chapter 7 Page 1

7-2 Answer C
A propeller's forward flight power range occurs between 20° and 35° depending upon if it is a climb or cruise mode. 10-12° is a flight idle setting used on descent or for fast taxi. 85° is a feather position, producing no thrust and used only in emergency conditions.
Ref: Powerplant Handbook H-8083-32B-ATB Chapter 7 Page 2

7-3 Answer B
Pitch is not the same as blade angle but pitch is largely determined by blade angle. Geometric pitch is the distance the propeller should advance in one revolution with no slippage. Effective pitch is the distance the propeller actually advances. Thus, geometric pitch is theoretical. It is the effective pitch plus the slippage. Geometric pitch is usually expressed in inches.
Ref: Powerplant Handbook H-8083-32B-ATB Chapter 7 Page 2

7-4 Answer A
Propeller slip is the difference between geometric pitch of the propeller and its effective pitch. Geometric pitch is the distance the propeller should advance in one revolution with no slippage; effective pitch is the distance it actually advances. Thus, geometric pitch is based on no slippage. Effective (or actual) pitch recognizes propeller slippage in the air.
Ref: Powerplant Handbook H-8083-32B-ATB Chapter 7 Page 2

7-5 Answer B
Although blade angle and propeller pitch are closely related, blade angle is the angle between the chord of a blade section and the plane in which the propeller rotates. Therefore, blade angle, usually measured in degrees, is the angle between the chord line of the blade and the plane of rotation. Note that the plane of rotation is perpendicular to the crankshaft.
Ref: Powerplant Handbook H-8083-32B-ATB Chapter 7 Page 2, 3

7-6 Answer A
For purposes of analysis and maintenance, a propeller blade can be divided into segments that are located by station numbers in inches from the center of the blade hub. Thus, the station numbers increase from hub to tip.
Ref: Powerplant Handbook H-8083-32B-ATB Chapter 7 Page 3

7-7 AM.III.M.K1

The physical force which creates the largest amount of stress on a propeller is absorbed by which section of the propeller?

A. The blade root section.

B. The propeller hub.

C. The blades trailing edge.

7-8 AM.III.M.K1

What operational force causes propeller blade tips to lag in the opposite direction of rotation?

A. Thrust Bending

B. Aerodynamic Twisting

C. Torque Bending

7-9 AM.III.M.K1

What operational force tends to bend the propeller blades forward at the tips?

A. Torque Bending Force

B. Centrifugal-Twisting Force

C. Thrust Bending Force

7-10 AM.III.M.K1

How does the aerodynamic twisting force affect operating propeller blades?

A. It tends to turn the blades to a high blade angle.

B. It tends to bend the blades forward.

C. It tends to turn the blades to a low blade angle.

7-11 AM.III.M.K1

The centrifugal twisting force of an operating propeller tends to

A. increase the pitch angle.

B. reduce the pitch angle.

C. bend the blades in the direction of rotation.

7-12 AM.III.M.K1

The angle of attack of a rotating propeller blade is measured between the blade chord or face and which of the following?

A. Plane of blade rotation.

B. Full low-pitch blade angle.

C. Relative airstream.

PROPELLERS

ANSWERS

7-7 Answer B
The largest operational force on a propeller is centrifugal force, trying to pull the blades from the hub. Thus the component of the propeller which requires its greatest strength and significant scrutiny during inspection is the hub.
Ref: Powerplant Handbook H-8083-32B-ATB Chapter 7 Page 4

7-8 Answer C
Torque bending force, in the form of air resistance, tends to bend the propeller blade in the direction opposite that of rotation.
Ref: Powerplant Handbook H-8083-32B-ATB Chapter 7 Page 3

7-9 Answer C
Thrust bending force is the thrust load that tends to bend propeller blades forward as the aircraft is pulled through the air.
Ref: Powerplant Handbook H-8083-32B-ATB Chapter 7 Page 3

7-10 Answer A
Aerodynamic twisting force tends to turn the blades to a high blade angle.
Ref: Powerplant Handbook H-8083-32B-ATB Chapter 7 Page 3

7-11 Answer B
Centrifugal twisting force, being greater than aerodynamic twisting force tends to force the blades towards a lower blade angle and thus a reduced pitch.
Ref: Powerplant Handbook H-8083-32B-ATB Chapter 7 Page 3

7-12 Answer C
The angle at which the air, the relative wind, strikes the propeller blade is called the Angle Of Attack (AOA).
Ref: Powerplant Handbook H-8083-32B-ATB Chapter 7 Page 4

7-13 AM.III.M.K1
The thrust produced by rotating a propeller is a result of
A. an area of low pressure behind the propeller blades.
B. an area of decreased pressure immediately in front of the propeller blades.
C. the angle of the relative wind and rotational velocity of the propeller.

7-16 AM.III.M.K4
A constant-speed propeller provides maximum efficiency by
A. increasing blade pitch as the aircraft speed decreases.
B. adjusting blade angle for most conditions encountered in flight.
C. increasing the lift coefficient of the blade.

7-14 AM.III.M.K2
What is the purpose of a test club?
A. To identify harmonics produced by an engine/propeller combination.
B. To identify propeller pitch settings related to an engine's power output.
C. To provide an artificial load when ground running an engine.

7-17 AM.III.M.K4
Counterweights on constant-speed propellers are generally used to aid in
A. increasing blade angle.
B. decreasing blade angle.
C. un-feathering the propellers.

7-15 AM.III.M.K4
What are the rotational speed and blade pitch angle requirements of a constant-speed propeller during takeoff?
A. Low speed and high pitch angle.
B. High speed and low pitch angle.
C. High speed and high pitch angle.

7-18 AM.III.M.K4
In case of an engine failure, what holds a feathering propeller in the feathered position while in flight?
A. Centrifugal force
B. Counter weights
C. Aerodynamic force

PROPELLERS

ANSWERS

7-13 Answer B
The shape of the propeller blade creates thrust because it is shaped like a wing. As the air flows past the propeller, the pressure on one side is less than that on the other. As in a wing, this difference in pressure produces a reaction force in the direction of the lesser pressure. The area above a wing has less pressure and the force, lift, is upward. The area of decreased pressure is in front of a propeller which is mounted in a vertical instead of horizontal position. Thus, the force, thrust, is in a forward direction.
Ref: Powerplant Handbook H-8083-32B-ATB Chapter 7 Page 4

7-16 Answer B
To provide an efficient propeller, the engine speed is kept as constant as possible. If the throttle setting is changed, instead of changing the speed of the aircraft by climbing or diving, the blade angle increases or decreases as required to maintain a constant engine RPM. The power output, not the RPM, changes in accordance with changes in throttle setting. The constant-speed propeller changes the blade angle automatically keeping engine RPM constant.
Ref: Powerplant Handbook H-8083-32B-ATB Chapter 7 Page 7

7-14 Answer A
A test club is a shortened propeller (typically wood) used to test or break in reciprocating engines. They are made to provide the correct amount of load on the engine during the test break-in period and to provide extra cooling air flow during testing.
Ref: Powerplant Handbook H-8083-32B-ATB Chapter 7 Page 6

7-17 Answer A
Each constant-speed propeller has an opposing force that operates against oil pressure from the governor. Flyweights (counterweights) mounted to the blades move the blades in the high pitch direction as the propeller turns. Other forces used to move the blades toward the high pitch direction include air pressure (contained in the front dome), springs, and aerodynamic twisting moment.
Ref: Powerplant Handbook H-8083-32B-ATB Chapter 7 Page 8

7-15 Answer B
During takeoff, when maximum power and thrust are required, the constant-speed propeller is at low propeller blade angle or pitch. The low blade angle keeps the AOA small and efficient with respect to the relative wind. This light load allows the engine to turn at high speed, and convert the maximum amount of fuel into heat energy. The high RPM also creates maximum thrust. The mass of air handled per revolution of the propeller is small due to the low blade angle, however, with high RPM, the slipstream velocity is high and, combined with the low speed of the aircraft, thrust is at maximum.
Ref: Powerplant Handbook H-8083-32B-ATB Chapter 7 Page 2, 7

7-18 Answer C
When a feathered propeller stops turning, the blades are held in position by aerodynamic forces. In normal operation, oil pressure holds the blades in a low pitch position, and counterweights or springs hold it in a high pitch positions.
Ref: Powerplant Handbook H-8083-32B-ATB Chapter 7 Page 8

7-19 AM.III.M.K4
How do small feathering propellers prevent feathering when the engine is shut down?
- A. Latches lock the propeller in low pitch to prevent excess load on the engine at start-up.
- B. Oil pressure is held against the pitch change mechanism.
- C. Aerodynamic twisting movement prevents feathering.

7-20 AM.III.M.K5
Reverse pitch propellers
- A. turn in the opposite direction than that of the crankshaft.
- B. produce a negative blade angle to slow the aircraft after touchdown.
- C. go beyond feathering position to provide thrust for stopping.

7-21 AM.III.M.K4
The propeller governor cockpit control
- A. adjusts tension on the speeder spring.
- B. opens and closes the pilot valve.
- C. adjusts the position of counter weights.

7-22 AM.III.M.K4
During the on-speed condition of a propeller, the
- A. centrifugal force acting on the governor flyweights is greater than the tension of the speeder spring.
- B. tension on the speeder spring is less than the centrifugal force acting on the flyweights.
- C. centrifugal force of the governor flyweights is equal to the speeder spring tension.

7-23 AM.III.M.K4
When the centrifugal force acting on the propeller governor flyweights overcomes the tension on the speeder spring, a propeller is in what speed condition?
- A. On-speed.
- B. Under-speed.
- C. Over-speed.

7-24 AM.III.M.K2
A fixed pitch metal propeller is stamped with the model number 1B50-CM-71-44. What does the CM stand for?
- A. The type of hub to which it may be mounted.
- B. The manufacturer designation.
- C. Its vibration characteristics.

PROPELLERS

ANSWERS

7-19 Answer A
Almost all small feathering propellers use oil pressure to take the propeller to low pitch and blade flyweights, springs and compressed air to take the blades to high pitch. Since the blades would go to feather position during shutdown, latches lock the propeller in the low pitch position as the propeller slows down at shutdown. The latches are needed to prevent excess load on the engine at start up.
Ref: Powerplant Handbook H-8083-32B-ATB Chapter 7 Page 8

7-20 Answer B
The purpose of the reversible pitch feature is to produce a negative blade angle that produces thrust opposite to the normal forward direction. Normally, when the landing gear is in contact with the runway after landing, the propeller blades can be moved to negative pitch (reversed), which creates thrust opposite of the aircraft direction and slows the aircraft. Engine power can be applied to increase the negative thrust.
Ref: Powerplant Handbook H-8083-32B-ATB Chapter 7 Page 8

7-21 Answer A
A governor is set to a specific RPM via the cockpit propeller control which compresses or releases tension on the governor speeder spring, thus regulating oil flow into a hydraulic cylinder.
Ref: Powerplant Handbook H-8083-32B-ATB Chapter 7 Page 8

7-22 Answer C
In an on-speed condition, the centrifugal force acting on the flyweights is balanced by the speeder spring and the pilot valve is neither directing oil to or from the propeller hydraulic cylinder.
Ref: Powerplant Handbook H-8083-32B-ATB Chapter 7 Page 11

7-23 Answer C
In an over-speed condition, the centrifugal force acting on the flyweights is greater than the speeder spring force. Therefore, the flyweights tilt outward. This raises the pilot valve and allows oil to flow to the piston so as to increase blade pitch and reduce RPM.
Ref: Powerplant Handbook H-8083-32B-ATB Chapter 7 Page 11

7-24 Answer A
CM represents the physical shape of the hub (to what type of hub it will attach and tip shape (square or elliptical). 1B50 represents the manufacturer's model number or basic design number. 71 represents its diameter. 44 represents its pitch angle at .75 radius.
Ref: Powerplant Handbook H-8083-32B-ATB Chapter 7 Page 14

7-25 AM.III.M.K4

What normally prevents a constant speed feathering propeller from going into feather when the engine is shut down on the ground?
- A. Counterweight springs
- B. Latching mechanisms
- C. Residual oil pressure

7-26 AM.III.M.K10

The proper operation of an electric deicing system and its timers may be monitored onboard with the use of a(n)
- A. amp meter.
- B. ohm meter.
- C. volt meter.

7-27 AM.III.M.K10

Propeller fluid anti-icing systems generally use which of the following?
- A. Ethylene Glycol
- B. Isopropyl Alcohol
- C. Ethyl Alcohol

7-28 AM.III.M.K10

Propeller deicer boots are
- A. "ON" continuously in icing conditions.
- B. used to prevent ice before it builds on the propeller surfaces.
- C. energized for short periods by a cycling timer.

7-29 AM.III.M.K9

What is the function of the automatic propeller synchronizing system on multiengine aircraft?
- A. To control the tip speed of all propellers.
- B. To control engine RPM and reduce vibration.
- C. To control the power output of all engines.

7-30 AM.III.M.K6

How can a steel propeller hub be tested for cracks?
- A. By anodizing.
- B. By magnetic particle inspection.
- C. By etching.

PROPELLERS

ANSWERS

7-25 Answer B
In order to prevent feathering spring and counterweights from feathering the propeller when the engine is shut down and the engine stopped, automatically removable high-pitch stops were incorporated in the design. These consist of spring-loaded latches fastened to the stationary hub that engage high-pitch stop plates bolted to the movable blade clamps.
Ref: Powerplant Handbook H-8083-32B-ATB Chapter 7 Page 16

7-26 Answer A
An ammeter or load meter allows each circuit to be monitored for when it is operational and drawing current. The gauge can be seen to fluctuate as the timer cycles as each circuit is turned on and off.
Ref: Powerplant Handbook H-8083-32B-ATB Chapter 7 Page 19

7-27 Answer B
Isopropyl alcohol is used in some anti-icing systems because of its availability and low cost. Phosphate compounds are comparable to isopropyl alcohol in performance and have reduced flammability, however, they are more expensive.
Ref: Powerplant Handbook H-8083-32B-ATB Chapter 7 Page 17

7-28 Answer C
Electric deicing systems are usually designed for intermittent application of power to the heating elements to remove ice after formation but before excessive accumulation. Cycling timers are used to energize the heating element circuits for periods of 15 to 30 seconds, with a complete cycle time of 2 minutes. A cycling timer is an electric motor driven contactor that controls power contactors in separate sections of the circuit.
Ref: Powerplant Handbook H-8083-32B-ATB Chapter 7 Page 18

7-29 Answer B
Most multiengine aircraft are equipped with propeller synchronization systems. Synchronization systems provide a means of controlling and synchronizing engine RPM. Synchronization reduces vibration and eliminates the unpleasant beat produced by unsynchronized propeller operation.
Ref: Powerplant Handbook H-8083-32B-ATB Chapter 7 Page 19

7-30 Answer B
The inspection of steel blades may be accomplished by either visual, fluorescent penetrant, or magnetic particle inspection. The full length of the leading edge (especially near the tip), the full length of the trailing edge, the grooves and shoulders on the shank, and all dents and scars should be examined with a magnifying glass to decide whether defects are scratches or cracks.
Ref: Powerplant Handbook H-8083-32B-ATB Chapter 7 Page 20

7-31 AM.III.M.K6
If a delamination is suspected on a composite propeller blade, the extent of damage
  A. can be confirmed by a coin tap test.
  B. can be confirmed by eddy current inspection.
  C. can be confirmed by ultrasonic inspection.

7-32 AM.III.M.K6
If an apparent propeller vibration occurs only at cruise RPM ranges, the problem is most likely caused by
  A. incorrect propeller for the engine.
  B. an out of track propeller.
  C. an out of balance propeller.

7-33 AM.III.M.K6
Propeller blade tracking is the process of determining
  A. the plane of rotation of the propeller with respect to the aircraft longitudinal axis.
  B. that the blade angles are within the specified tolerance of each other.
  C. the positions of the tips of the propeller blades relative to each other.

7-34 AM.III.M.K6
Which of the following functions requires the use of a propeller blade station?
  A. Measuring Blade Angle
  B. Indexing Blades
  C. Propeller Balancing

7-35 AM.III.M.K6
Propeller aerodynamic (thrust) imbalance can be largely eliminated by
  A. correct blade contouring and angle setting.
  B. static balancing.
  C. keeping the propeller blades within the same plane of rotation.

7-36 AM.III.M.K6
An out of balance propeller is typically corrected by
  A. lightening the weight of the heavy side.
  B. adding weight on the light side.
  C. modifying its aerodynamic aspects to compensate for the imbalance.

PROPELLERS

ANSWERS

7-31 Answer C
A suspected delamination may be observed through a coin tab test. If this occurs, a confirmation of this damage and its severity may be confirmed by ultrasound inspection. Once conformed, only the propeller manufacturer or a certified propeller repair station may perform the repair.
Ref: Powerplant Handbook H-8083-32B-ATB Chapter 7 Page 21

7-32 Answer A
If a propeller vibrates due to balance, angle, or track problems, the vibration usually occurs at all RPM settings. Particularly with metal propellers, if the apparent vibration is limited to only certain RPM ranges, then the problem is typically a mismatch of the wrong propeller for the engine it is installed on.
Ref: Powerplant Handbook H-8083-32B-ATB Chapter 7 Page 22

7-33 Answer C
Blade tracking is the process of determining the positions of the tips of the propeller blades relative to each other (blades rotating in the same plane of rotation). An out of track propeller may be due to one or more of the blades being bent, a bent propeller flange, or propeller mounting bolts that are improperly torqued.
Ref: Powerplant Handbook H-8083-32B-ATB Chapter 7 Page 22

7-34 Answer A
Due to the twist of most propellers, blade angle must be measured at the same blade station on each blade to ensure comparable readings. The manufacturer's instructions are used to obtain the blade angle setting and the station at which the blade angle is checked.
Ref: Powerplant Handbook H-8083-32B-ATB Chapter 7 Page 23

7-35 Answer A
Dynamic imbalance of a propeller resulting from improper mass distribution is negligible provided the track tolerance requirements are met. Aerodynamic unbalance, however, results when the thrust (or pull) of the blades is unequal. This type of unbalance can be largely eliminated by checking blade contour and blade angle setting.
Ref: Powerplant Handbook H-8083-32B-ATB Chapter 7 Page 24

7-36 Answer B
A propeller weight imbalance is corrected by adding weights to the side of the propeller hub of the lighter blade up to a maximum weight as stated by the manufacturer.
Ref: Powerplant Handbook H-8083-32B-ATB Chapter 7 Page 24, 25

7-37 AM.III.M.K6
When lubricating a Hartzell® propeller blade with grease, to prevent damage to the blade seals, the service manual may recommend on some models to
    A. pump grease into both zerk fittings for the blade simultaneously.
    B. remove the seals prior to greasing and reinstall them afterwards.
    C. remove one of the two zerk fittings for the blade and grease the blade through the remaining fitting.

7-38 AM.III.M.K6
When charging a propeller air dome to the manufacturer's specifications, which factor must be considered when determining the proper air pressure?
    A. Density altitude
    B. Humidity
    C. Temperature

7-39 AM.III.M.K6
Cold straightening of a bent aluminum propeller blade
    A. may be accomplished by any certified powerplant mechanic.
    B. requires specialized tooling and precision measuring equipment.
    C. renders it unairworthy.

7-40 AM.III.M.K6
How is a propeller controlled in a large aircraft with a turboprop installation?
    A. Independently of the engine.
    B. By varying the engine RPM except for propeller feathering and propeller reverse pitch.
    C. By the engine power lever.

7-41 AM.III.M.K6
On a typical turboprop engine such as a Pratt & Whitney PT-6, oil for the governor is supplied by
    A. a separate reservoir from the main engine oil supply.
    B. the aircraft hydraulic system.
    C. the engine oil supply.

7-42 AM.III.M.K4
In what way do hydromatic propeller systems differ from other constant speed propeller systems?
    A. The hydromatic system does not include counterweights.
    B. Oil pressure is applied on only one side of the propeller piston.
    C. The hydromatic system has a limited blade angle range compared to others.

PROPELLERS

ANSWERS

7-37 Answer C
Redistribution of grease may result in voids in the blade bearing area where moisture can collect. Remove one of the lubrication fittings for each blade hub. Pump grease into the fitting located nearest the leading edge of the blade on a tractor propeller installation, or nearest the trailing edge on a pusher installation, until grease emerges from the hole where the fitting was removed. Always follow specific manufacturer's instructions for the specified model propeller undergoing maintenance.
Ref: Powerplant Handbook H-8083-32B-ATB Chapter 7 Page 28

7-38 Answer C
The correct charge pressure is determined by a chart which is typically attached to the air dome. The outside temperature is used to find the correct pressure to charge the hub.
Ref: Powerplant Handbook H-8083-32B-ATB Chapter 7 Page 27

7-39 Answer B
Occasionally, blade straightening is required during propeller overhaul. The manufacturer's specifications dictate certain allowable limits within which damaged blades can be straightened and returned to airworthy condition. Specialized tooling and precision measuring equipment permit pitch changes or corrections of less than one-tenth of one degree.
Ref: Powerplant Handbook H-8083-32B-ATB Chapter 7 Page 29

7-40 Answer C
The turboprop engine produces thrust indirectly because the compressor and turbine assembly furnish torque to a propeller producing the major portion of the propulsive force that drives the aircraft. The turboprop fuel control and the propeller governor are connected and operate in coordination with each other. The power lever directs a signal from the cockpit to the fuel control for a specific amount of power from the engine. The fuel control and the propeller governor together establish the correct combination of RPM, fuel flow, and propeller blade angle to create sufficient propeller thrust to provide the desired power.
Ref: Powerplant Handbook H-8083-32B-ATB Chapter 7 Page 30, 31

7-41 Answer C
Engine oil is supplied to the propeller governor from the engine oil supply. A gear pump mounted at the base of the governor increases flow and pressure as demanded.
Ref: Powerplant Handbook H-8083-32B-ATB Chapter 7 Page 31, 32

7-42 Answer A
A Hydromatic propeller has a double acting governor that uses oil pressure on both sides of the propeller piston. In the pitch changing mechanism, no counterweights are used. Engine oil pressure on one side of the piston is used against propeller governor oil on the other side of the piston to change blade angle or pitch. Hydromatic propellers can be found on some older radial engines but also on large new turboprop systems.
Ref: Powerplant Handbook H-8083-32B-ATB Chapter 7 Page 34

7-43 AM.III.M.K4

How does the propeller overspeed governor on a turboprop engine decrease propeller RPM?

A. When oil pressure is decreased, the return spring and counterweights force the oil out of the servo piston.

B. As oil pressure increases, the servo piston is pushed forward, and the feather spring is compressed.

C. When oil pressure is increased, the return spring and counterweights force the oil out of the servo piston.

7-44 AM.III.M.K10

How is anti-icing fluid ejected from the slinger ring on a propeller?

A. By pump pressure.

B. By centripetal force.

C. By centrifugal force.

7-45 AM.III.M.K6

Inspection of aluminum propeller blades by dye penetrant inspection is accomplished to detect

A. fatigue failure.

B. material debond.

C. warpage.

7-46 AM.III.M.K6

When measuring a propeller's blade angle with a universal protractor, first position the propeller so that the blade to be measured is

A. horizontal to the wing with the leading edge up.

B. horizontal to the wing with the leading edge down.

C. perpendicular to the wing with the blade in ground idle position.

7-47 AM.III.M.K6

Propellers exposed to salt spray should be flushed with

A. engine oil.

B. fresh water.

C. soapy water.

7-48 AM.III.M.K7

If a flanged propeller shaft has dowel pins,

A. install the propeller so the blades are positioned for hand propping.

B. the propeller can only be installed in a given position.

C. the front cone should be checked for bottoming against the pins.

PROPELLERS

7-43 Answer B
When the engine speed increases above the RPM for which the governor is set, the counter weights move outward against the force of the speeder spring raising the pilot valve. The pilot valve then opens a metering port allowing governor oil flow from the propeller piston and so allowing the counterweights on the blades to increase pitch and slow the engine.
Ref: Powerplant Handbook H-8083-32B-ATB Chapter 7 Page 11

7-44 Answer C
Anti-icing fluid is transferred from a stationary nozzle on the engine nose case into a circular U-shaped channel (slinger ring) mounted on the rear of the propeller assembly. The fluid under pressure of centrifugal force is then transferred to each blade shank.
Ref: Powerplant Handbook H-8083-32B-ATB Chapter 7 Page 17

7-45 Answer A
Inspect aluminum propeller blades for cracks which are often caused by metal fatigue. A transverse crack of any size is cause for rejection. Use dye penetrant to confirm and suspected crack found in the propeller.
Ref: Powerplant Handbook H-8083-32B-ATB Chapter 7 Page 21

7-46 Answer A
If you suspect an improper blade angle, prior to an on-aircraft inspection with a universal protractor, position the blade in a horizontal position, parallel with the wing and with the leading edge up.
Ref: Powerplant Handbook H-8083-32B-ATB Chapter 7 Page 23

7-47 Answer B
If a propeller has been subjected to salt spray, as soon as possible flush it with fresh water until all traces of salt have been removed. After flushing thoroughly dry all parts and coat metal parts with clean engine oil or a suitable equivalent.
Ref: Powerplant Handbook H-8083-32B-ATB Chapter 7 Page 27

7-48 Answer B
A flange propeller has six studs configures in a four inch circle. Two special studs that also function as dowel pins are provided to transfer torque and index the propeller with respect to the engine crankshaft. Make certain to align the dowel studs in the propeller flange with the corresponding holes in the engine mounting flange in that stated position or 180° from that position.
Ref: Powerplant Handbook H-8083-32B-ATB Chapter 7 Page 27

ORAL EXAM

7-1(O).   How does a propeller function?

7-2(O).   Why are constant speed propellers used?

7-3(O).   What are the components of a propeller governor and how does it operate?

7-4(O).   What is a test club propeller? When and why is it used?

7-5(O).   What is the maximum interval between lubrication of a propeller and where does the technician find the proper procedures for lubrication of a particular propeller?

7-6(O).   How is the angle of a propeller blade measured while the propeller is mounted on the engine?

7-7(O).   In general, what is the procedure for removing a propeller?

7-8(O).   What is the function of a typical propeller synchronization system and how does it operate?

7-9(O).   Explain why is ice a problem for propeller operation. Then, name a means for anti-icing and a means of deicing aircraft propellers.

PROPELLERS

ANSWERS

ORAL EXAM

7-1(O).   A propeller is essentially a rotating wing. As the engine turns it, the air moving past the curved forward surface of the propeller causes a low pressure when compared to the area on the aft side of the propeller, which is relatively flat. As in a wing, the difference in pressure causes a reactive force in the direction of the lesser pressure. On a wing, this force is upward and is called lift. On a propeller, this force is forward and is called thrust. It is this force that moves the aircraft.
Ref: Powerplant Handbook H-8083-32B-ATB Chapter 7

7-2(O).   To obtain maximum efficiency from the propeller by rotating it at a constant speed and to keep the engine RPM constant while adjusting the power output with the throttle lever.
Ref: Powerplant Handbook H-8083-32B-ATB Chapter 7

7-3(O).   A typical propeller governor consists of a drive gear to engage the engine, an oil pump, a pilot valve controlled by flyweights, a relief valve system, a piston connected mechanically to the blades, a speeder spring, and an adjusting rack for control from the flight deck. The governor senses the RPM of the engine/propeller assembly via the flyweights. The force of the flyweights is counterbalanced against the force of the speeder spring that is set via the adjusting rack. If the speed of the engine and propeller increase, the flyweight force increases and they move outward. This opens the pilot valve and oil is pumped against the piston. The piston motion transmits the force to the blades which increase pitch angle. At a higher pitch angle, the force of the air striking the blades increases. This increases the load on the engine and serves to suppress engine RPM and keep it constant.
Ref: Powerplant Handbook H-8083-32B-ATB Chapter 7

7-4(O).   A test club propeller is a four-bladed, fixed pitch propeller used during ground testing or break-in of a reciprocating engine. The blades are short and designed to put the correct amount of load on the engine during the test break-in period. The multi-blade design also provides additional cooling airflow.
Ref: Powerplant Handbook H-8083-32B-ATB Chapter 7

7-5(O).   Propellers must be lubricated every 100 hours or at 12 calendar months, whichever occurs first. If annual operation is significantly less than 100 hours, calendar lubrication intervals should be reduced 6 months. Also, if the propeller is exposed to adverse atmospheric conditions, such as high humidity and, salt air, the calendar interval should be shortened to 6 months. The manufacturer's instructions should be consulted for the proper propeller lubrication procedures as well as oil and grease specifications.
Ref: Powerplant Handbook H-8083-32B-ATB Chapter 7

7-6(O).   Propeller blade angle is measure at a blade station(s) specified by the manufacturer. Blade stations are measured in inches from the base of the blade toward the tip. Using a propeller or universal protract placed at the correct blade station, follow the manufacturer's instruction. The angle between the plane of rotation and the propeller blade face at the specified station is what is being measured.
Ref: Powerplant Handbook H-8083-32B-ATB Chapter 7

7-7(O).   Always follow manufacturer's instruction. In general, remove the spinner dome. Then cut and remove the safety wire on the propeller mounting studs. Support the propeller assembly with a sling. Make an alignment mark on the hub and engine flange to maintain dynamic balance during reinstallation. Unscrew the four mounting bolts from the engine bushings. Unscrew the two mounting nuts and the attached studs from the engine bushings. If the propeller is removed between overhauls, mounting studs, nuts, and washers may be reused if not damaged or corroded. Using care and supporting the weight of the propeller assembly with the sling, remove the propeller from the mounting flange.
Ref: Powerplant Handbook H-8083-32B-ATB Chapter 7

ORAL EXAM

7-8(O).   Propeller synchronization is used to eliminate the unpleasant beat produced by unsynchronized propeller operation. A typical synchrophasing system is an electronic system. It functions to match the RPM of both engines and establish a blade phase relationship between the left and right propellers to reduce cabin noise. A switch on the flight deck controls the system. When in the "ON" position, pick-ups on each propeller send a signal to a control box. The control box sends a command signal to an RPM trimming coil on the propeller governor of the slow engine to adjust the RPM to equal that of the other propeller.
Ref: Powerplant Handbook H-8083-32B-ATB Chapter 7

7-9(O).   Ice formation on a propeller blade in effect produces a distorted blade airfoil section and makes the propeller inefficient. Ice collects asymmetrically and produces propeller unbalance resulting in destructive vibration and increased blade weight. A typical propeller anti-icing system includes an on-board reservoir of anti-icing fluid that is pumped to a slinger ring mounted on the rear of the assembly and distributed to the blades by centrifugal force. A typical propeller de-icing system includes electric heating elements adhered to the leading edge of each blade. Power is transferred to the propeller elements through brushes and a slip ring. A timer cycles the elements on and off in sequence or this can be controlled by the pilot.
Ref: Powerplant Handbook H-8083-32B-ATB Chapter 7

PROPELLERS

QUESTIONS

PRACTICAL EXAM

7-1(P).   Given an actual aircraft propeller or mockup, appropriate publications, and tooling inspect a propeller installation and make a minor repair on an aluminum propeller and record maintenance. [Level 3]

7-2(P).   Given an appropriate type certificate data sheet determine what minor propeller alterations are acceptable. [Level 2]

7-3(P).   Given an actual aircraft propeller or mockup, appropriate publications, and tooling service a constant speed propeller with lubricant and record maintenance. [Level 2]

7-4(P).   Given an actual aircraft propeller or mockup, appropriate publications, a propeller protractor determine correct blade angle and record findings. [Level 3]

7-5(P).   Given an actual aircraft propeller or mockup, appropriate publications, and tooling leak check a constant speed propeller installation and record findings. [Level 3]

7-6(P).   Given an actual aircraft propeller or mockup, appropriate publications, and tooling install a fixed pitch propeller and check the tip tracking and record maintenance. [Level 3]

7-7(P).   Given an actual aircraft propeller or mockup, appropriate publications, and tooling inspect a spinner/bulkhead for defects and proper alignment and installation and recording findings. [Level 3]

7-8(P).   Given an actual aircraft propeller or mockup, appropriate publications, and dye-penetrant complete an inspection the propeller to determine the amount of any damage and record findings. [Level 2]

7-9(P).   Given an actual aircraft propeller or mockup, appropriate publications, and tooling inspect a propeller governor and record findings. [Level 3]

7-10(P).   Given an actual aircraft propeller or mockup, appropriate publications, and tooling adjust a propeller governor and record maintenance. [Level 3]

7-11(P).   Given an actual aircraft propeller or mockup, appropriate publications, and tooling inspect a wood propeller and record findings. [Level 3]

7-12(P).   Given an actual aircraft propeller or mockup, appropriate publications, and tooling troubleshoot a propeller system and record findings. [Level 3]

ENGINE REMOVAL AND REPLACEMENT

CHAPTER 8

General Procedures, Inspection and Replacement of External Systems,
Mounting Engines for Replacement, Rigging and Adjustments

QUESTIONS

8-1 AM.III.C.K1
What is the responsibility of the FAA in determining the TBO
(Time Before Overhaul) number of hours of a particular
aircraft engine?
A. The FAA requires a minimum number of TBO hours of
   which the manufacturer's design team must comply.
B. The FAA determines TBO hours based on the
   manufacturer's specifications and historical data.
C. The FAA ensures that the manufacturer has determined
   this number.

8-2 AM.III.A.K8
If following a sudden reduction in engine speed due to a prop
strike, small filings of metal are found in the oil screen, where
is the most likely damaged?
A. The crankshaft.
B. The crankshaft bearings.
C. A connecting rod.

8-3 AM.III.C.K5
A ground incident that results in propeller sudden stoppage
may require a crankshaft run-out inspection. What publication
would be used to obtain crankshaft run-out tolerance?
A. current manufacturer's maintenance instructions
B. type certificate data sheet
C. AC43.13-1A Acceptable Methods, Techniques, and
   Practices Aircraft Inspection and Repair

8-4 AM.III.G.K6
When conducting spectrometric oil analysis, regarding a
specific particle type, which is of the greatest concern?
A. The amount of particles found in the oil.
B. The amount of particles found compared to the
   last test.
C. The size of the particles found in the oil.

8-5 AM.III.C.K7
The QECA system of engine replacement is primarily used
A. during unexpected engine replacements.
B. during scheduled engine replacements.
C. when the same engine will be removed, serviced,
   and reinstalled.

8-6 AM.III.C.K7
In addition to its primary purpose of confining a potential fire
to the engine compartment, the engine firewall also
A. provides mounting surfaces for the engine
   and accessories.
B. acts as a heat sink for the engine nacelle.
C. is used as a ground plain for radio antenna reception.

ENGINE REMOVAL AND REPLACEMENT

ANSWERS

8-1 Answer C
Engine life is dependent upon such factors as operational use, the quality of manufacture or overhaul, the type of aircraft in which the engine is installed, the kind of operation being carried out, and the degree to which maintenance is accomplished. Thus, the engine manufacturer sets engine removal times. Based on service experience, it is possible to establish a maximum expected Time Before Overhaul (TBO) or span of time within which an engine needs to be overhauled. Regardless of condition, an engine should be removed when it has accumulated the recommended maximum allowable time since the last overhaul or since new.
Ref: Powerplant Handbook H-8083-32B-ATB Chapter 8 Page 1

8-4 Answer B
It is normal for particles of wear metals to be found in oil. When these test are performed regularly in a healthy engine, the amount of any particular particle will remains roughly the same. However when a marked increase in the amount of a specific type of particle occurs, it is a sign that a component is near failure and that action must be taken before that actual failure occurs.
Ref: Powerplant Handbook H-8083-32B-ATB Chapter 8 Page 2

8-2 Answer B
Following a sudden slowdown, if there are no heavy metal particles found in the oil, restart the engine and then check for particles in the oil screen. If these are now found, the likely source are failing crankshaft bearings.
Ref: Powerplant Handbook H-8083-32B-ATB Chapter 8 Page 2

8-5 Answer B
After the decision has been made to remove an engine, the preparation of the replacement engine must be considered. Commercial operators, whose maintenance requires the most efficient and expeditious replacement of aircraft engines, usually rely on a system that utilizes the quick-engine-change-assembly, also sometimes referred to as the engine power package. The QECA is essentially a powerplant and the necessary accessories installed with the engine.
Ref: Powerplant Handbook H-8083-32B-ATB Chapter 8 Page 3

8-3 Answer A
When sudden stoppage occurs, the engine usually requires replacement or disassembly and inspection as per manufacturer's instructions. When a crankshaft or propeller drive shaft run-out is performed, consult the applicable manufacturer's instructions for permissible limits.
Ref: Powerplant Handbook H-8083-32B-ATB Chapter 8 Page 2

8-6 Answer A
The engine firewall also provides a mounting surface for units within the engine nacelle and a point of disconnect for lines, linkages, and electrical wiring that are routed between the engine and aircraft.
Ref: Powerplant Handbook H-8083-32B-ATB Chapter 8 Page 3, 4

8-7 AM.III.A.K6
When depreserving an opposed cylinder engine, after draining corrosion prevention compound you notice that small amounts remain clinging to the cylinder walls. What must be done?
   A. Wash out the remaining compound with Avgas.
   B. Nothing; small quantities are acceptable.
   C. Remove the cylinder head and clean it off manually.

8-8 AM.III.A.K8
If a reciprocating engine has suffered a major internal failure and must be replaced, which of the following appliances must always also be replaced, rather than simply cleaned and inspected?
   A. Oil cooler and propeller governor.
   B. Alternator and starter.
   C. Carburetor or fuel injection system components.

8-9 AM.III.A.K8
When preparing to remove an engine, fuel valves must be
   A. removed first.
   B. fully opened.
   C. fully closed even if they are solenoid operated.

8-10 AM.III.A.K8
When mounting an engine to an airframe; after all mounting bolts have been installed and properly torqued, what is typically the next step?
   A. Install intake components.
   B. Install the propeller.
   C. Install bonding strips.

8-11 AM.III.C.K7
When tightening the exhaust system clamps,
   A. torque the clamp nuts, run the engine, and then torque the nuts again.
   B. tapping the clamps with a rawhide mallet prevents binding.
   C. tighten the nuts, back them off and tighten them again.

8-12 AM.III.C.K7
Upon an engine installation, when adjusting the throttle linkage and other controls, set the control travel to
   A. precisely match the movement of the throttle arm stops.
   B. slightly exceed the movement of the throttle arm stops.
   C. be slightly less than the movement of the throttle arm stops.

ENGINE REMOVAL AND REPLACEMENT

ANSWERS

8-7 Answer B
While less critical than with radial engines, drain as much as possible. If larger puddles of compound exist, remove with a hand pump. Otherwise light coatings or small droplets remaining are not an issue and will quickly burn out when the engine is started.
Ref: Powerplant Handbook H-8083-32B-ATB Chapter 8 Page 4

8-8 Answer A
If an engine has been removed for internal failure, usually some units in the oil system must be replaced and others thoroughly cleaned and inspected. The oil cooler and temperature regulator must be removed and sent to a repair facility for overhaul. The propeller governor and feathering pump mechanism must also be replaced if these units are operated by oil pressure. There is a high probability that contaminants from the internal engine failure may have lodged in these parts.
Ref: Powerplant Handbook H-8083-32B-ATB Chapter 8 Page 5

8-9 Answer C
When preparing to remove an engine, check to see that all fuel selectors or solenoid operated fuel shutoff valves are closed. The fuel selector valves are either manually or solenoid operated. If solenoid operated fuel shutoff valves are installed, it may be necessary to turn the battery switch ON to close the valves. These valves close the fuel line at the firewall between the engine and the aircraft. After ensuring all fuel to the engine is shut off, disconnect the battery to eliminate the possibility of a hot wire starting a fire.
Ref: Powerplant Handbook H-8083-32B-ATB Chapter 8 Page 6

8-10 Answer C
After all mounting bolts are secured and safetied, bonding strips should be installed across each engine mount to provide an electrical path from the mount to the airframe. Beyond this, there are no specific rules for the order in which components should be installed. It is typically determined for each specific installation by checklists, experience, and convenience.
Ref: Powerplant Handbook H-8083-32B-ATB Chapter 8 Page 9-10

8-11 Answer B
During assembly of the exhaust system, the nuts should be gradually and progressively tightened to the correct torque. The clamps should be tapped with a rawhide mallet as they are being tightened to prevent binding at any point.
Ref: Powerplant Handbook H-8083-32B-ATB Chapter 8 Page 10

8-12 Answer B
Set control movements so there is a slight cushion between the control stop and the actuator stop. The presence of this cushion ensures that the travel of the throttle valve is not limited by the travel of the throttle control and that they are fully opened or closed when the control is at its stop. On multi engine aircraft, be sure this amount of cushion is equal for each engine so that each is aligned with any specific setting chosen.
Ref: Powerplant Handbook H-8083-32B-ATB Chapter 8 Page 11

8-13 AM.III.G.K4
How may it be determined that a reciprocating engine with a dry sump is pre-oiled sufficiently?
- A. The engine oil pressure gauge will indicate normal oil pressure
- B. Oil will flow from the engine return line or indicator port
- C. When the quantity of oil specified by the manufacturer has been pumped into the engine

8-16 AM.III.G.K6
When evaluating the results of a spectrometric oil analysis, which of the following is of the greatest concern?
- A. an indicator which is above normal
- B. an indicator which has risen since the last analysis
- C. an indicator which has risen at a faster rate than in its last analysis

8-14 AM.III.M.K7
Once an engine has been installed satisfactorily, the propeller can be installed. It should be
- A. tested before, during, and after the engine has been ground operated.
- B. mounted with the blades in the feathered position.
- C. a low pitch test propeller during ground test operation of the engine.

8-17 AM.III.I.K8
After a turbofan engine has been replaced, it must be trimmed. What other actions or conditions mandate that a turbofan engine be re-trimmed?
- A. annual inspection or replacement of the fuel control.
- B. replacement of the fuel control or after an in-flight shutdown.
- C. replacement of fuel control, engine not developing maximum thrust, or excessive throttle stagger.

8-15 AM.III.C.K8
Typical engine mounts on a reciprocating engine
- A. bolt firmly to the frame so vibration is kept to a minimum.
- B. are studs mounted in the rear of the engine and bolts used in the front of the engine.
- C. utilize a rubber shock mount to reduce vibration.

8-18 AM.III.I.K8
When trimming a turbine engine, from what point on the engine are measurements taken?
- A. Fuel flow sensor.
- B. Turbine inlet temperature sensor.
- C. Turbine discharge pressure line.

ENGINE REMOVAL AND REPLACEMENT

ANSWERS

8-13 Answer B
In using some types of pre-oilers, the oil line from the inlet side of the engine oil pump must be disconnected to permit the pre-oiler tank to be connected at this point. Then, a line must be disconnected, or an opening made in the oil system at the nose of the engine to allow oil to flow out of the engine. Oil flowing out of the engine indicates the completion of the pre-oiling operation since the oil has now passed through the entire system.
Ref: Powerplant Handbook H-8083-32B-ATB Chapter 8 Page 12

8-14 Answer A
The propeller must be checked before, during, and after the engine has been ground operated. The propeller should be checked for proper torque on the mounting bolts, leaks, vibration, and for correct safety. A propeller whose pitch-changing mechanism is electrically actuated may be checked before the engine is operated. Propellers whose pitch-changing mechanisms are oil actuated must be checked during engine operation after the normal operating temperature of the oil has been reached. In addition to checking the increase or decrease in RPM, the feathering cycle of the propeller should also be checked.
Ref: Powerplant Handbook H-8083-32B-ATB Chapter 8 Page 13

8-15 Answer C
Most reciprocating engines are bolted to the engine mount with the use of rubber engine mount pads. This helps dissipate the vibration developed by the engine.
Ref: Powerplant Handbook H-8083-32B-ATB Chapter 8 Page 16

8-16 Answer C
The existence of wear metals in oil is normal, and some engines will exhibit this wear at a greater rate than others. While all abnormal indications are cause for concern, an accelerated rate of change between one analysis and the next indicates that something in the engine's operation has changed which is then likely to accelerate further until an engine failure occurs.
Ref: Powerplant Handbook H-8083-32B-ATB Chapter 8 Page 2

8-17 Answer C
The fuel control of the engine is adjusted to trim the engine to obtain maximum thrust output of the engine when desired. The engine must be re-trimmed after a fuel control unit is replaced, the engine does not develop maximum thrust, engine change, or excessive throttle stagger.
Ref: Powerplant Handbook H-8083-32B-ATB Chapter 8 Page 14

8-18 Answer C
With the aircraft faced into the wind and the exhaust area clear, install an engine trim gauge to the T-fitting in the turbine discharge pressure line. Then run the engine for 5+ minutes to stabilize and refer your measurements to the manufacturer's correct trim values.
Ref: Powerplant Handbook H-8083-32B-ATB Chapter 8 Page 14, 15

8-19 AM.III.I.K8
For what primary purpose is a turbine engine fuel control unit trimmed?
  A. to obtain maximum thrust output when desired
  B. to properly position the thrust levers
  C. to adjust idle RPM

8-22 AM.III.C.K8
The engine mounts on a turbofan engine
  A. are solid steel due to the weight of the engine.
  B. isolate the aircraft structure from adverse engine vibrations.
  C. block the centrifugal force of the rotating fan mass.

8-20 AM.III.I.K8
Which two atmospheric factors must be primarily considered when checking and performing trim adjustments of a turbine engine?
  A. Ambient temperature and airport elevation.
  B. Ambient temperature and barometric pressure.
  C. Ambient temperature and humidity.

8-23 AM.III.A.K6
Engines that are not flown regularly may not achieve normal service life due to corrosion
  A. of the interior parts of the carburetor.
  B. of the crankshaft and bearing journals.
  C. in and around the cylinders.

8-21 AM.III.C.K8
A characteristic of Dyna-focal engine mounts as applied to aircraft reciprocating engines is that the
  A. shock mounts eliminate the torsional flexing of the powerplant.
  B. engine attached to the shock mounts at the engine's center of gravity.
  C. shock mounts point towards the engines center of gravity.

8-24 AM.III.A.K6
An aircraft engine having at least one continuous hour of operation with an oil temperature of at least 165°F within 30 days is said to be in
  A. temporary storage.
  B. active storage.
  C. indefinite storage.

ENGINE REMOVAL AND REPLACEMENT

ANSWERS

8-19 Answer A
All of the above are accomplished when trimming an engine. However, the primary purpose the fuel control unit of the engine is adjusted to trim the engine is to obtain maximum thrust output of the engine when desired.
Ref: Powerplant Handbook H-8083-32B-ATB Chapter 8 Page 14

8-20 Answer B
An actual trim check is done based on barometric pressure and temperature. For given temperatures and pressures, target parameter values vary slightly. A chart is developed by the manufacturer for use during the trim check and the values are checked against the tolerances given on the chart.
Ref: Powerplant Handbook H-8083-32B-ATB Chapter 8 Page 15

8-21 Answer C
Dyna-focal engine mounts, or vibration isolators, are units that give directional support to the engines. Dyna-focal engine mounts have the mounting pad angled to point to the CG (Center of Gravity) of the engine mass.
Ref: Powerplant Handbook H-8083-32B-ATB Chapter 8 Page 16, 17

8-22 Answer B
Vibration isolator engine mounts are used on turbofan engines. They isolate the airplane structure from adverse engine vibrations. Vibration isolators consist of a resilient material permanently enclosed in a metal case. As an engine vibrates, the resilient material deforms slightly, thereby dampening the vibrations before they reach the airplane structure. If complete failure or loss of the resilient material occurs, the isolators will continue to support the engine.
Ref: Powerplant Handbook H-8083-32B-ATB Chapter 8 Page 17

8-23 Answer C
An engine must receive daily care and attention to detect and correct early stages of corrosion.
Engines that are not flown regularly may not achieve normal service life because of corrosion in and around the cylinders. The normal combustion process creates moisture and corrosive byproducts that attack the unprotected surfaces of the cylinder walls, valves, and any other exposed areas that are unprotected.
Ref: Powerplant Handbook H-8083-32B-ATB Chapter 8 Page 18

8-24 Answer B
There are three types of engine storage: active, temporary and indefinite. Active storage is defined as having at least one continuous hour of operation with an oil temperature of at least 165°F to 200°F and storage time not to exceed 30 days. Temporary storage describes an aircraft and engine that is not flown for 30 to 90 days. Indefinite storage is for an aircraft not to be flown for over 90 days or is removed from the aircraft for extended time.
Ref: Powerplant Handbook H-8083-32B-ATB Chapter 8 Page 19

8-25 AM.III.A.K6

Light corrosion preventative compounds

A. are intended to preserve an engine for less than 30 days and to spray cylinders.

B. can be used to dip metal parts in for long-term storage.

C. do not mix with the oil but cover surfaces where oil has been removed.

8-26 AM.III.A.K6

To prevent moisture from aiding in corroding engine cylinders when stored or shipped, spark plugs are remove and dehydrator plugs installed. When the dehydrator plugs are blue, it is an indication

A. of high humidity with corrosion likely.

B. of low humidity with corrosion unlikely.

C. the limited life of the desiccant has been reached.

8-27 AM.III.A.K6

When preparing an engine for indefinite storage

A. replace the oil with a corrosion prevention mixture; then run the engine at normal operating temperatures for one hour.

B. run the engine until reaching normal operating temperatures; then drain and replace the oil with the manufacturer's recommended corrosion prevention mixture.

C. drain and replace the engine oil with a corrosion prevention mixture without starting the engine.

8-28 AM.III.A.K6

Which is considered as the most critical function of a shipping or storage container for an aircraft engine?

A. Proper ventilation.

B. Filtering of dust and debris.

C. Elimination of humidity.

8-29 AM.III.C.K7

Before removing a fuel hose from an engine, a solenoid operated fuel valve is placed in the closed position by

A. moving the fuel selector to fuel cut off position.

B. Switching off all fuel pumps.

C. Closing the solenoid fuel valves with battery power and then disconnecting battery.

8-30 AM.III.B.K9

When a turbine engine is sealed in a container during long term storage, periodic checks must be made every 30 days for

A. corrosion.

B. humidity.

C. temperature.

ENGINE REMOVAL AND REPLACEMENT

ANSWERS

8-25 Answer A
Corrosion preventative compounds are petroleum-based products that form a wax-like film over metal to which they are applied. Several types are manufactured according to different specifications to fit various aviation needs. The type mixed with engine oil is a relatively light compound that readily blends with the oil when the mixture is heated. The light mixture is intended for use when a preserved engine is to remain inactive for less than 30 days. It is also used to spray cylinders and other designated areas.
Ref: Powerplant Handbook H-8083-32B-ATB Chapter 8 Page 18

8-26 Answer B
Cobalt chloride is added to the silica gel used in dehydrator plugs. This makes it possible for the plugs to indicate moisture content in the cylinders. The cobalt chloride treated silica gel remains a bright blue color with low relative humidity. As humidity increases, the shade of blue becomes progressively lighter, becoming lavender at 30 percent humidity and fading through various shades of pink until at 60 percent humidity, the dehydrator plug is natural or white in color. When humidity is less than 30 percent, corrosion does not normally take place.
Ref: Powerplant Handbook H-8083-32B-ATB Chapter 8 Page 18

8-27 Answer A
Before an engine is placed in temporary or indefinite storage, it should be operated and filled with a corrosion-preventative oil mixture added in the oil system to retard corrosion by coating the engine's internal parts. Drain the normal lubricating oil from the sump or system, and replace with a preservative oil mixture according to the manufacturer's instructions. Operate the engine until normal operating temperatures are obtained for at least one hour.
Ref: Powerplant Handbook H-8083-32B-ATB Chapter 8 Page 18, 19

8-28 Answer C
When lowering a wooden shipping case cover into position, be sure the humidity indicator card is placed so it can be seen through the inspection window. Engines in wooden shipping containers typically have an envelope that is vacuumed to remove excess air. Metal shipping containers are sealed and pressurized to about 5 psi with dehydrated air. However, a humidity indicator should be fastened inside the container at the inspection window provided.
Ref: Powerplant Handbook H-8083-32B-ATB Chapter 8 Page 21

8-29 Answer C
The fuel selector valves are either manually or solenoid operated. If solenoid-operated fuel shutoff valves are installed, it may be necessary to turn the battery switch on before the valves can be closed, since the solenoid depends on electricity for operation.
Ref: Powerplant Handbook H-8083-32B-ATB Chapter 8 Page 6

8-30 Answer B
The onset of corrosion may occur if humidity levels increase above an acceptable range. Therefore humidity indicators are included with all storage containers and their levels must checked on a regular basis, typically every 30 days.
Ref: Powerplant Handbook H-8083-32B-ATB Chapter 8 Page 21

ORAL EXAM

8-1(O).   What procedures are required after the installation of a turbine engine?

8-2(O).   What are the reasons a turbine engine would require a trim check?

8-3(O).   What is the procedure required to adjust (trim) a fuel control unit (FCU)?

8-4(O).   Name three reasons for removal of an engine and what are the required inspections after a potentially damaging event occurs.

8-5(O)   Prior to removing a turbofan engine from an aircraft, what are the 6 component groups that must first be removed or disconnected?

8-6(O)   Prior to starting a new reciprocating engine for the first time, name 4 steps which must be taken?

ENGINE REMOVAL AND REPLACEMENT

ANSWERS

ORAL EXAM

8-1(O).   After installation, an engine run-up should be performed. On newer engines with electronic engine controls, verification of correct engine instrument indications is required. On engines with hydromechanical fuel controls, the engine must be manually trimmed. This is the process of adjusting the idle and maximum RPM and EPR settings in accordance with temperature and pressure adjusted values provided by the manufacturer.
Ref: Powerplant Handbook H-8083-32B-ATB Chapter 8

8-2(O).   It has a hydromechanical fuel control and the engine or fuel control has just been changed. Also, if the engine is not developing maximum thrust or if there is excessive throttle stagger the engine should be trimmed.
Ref: Powerplant Handbook H-8083-32B-ATB Chapter 8

8-3(O).   Ideally, trimming an engine should be done under conditions of no wind and clear, moisture-free air. Never trim when icing conditions exist because of the adverse effect on trimming accuracy. If there is wind, face the engine intake into the wind to avoid re-ingestion of the exhaust gases. Accurate ambient temperature and pressure readings need to be taken. These are used to compute the desired EPR indication(s) from charts in the maintenance manual. Idle RPM and maximum speed adjustments are made as well as acceleration and deceleration checks according to the specific instructions provided by the manufacturer.
Ref: Powerplant Handbook H-8083-32B-ATB Chapter 8

8-4(O).   Reasons for removal of an engine include: Engine or components lifespan exceeded; sudden stoppage; sudden reduction in speed; metal particles in oil; negative spectrometric oil analysis; operational problems such as excessive vibration; low power output caused by low compression or internal engine deterioration or damage; turbine engine parameters exceeded; and, turbine engine condition monitoring program trends. A sudden reduction does not automatically result in an engine change. Additional test such as a complete visual inspection should be performed - especially of the engine mounts and the nose section of the engine, crankshaft run-out, and oil filter, sump, and screen checks for metal in the oil. If these all prove negative, the engine may be able to stay in service. Also, just the presence of metal in the oil does not mean the engine has to be removed. The quantity and type of metal particles must be further analyzed. Any ferrous metal in an oil screen is cause for concern. Small non-ferrous particles could be normal. A complete oil and filter/screen change should be performed and the engine should be ground-run and filters and screens rechecked.
Ref: Powerplant Handbook H-8083-32B-ATB Chapter 8

8-5(O).   (A) Engine mount access plates; (B) Pneumatic ducts; (C) Electrical connections; (D) Thermocouple leads; (E) Fuel lines; (F) Hydraulic lines.
Ref: Powerplant Handbook H-8083-32B-ATB Chapter 8

8-6(O).   (A) A thorough ground check is performed; (B) Pre-oil the engine by rotating it with the starter with a spark plug removed from each cylinder; (C) Bleed the fuel system to eliminate air bubbles and traces of preservative oil; (D) Check propeller bolt torque and electrical operation or oil flow if applicable.
Ref: Powerplant Handbook H-8083-32B-ATB Chapter 8

PRACTICAL EXAM

8-1(P).   Given an actual aircraft engine or mockup, appropriate publications, and tooling, perform a crankshaft run-out on a reciprocating engine installation and record findings. [Level 3]

8-2(P).   Given an actual aircraft engine or mockup, appropriate publications, and tooling, inspect a reciprocating aircraft engine as though it had experienced a sudden reduction in speed during operation and record findings. [Level 3]

8-3(P).   Given an actual aircraft engine or mockup, appropriate publications, and tooling, inspect a reciprocating engine for suspected internal engine damage and record findings. [Level 3]

8-4(P).   Given an actual aircraft engine or mockup, appropriate publications, and tooling, inspect an engine mounting frame assembly and mounting bolts for serviceability and record findings. [Level 3]

8-5(P).   Given an actual aircraft engine or mockup, appropriate publications, and required tooling, prepare an engine for removal. [Level 3]

8-6(P).   Given an actual aircraft engine or mockup, appropriate publications, and tooling, inspect the intake ducting and exhaust system of an aircraft engine and record findings. [Level 3]

8-7(P).   Given an actual aircraft engine or mockup, appropriate publications, and tooling, disconnect and inspect the engine controls including control rods, cables, pulleys, bell cranks, and linkages. Record findings. [Level 3]

8-8(P).   Given an actual aircraft engine or mockup, appropriate publications, and tooling, properly remove an aircraft engine from the aircraft or test stand. [Level 3]

8-9(P).   Given an actual aircraft engine or mockup, appropriate publications, and tooling, properly mount an aircraft engine to the aircraft or a test stand. [Level 3]

8-10(P).   Given an actual aircraft engine or mockup, appropriate publications, and tooling, properly connect the engine controls to a newly mounted engine and record the maintenance activity. [Level 3]

8-11(P).   Given an actual aircraft engine or mockup, appropriate publications, and tooling, inspect and connect electrical wiring to engine mounted components on a newly mounted engine and record maintenance activity. [Level 3]

8-12(P).   Given an actual aircraft engine or mockup, appropriate publications, and tooling, properly connect all fluid lines to a newly mounted engine and record the maintenance activity. [Level 3]

8-13(P).   Given an actual aircraft engine or mockup, appropriate publications, and tooling, properly connect all intake ducting and the exhaust system to a newly mounted engine and record the maintenance activity. [Level 3]

8-14(P).   Given an actual aircraft engine or mockup, appropriate publications, and tooling, perform the final inspection and preparation of a newly installed engine for run-up and record the maintenance activity. [Level 3]

ENGINE REMOVAL AND REPLACEMENT

PRACTICAL EXAM

8-15(P).   Given an actual aircraft engine or mockup, appropriate publications, and tooling, run-up a newly installed engine. Check and record all performance parameters per manufacturer's data . [Level 3]

8-16(P).   Given an actual aircraft engine or mockup, appropriate publications, and tooling, perform a post run-p inspection of a newly installed engine and record findings. [Level 3]

8-17(P).   Given an actual aircraft engine or mockup, appropriate publications, and tooling, perform fuel control rigging, adjustments, and trimming of a turbine engine. Record the maintenance activity. [Level 3]

ENGINE FIRE PROTECTION SYSTEMS

Engine Fire Detection, Extinguishers, Troubleshooting, Fire Detection System Maintenance

CHAPTER
9

9-1 AM.III.E.K2
In a thermal switch type fire detection system, heat sensitive switches are placed in _____ with each other, and in _____ with the flight deck indicator lights.
   A. parallel; series
   B. series; parallel
   C. series; series

9-2 AM.III.E.K2
Which of the following fire detection systems are commonly used in large aircraft engine nacelles?
   A. Optical sensors.
   B. Thermocouple detector.
   C. Kidde continuous-loop.

9-3 AM.III.E.K2
What is the operating principle of the spot detector sensor in a fire detection system?
   A. Resistant core material that prevents current flow at normal temperatures.
   B. If conventional thermocouple that produces a current flow.
   C. A bimetallic thermal switch that closes when heated to a high temperature.

9-4 AM.III.E.K2
Which of the following fire detection systems measure temperature rise compared to a reference temperature?
   A. Thermocouple
   B. Thermal Switch
   C. Lindberg Continuous Element

9-5 AM.III.E.K2
Optical fire detection systems
   A. can be infrared or ultraviolet.
   B. must be used out of the way of direct sunlight.
   C. give a false alarm if not disarmed before an incandescent light strikes the sensor.

9-6 AM.III.E.K2
A fire detection system operates on the principle of a buildup of gas pressure within a tube proportional to temperature. Which of the following systems does this statement define?
   A. Kidde Continuous-Loop System
   B. Pneumatic Thermal Detectors
   C. Thermal Switch System

ENGINE FIRE PROTECTION SYSTEMS

ANSWERS

9-1 Answer A
A thermal switch has one or more heat sensitive switches energized by the aircraft power system which close when the temperature reaches a certain point. They are connected in parallel to each other for independent operation, but in series with the flight deck warning lights.
Ref: Powerplant Handbook H-8083-32B-ATB Chapter 9 Page 2

9-2 Answer C
Large commercial aircraft almost exclusively use continuous thermal sensing elements for powerplant protection since these systems offer superior detection performance and proven ruggedness to survive in the harsh environment of an engine nacelle.
Ref: Powerplant Handbook H-8083-32B-ATB Chapter 9 Page 3, 4

9-3 Answer C
Thermal switches are heat sensitive units that complete electrical circuits at a certain temperature. They are connected in parallel with each other, but in series with the indicator lights. If the temperature rises above a set value in any area where a thermal switch is located, the switch closes completing the light circuit to indicate a fire or overheat condition.
Ref: Powerplant Handbook H-8083-32B-ATB Chapter 9 Page 2

9-4 Answer A
A thermocouple depends on the rate of temperature rise and does not give a warning when an engine slowly overheats or a short circuit develops. The thermocouple is constructed of a junction of two dissimilar metals that produce current flow when heated. In addition to the thermocouple sensors, there is a reference junction of dissimilar metals enclosed in a dead air space between two insulation blocks. This reference junction box is in the engine nacelle. Current flow of the thermocouple sensor(s) is compared to the current flow at the reference junction. Only the sensor temperature increasing a faster rate than the reference junction temperature produces enough resultant current flow to close the fire warning indicator circuit.
Ref: Powerplant Handbook H-8083-32B-ATB Chapter 9 Page 2

9-5 Answer A
Optical sensors are often referred to as flame detectors. They are designed to alarm when they detect the presence of prominent, specific radiation emissions from hydrocarbon flames. The two types of optical sensors available are infrared (IR) and ultraviolet (UV), based on the specific emission wavelengths they are designed to detect. A window in the unit allows light to strike a detector. The processing electronics are tailored exactly to the time signature of all known hydrocarbon flame sources and ignores false alarms sources such as incandescent lights and sunlight.
Ref: Powerplant Handbook H-8083-32B-ATB Chapter 9 Page 3

9-6 Answer B
Pneumatic detectors are based on the principle of gas laws. The sensing element consists of a closed helium-filled tube connected at one end to a responder assembly. As the element is heated, the gas pressure inside the tube increases until the alarm threshold is reached. An internal switch in the responder closes and an alarm is reported on the flight deck. Thermal switches are spot detectors and the Kidde continuous-loop system consists of two wires embedded in an inconel tube with a thermistor core material. Therefore, the gas-filled continuous element, sometimes called Lindberg from the name of its long-time manufacturer, is the answer.
Ref: Powerplant Handbook H-8083-32B-ATB Chapter 9 Page 3

9-7 AM.III.E.K2

What is the principle of operation of the continuous loop fire detection system sensor?
  A. Fuse material which melts at high temperatures.
  B. Core resistance material which prevents current flow at normal temperatures.
  C. A bimetallic thermo-switch which closes when heated to a high temperature.

9-10 AM.III.E.K4

In the event of a fire caused by a false start of a turbine engine which is not blown out by continued starting attempts, which agent is first used as an extinguishant?
  A. Carbon Dioxide (CO_2)
  B. Halon 1301
  C. HCL-125

9-8 AM.III.E.K4

Which of the following is the safest fire-extinguishing agent to use from a standpoint of toxicity and corrosion hazards?
  A. Dibromodiflouromethane (Halon 1202)
  B. Bromochlorodiflouromethane (Halon 1211)
  C. Bromotriflouromethane (Halon 1301)

9-11 AM.III.E.K5

A common visual check of fire detection elements includes
  A. the contact points in the control box.
  B. cracked or broken sections.
  C. the color of missing blowout disks.

9-9 AM.III.E.K4

How is the fire extinguishing agent distributed in the engine section?
  A. Spray nozzles and fluid pump.
  B. Nitrogen pressure and slinger rings.
  C. Spray nozzles and perforated tubing.

9-12 AM.III.E.K5

If a continuous-loop fire detection system is giving a false alarm, how can it be determined if the problem is in the control unit or in the sensing loop?
  A. By disconnecting the loop from the control box and observing if the false alarm stops.
  B. By connecting a voltmeter across the connected loop terminals.
  C. By resetting the warning lights and timing the interval until the next false alarm.

ENGINE FIRE PROTECTION SYSTEMS

ANSWERS

9-7 Answer B
In the Kidde continuous-loop system, two wire conductors are embedded in an inconel tube filled with a thermistor core material. One conductor has a ground connection to the tube, the other conductor connects to the fire detection control unit. As the temperature of the core increases, electrical resistance of the thermistor core decreases. Current can flow to ground completing the overheat or fire warning circuit which warns the crew on the flight deck.
Ref: Powerplant Handbook H-8083-32B-ATB Chapter 9 Page 3, 4

9-8 Answer C
The most common extinguishing agent still used today is Halon 1301 because of its effective firefighting capability and relatively low toxicity. Noncorrosive Halon 1301 does not effect the material it contacts and requires no clean-up when discharged.
Ref: Powerplant Handbook H-8083-32B-ATB Chapter 9 Page 7

9-9 Answer C
Many systems use perforated tubing or discharge nozzles to distribute the extinguishing agent. High rate of discharge (HRD) systems use open-end tubes to deliver a large quantity of extinguishing agent in 1 to 2 seconds.
Ref: Powerplant Handbook H-8083-32B-ATB Chapter 9 Page 7

9-10 Answer B
Halon 1301 is the current extinguishing agent for commercial aircraft. Never use CO_2 as its cooling effect can damage the engine. HCL-125 is currently experimental for military use only.
Ref: Powerplant Handbook H-8083-32B-ATB Chapter 9 Page 79

9-11 Answer B
An inspection and maintenance program for all types of continuous-loop systems should include the following visual checks and others. 1) Inspect for cracked or broken sections caused by crushing or squeezing between inspection plates, cowl panels, or engine components, 2) Inspect for abrasion caused by rubbing of the element on the cowling, accessories, or structural members, 3) Check the condition of rubber grommets in mounting clamps which may be softened from exposure to oils or hardened from excessive heat, 4) Look for dents and kinks in sensing element sections.
Ref: Powerplant Handbook H-8083-32B-ATB Chapter 9 Page 10

9-12 Answer A
Fire alarms and warning lights can occur when no engine fire or overheat condition exists. Such false alarms can most easily be located by disconnecting the engine sensing loop from the control unit. If the false alarm ceases when the engine sensing loop is disconnected, the fault is in the disconnected sensing loop.
Ref: Powerplant Handbook H-8083-32B-ATB Chapter 9 Page 11, 12

9-13 AM.III.E.K4
Generally speaking, as air temperature increases, the allowable pressure range inside a fire extinguisher container
A. goes up.
B. goes down.
C. remains constant.

9-16 AM.III.E.K4
Within an engine fire extinguisher system what causes the extinguishant to be transported to the fire?
A. An explosive charge.
B. Pressurized gas.
C. Pressure differentials caused by the fire.

9-14 AM.III.E.K5
Using the chart below (Figure 9-18) what are the fire extinguisher container pressure limits when the temperature is 40°F?
A. 448 psi minimum and 598 psi maximum.
B. 405 psi minimum and 560 psi maximum.
C. 477 psi minimum and 650 psi maximum.

9-17 AM.III.E.K4
How is the fire extinguishing agent discharged on most transport category aircraft?
A. By pulling the fire handle.
B. By pulling the fire handle and rotating it to the mechanic stop.
C. By pressing the extinguisher discharge button on the fire control panel.

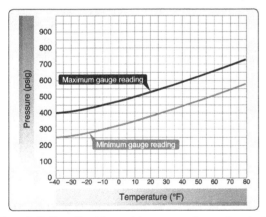

Figure 9-18. Fire extinguisher container pressure-temperature chart.

9-15 AM.III.E.K5
Engine fire detection on a Boeing 777 aircraft is accomplished with two loops which are monitored by the fire detection card file. When is a BITE test performed?
A. When one of the loops fails to have continuity and the other one has continuity.
B. Before starting the engine and before it is shut down.
C. When power is applied, after a power interrupt, and every 5 minutes of operation.

9-18 AM.III.E.K4
In which situation will the fire extinguishing system of Auxiliary Power Unit (APU) discharge automatically?
A. When both optical and heat sensors detect a fire.
B. When the aircraft weight on wheels sensor is activated.
C. When neither of the aircraft's main engines are running.

ENGINE FIRE PROTECTION SYSTEMS

ANSWERS

9-13 Answer A
Fire extinguisher containers are checked periodically to insure that the pressure is between the prescribed minimum and maximum limits. Changes of pressure with ambient temperatures must also fall within prescribed limits.
Ref: Powerplant Handbook H-8083-32B-ATB Chapter 9 Page 12, Figure 9-18

9-14 Answer A
To find the answer on the chart, locate the temperature on the bottom (horizontal) scale: 40°F. Go straight up the 40°F line until you intersect with the green arc. Follow this intersection point across to the vertical scale to obtain the minimum pressure reading (448 psi). Now continue up the 40°F line until it intersects with the blue arc. This is the maximum pressure allowed in the extinguisher bottle at 40°F. From this intersection point, move horizontally to the vertical scale to obtain the maximum psi allowed in the bottle (598 psi). So on a day where the temperature is 40°F, the pressure in the fire extinguisher bottle should between 448 psi and 598 psi. If it is not, the bottle should be replaced.
Ref: Powerplant Handbook H-8083-32B-ATB Chapter 9 Page 12

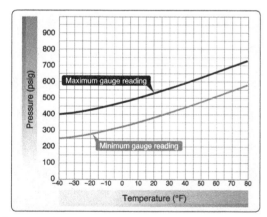

Figure 9-18. Fire extinguisher container pressure-temperature chart.

9-15 Answer C
The 777 has continuous fault monitoring of the fire detection loops. Built-In-Test-Equipment (BITE) performs a test of the engine fire detection system for these conditions: 1) when the system first gets power, 2) after a power interrupt, and 3) every 5 minutes of operation.
Ref: Powerplant Handbook H-8083-32B-ATB Chapter 9 Page 14

9-16 Answer B
When a fire extinguishing system is activated an explosive device called a squib is electrically activated, braking the seal of a pressurized bottle containing nitrogen. The escaping nitrogen sends the extinguishant to the fire.
Ref: Powerplant Handbook H-8083-32B-ATB Chapter 9 Page 16

9-17 Answer B
When the fire switch is pulled, the push-pull switch contacts operate electrical circuits that stop the engine and isolate it from the airplane systems. With the switch pulled, it can be rotated to left or right to a mechanical stop at the discharge position. The rotary switch contacts close and operate the fire extinguishing system (discharges the agent).
Ref: Powerplant Handbook H-8083-32B-ATB Chapter 9 Page 16

9-18 Answer C
Because the APU is often operated with no personnel on board, its fire protection system can operate in an unattended mode. This mode is activated when the aircraft is on the ground and neither of the main engines are running, thus signifying that the flight deck is unoccupied.
Ref: Powerplant Handbook H-8083-32B-ATB Chapter 9 Page 18

ORAL EXAM

9-1(O). How would a technician verify proper operation of a fire extinguishing system?

9-2(O). How would a technician troubleshoot an engine fire detection system?

9-3(O). What are the basic inspection requirements for an engine fire extinguisher squib and the safety practices and precautions to be followed?

9-4(O). What are the components of a typical fire detection system?

9-5(O). Maintenance procedures for fire detection systems include extensive visual inspection of the components. Name three common items to look for on a visual inspection of a fire detection system.

ENGINE FIRE PROTECTION SYSTEMS

ANSWERS

ORAL EXAM

9-1(O).   By inspection and good maintenance practices. The fire extinguishing system contains agent containers that must be verified as fully charged by checking the pressure gauge mounted in each bottle against a chart containing temperature-adjusted values. The extinguisher bottle squib, which fires to discharge the agent, has a limited service life and must be changed if the date on the squib has been exceeded. The pressure switch mounted on the bottle sends a signal for an indication on the flight deck when low pressure exists in the bottle due to leakage or discharge. This indication should not be illuminated. An electrical wiring continuity check can also be performed to ensure that power will arrive at the squib when the switch on the flight deck is closed.
Ref: Powerplant Handbook H-8083-32B-ATB Chapter 9

9-2(O).   A push-to-test button is provided on most fire detection systems. It should light all warning lights and sound the aural alarms. Failure to do so requires further investigation. A faulty test switch or control unit is possible. Also, lack of electric power, an inoperative indicator light, or opening in the sensor element or connecting wiring are possible. Continuity of the sensing element can be checked by measuring the resistance. Intermittent alarms can be traced by visual inspection and moving wires and the sensors in suspected areas to recreate the fault. Also, by disconnecting the sensing elements from the control unit, the fault can be isolated to the sensing elements if the false alarm stops.
Ref: Powerplant Handbook H-8083-32B-ATB Chapter 9

9-3(O).   The squib must be inspected to insure it is within its serviceable life. It must be replaced if it is not. The date is stamped on the outside of the squib. Power to the discharge valve assembly should be disconnected when disassembled to access the squib. A discharge cartridge (squib) removed from an assembly should not be used in another discharge valve assembly. The distance that the contact points protrude may vary. The wrong length of protrusion could result in a loss of electrical continuity required to fire the squib and discharge the agent.
Ref: Powerplant Handbook H-8083-32B-ATB Chapter 9

9-4(O).   There are different types of fire detection systems. All types have some sort of detection device and indication devices on the flight deck. Thermal switch systems are simple and typically will also contain a test switch, test relay, and a dimming relay for the indicator light(s). Thermocouple detection systems contain a control box with relays and a thermal test unit. Optical fire detection systems contain an amplifier and comparative circuits to decipher sensing data. Continuous loop systems also contain control boxes which decipher the analog signal from the sensor loops and signal warnings or supply the Aircraft In-flight Monitoring System. The most sophisticated systems contain a control module that uses control cards with various interpretive circuitry to decipher signals from each area where sensors are located. Some systems will initiate extinguishing automatically from the control module.
Ref: Powerplant Handbook H-8083-32B-ATB Chapter 9

9-5(O).   Cracked or broken loop sections, abrasion of elements by rubbing, loose metal that might short a spot detector, condition of rubber grommets and mounting clamps, dents and kinks in loop elements, secure connections at the end of the sensing elements, integrity of shielded leads, and, proper routing and support of elements.
Ref: Powerplant Handbook H-8083-32B-ATB Chapter 9

PRACTICAL EXAM

9-1(P).   Given an actual aircraft engine or mockup, appropriate publications, and tooling check an engine fire detection system for proper operation and record findings. [Level 2]

9-2(P).   Given an actual aircraft engine or mockup, appropriate publications, and tooling check an engine fire extinguishing system for proper operation and record findings. [Level 2]

9-3(P).   Given an actual aircraft engine or mockup, appropriate publications, and tooling accomplish a weight and pressure inspection of an engine fire bottle, verify hydrostatic inspection date and record findings. [Level 2]

9-4(P).   Given an actual aircraft engine or mockup, appropriate publications, and tooling repair an engine fire detector heat sensing loop malfunction and record maintenance. [Level 3]

9-5(P).   Given an actual aircraft engine or mockup, appropriate publications, and tooling check operation of firewall shut-off valve after a fire handle is pulled and record findings. [Level 2]

9-6(P).   Given an actual aircraft engine or mockup, appropriate publications, and tooling troubleshoot an engine fire detection and record findings. [Level 2]

9-7(P).   Given an actual aircraft engine or mockup, appropriate publications, and tooling troubleshoot an engine fire extinguishing system and record findings. [Level 2]

9-8(P).   Given an actual aircraft engine or mockup, appropriate publications, and tooling inspect an engine fire detection and record findings. [Level 3]

9-9(P).   Given an actual aircraft engine or mockup, appropriate publications, and tooling inspect an engine fire extinguishing system and record findings. [Level 3]

PAGE LEFT BLANK INTENTIONALLY

QUESTIONS

10-1 AM.III.C.K7
A certified technician with only a powerplant rating may NOT perform or supervise a major overhaul of an engine
  A. if it is operated for commercial purposes.
  B. if it has been operated beyond its scheduled TBO time.
  C. if it is equipped with a supercharger.

10-2 AM.III.C.K7
In the sequence tasks to be performed in a major engine overhaul, which is done first?
  A. Clean the engine.
  B. Drain all fluids.
  C. Visually inspect the engine.

10-3 AM.III.C.K7
Indentations on bearing races caused by high static loads are known as
  A. fretting.
  B. brinelling.
  C. galling.

10-4 AM.III.C.K7
What type of defect is most likely to be found on a ball bearing assembly?
  A. Burnishing
  B. Fretting
  C. Galling

10-5 AM.III.C.K7
Which component of a piston engine would be the most susceptible to the defect known as "pitting"?
  A. Bearing races.
  B. The piston dome.
  C. An exhaust valve.

10-6 AM.III.C.K7
During visual inspection while overhauling an engine, the piston heads were depressed. This is a sign that
  A. the engine was running normally.
  B. preignition had occurred.
  C. detonation had occurred.

ENGINE MAINTENANCE AND OPERATION

ANSWERS

10-1 Answer C
A certified technician with a powerplant rating may perform or supervise a major engine overhaul in all cases except if the engine contains a supercharger or a propeller reduction system other than with spur type gears.
Ref: Powerplant Handbook H-8083-32B-ATB Chapter 10 Page 1

10-2 Answer A
The first step of an engine overhaul is known as a receiving inspection. This inspection includes a check of all paper work, AD compliance, log books, cleaning of the exterior and mounting it on an overhaul stand. The disassembly process follows which includes draining all fluids, and then followed by a visual, structural (NDT) and dimensional inspection.
Ref: Powerplant Handbook H-8083-32B-ATB Chapter 10 Page 2

10-3 Answer B
Several terms are used to describe defects detected in engine parts during inspection. One common term is brinelling. Brinelling is one or more indentations on bearing races, usually caused by high static loads or application of force during installation or removal. Indentations are rounded or spherical due to the impression left by the contacting balls or rollers of the bearings.
Ref: Powerplant Handbook H-8083-32B-ATB Chapter 10 Page 3

10-4 Answer C
Ball bearing assemblies should be inspected for roughness, flat spots, and pitting. In addition the journals should be inspected for galling, scores, and misalignment. Fretting is caused by slight movement in rigidly attached surfaces. Burnishing is resembles polishing caused by movement of surfaces of differing hardness.
Ref: Powerplant Handbook H-8083-32B-ATB Chapter 10 Page 3, 4

10-5 Answer A
Pitting is the result of chemical or electrochemical corrosion which can be found in areas closely separated only by thin films of an electrolyte such as moisture or various hydrocarbons such as oil. Damage to piston domes and exhaust valves are most likely caused by physical stresses like burning or cracking.
Ref: Powerplant Handbook H-8083-32B-ATB Chapter 10 Page 3, 4

10-6 Answer C
When applicable, check for flatness of the piston head using a straight edge and thickness gauge. If a depression is found, check for cracks on the inside of the piston. A depression in the top of the piston usually means that detonation has occurred within the cylinder.
Ref: Powerplant Handbook H-8083-32B-ATB Chapter 10 Page 5

10-7 AM.III.A.K8

When cleaning aluminum and magnesium engine parts, it is inadvisable to soak them in solutions containing soap because

A. some of the soap will become impregnated in the surface of the material and subsequently cause engine oil contamination and foaming.
B. the soap can chemically alter the metals causing them to become more susceptible to corrosion.
C. the parts can be destroyed by dissimilar metal electrolytic action if they are placed together in the solution for more than a few minutes.

10-8 AM.III.A.K8

What is always the final step when degreasing a metal engine part with a soap and water or chemical solution?

A. Respray the part with oil.
B. Dry the part with clean rag to remove residue.
C. Rewash the part with clean water.

10-9 AM.III.C.K7

During inspection, If a rocker shaft is found with a bronze discoloration, what additional component should be inspected?

A. The rocker arm tips.
B. Alignment of the oil holes.
C. The rocker bushing.

10-10 AM.III.A.K8

On which part of the cylinder walls of a normally operating engine will the greatest amount of wear occur?

A. At the interface of the piston rings.
B. Near the top of the cylinder.
C. Near the bottom of the cylinder.

10-11 AM.III.A.K8

During overhaul, reciprocating engine exhaust valves are checked for stretch (Figure 10-8)

A. with a suitable inside spring caliper.
B. using a manufacturer's contour or radius gauge or by the stem diameter just behind the head.
C. by placing the valve on a surface plate and measuring its length with a vertical height gauge.

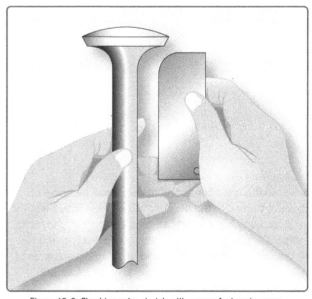

Figure 10-8. Checking valve stretch with a manufacturer's gauge.

ENGINE MAINTENANCE AND OPERATION

ANSWERS

10-7 Answer A
Degreasing can be done by spraying or immersing the part in a suitable commercial solvent. Extreme care must be used if any water-mixed degreasing solutions containing caustic compounds or soap are used. Such compounds, in addition to being potentially corrosive to aluminum and magnesium, may become impregnated in the pores of the metal and cause oil foaming when the engine is returned to service.
Ref: Powerplant Handbook H-8083-32B-ATB Chapter 10 Page 6

10-8 Answer A
Regardless of the method or type of degreasing solution used, always immediately respray the part with lubricating oil to prevent future corrosion. Washing with water is a middle step following the degreasing process.
Ref: Powerplant Handbook H-8083-32B-ATB Chapter 10 Page 6

10-9 Answer C
Rocker shafts are often found to be scored because of excessive turning in the cylinder head. There may be some bronze pickup on the shaft due to abrasion with the rocker bushing. Generally, this is caused by overheating and too little clearance between shaft and bushing. The clearance between the shaft and the bushing is most important.
Ref: Powerplant Handbook H-8083-32B-ATB Chapter 10 Page 8

10-10 Answer B
The cylinder is usually worn larger at the top than at the bottom. At the top of the piston stroke (top of the cylinder), the piston is subjected to greater heat and pressure and more erosive environment than at the bottom of the stroke. Also there is a greater freedom of movement at the top of the stroke. Under these conditions, the piston wears the cylinder more at the top of the cylinder.
Ref: Powerplant Handbook H-8083-32B-ATB Chapter 10 Page 7, 8

10-11 Answer B
Inspect a valve for stretch using a micrometer or a valve radius gauge. If a micrometer is used, stretch is found as a smaller diameter of the valve stem near the neck of the valve.
Ref: Powerplant Handbook H-8083-32B-ATB Chapter 10 Page 8, Figure 10-8

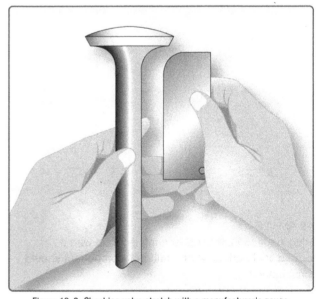

Figure 10-8. Checking valve stretch with a manufacturer's gauge.

10-12 AM.III.A.K8

Why is it improper to attempt to straighten a
bent crankshaft?

    A. Proper tolerances can rarely be restored.

    B. Damage will result to the hardened surfaces.

    C. The original bending and straightening will result in
       work hardening of the steel.

10-15 AM.III.A.K8

Checking the valve seat to valve face fit can be done with

    A. Prussian blue or by gently lapping the valve to the seat
       and examining the valve seat afterwards.

    B. gasoline by checking for leaks around the interface
       while the two surfaces are mated.

    C. a strong light held behind the valve head while examining
       the seat to valve interface from the other side.

10-13 AM.III.C.K7

In general, welding of engine parts is

    A. not acceptable.

    B. only allowed when approved by the manufacturer.

    C. can be accomplished if listed in 14 CFR, Part 43.

10-16 AM.III.A.K8

During overhaul, in order to obtain a more positive seal
(and thus less leakage) between a valve and its valve
seat _____.

    A. a narrower contact surface area is ground into the
       valve seat

    B. a wider contact surface area is ground into the
       valve created

    C. a narrower contact surface area is ground into the valve

10-14 AM.III.A.K8

When overhauling a certified reciprocating aircraft engine

    A. only steel valve seats can be used.

    B. new valve seats are required to be installed.

    C. steel valve seats can be wet or dry grinded.

10-17 AM.III.A.K8

Grinding the valves of a reciprocating engine to a feathered
edge is likely to result in

    A. normal operation and long life.

    B. excessive valve clearance.

    C. preignition and burned valves.

ENGINE MAINTENANCE AND OPERATION

ANSWERS

10-12 Answer B
A bent crankshaft should not be straightened. It must be discarded. Any attempt at straightening will result in a rupture and stresses of the nitride surfaces of the bearing journals, a condition which will lead to eventual failure.
Ref: Powerplant Handbook H-8083-32B-ATB Chapter 10 Page 9

10-13 Answer B
In general, welding of highly-stressed parts can be accomplished only when approved by the manufacturer. However, welding may be accomplished using methods that are approved by the engine manufacturer, and if it can be reasonably expected that the weld repair will not adversely affect the airworthiness of the engine.
Ref: Powerplant Handbook H-8083-32B-ATB Chapter 10 Page 12

10-14 Answer C
The valve seat inserts of an aircraft engine are usually in need of refacing at engine overhaul. They are refaced to provide a true, clean, and correct size seat for the valve. Steel valve seats are refaced by grinding equipment. It can be either wet or dry valve seat grinding equipment. The wet grinder uses a mixture of soluble oil and water to wash away the chips and to keep the stone and seat cool. This produces a smoother, more accurate job than the dry grinder. The grinding stones may be either silicon carbide or aluminum oxide.
Ref: Powerplant Handbook H-8083-32B-ATB Chapter 10 Page 13

10-15 Answer A
Prussian blue is used to check for contact transfer from one surface to another. To check the fit of the seat, spread a thin coat of Prussian blue evenly on the seat. Press the valve onto the seat. The blue transferred to valve indicates the contact surface. The contact surface should be one-third to two-thirds the width of the valve face and in the middle of the face. The same check may be made by lapping the valve lightly to the seat. Lapping is accomplished by using a small amount of lapping compound placed between the valve face and seat. The valve is then moved in a rotary motion back and forth until the lapping compound grinds slightly into the surface. After cleaning the lapping compound off, a contact area can be seen.
Ref: Powerplant Handbook H-8083-32B-ATB Chapter 10 Page 13

10-16 Answer C
The interference fit is used to obtain a more positive seal by means of a narrow contact surface between the valve face and the valve seat. Theoretically, there is a line contact between the valve and the seat. With this line contact, the load that the valve exerts against the seat is concentrated in a very small area, thereby increasing the unit load at any one spot. The interference fit is especially beneficial during the first few hours of operation after an overhaul because the positive seal prevents a burned valve or seat that a leaking valve might produce. Note that the interference angle is always cut into the valve and not the valve seat.
Ref: Powerplant Handbook H-8083-32B-ATB Chapter 10 Page 15

10-17 Answer C
After grinding, check the valve margin to be sure that the valve edge has not been ground too thin. A thin edge is called a feathered edge and can lead to preignition. The valve edge would burn away in a short period of time and the cylinder would have to be overhauled again.
Ref: Powerplant Handbook H-8083-32B-ATB Chapter 10 Page 16

10-18 AM.III.A.K8

Which is an advantage of a rough finish of the cylinder walls?
A. Allows improved lubrication of oil.
B. Allows better ring seating.
C. Allows improved cooling.

10-19 AM.III.A.K8

Once an aircraft cylinder wall is ground to an oversize, during overhaul,
A. it must be resurfaced or honed to the desired finish.
B. it is measured and installed on the engine.
C. a chemical finish is imparted to the cylinder walls.

10-20 AM.III.A.K8

After a piston engine is overhauled and reassembled, it must undergo a run-in procedure before being placed into service. What are primary purposes of this procedure?
A. Valve seating and crankshaft run-in.
B. Seating the piston rings and burnishing the crankshaft bearings.
C. Oil pressure leaks, checks, and adjustments.

10-21 AM.III.A.K9

What should be done In the event of a high carburetor air temperature reading after engine shutdown?
A. Fuel lines should be opened.
B. The carburetor heat door should be opened.
C. The engine should be rotated, (but not started).

10-22 AM.III.A.K8

Prior to starting a piston engine, which instrument can best suggest the amount of priming which should be used for a successful start?
A. The fuel pressure indicator.
B. The manifold pressure gauge.
C. The carburetor air temperature gauge.

10-23 AM.III.A.K8

Where in an oil system is the oil temperature measurement taken?
A. At the engine outlet.
B. At the engine inlet.
C. At the oil pump outlet.

ENGINE MAINTENANCE AND OPERATION

ANSWERS

10-18 Answer B
Some engine manufacturers specify a rough finish on the cylinder walls that allows the rings to seat even though they are not lapped to the cylinder. Others desire a smooth finish to which a lapped ring seats without much change in the ring or cylinder dimension.
Ref: Powerplant Handbook H-8083-32B-ATB Chapter 10 Page 17, 18

10-19 Answer A
The type of finish desired in the cylinder is an important consideration when ordering a regrind. Some engine manufacturers specify a fairly rough finish on the cylinder walls that allows the rings to seat even if they are not lapped to the cylinder. Other manufacturers desire a smooth finish to which a lapped ring seats without much change in ring or cylinder dimensions. Hones and deglazing hone are used to prepare the surface of the cylinder wall. Hones that remove material and change the dimension of the cylinder must be chosen before the cylinder is ground so that after it is honed the final dimension is correct.
Ref: Powerplant Handbook H-8083-32B-ATB Chapter 10 Page 18

10-20 Answer B
Engine run-in is as vital as any other phase of engine overhaul for it is the means by which the quality of a new or newly overhauled engine is checked and it is the final step in the preparation of an engine for service. Thus, the reliability and potential service life of an engine is in question until it has satisfactorily passed the test cell. The test serves a dual purpose. First, it accomplishes piston ring run-in and bearing burnishing. Second, it provides valuable information that is used to evaluate engine performance and determine engine condition.
Ref: Powerplant Handbook H-8083-32B-ATB Chapter 10 Page 19, 20

10-21 Answer A
After shutdown, a high carburetor air temperature is a warning that fuel trapped in the carburetor could expand and produce high internal pressure. When this condition is present, opening of the fuel line and manifold valves should be open so that fuel may pass back to the tank, and so relive this pressure.
Ref: Powerplant Handbook H-8083-32B-ATB Chapter 10 Page 21

10-22 Answer C
The carburetor air temperature gauge should be noted before starting and just after shutdown. The temperature before starting is the best indication of the temperature of the fuel in the carburetor body and tells whether vaporizing is sufficient for the initial firing or whether the mixture must be augmented by priming. If the engine has been shut down for only a short time, the residual heat in the carburetor may make it possible to rely on the vaporizing heat in the fuel and powerplant. Priming would then be unnecessary.
Ref: Powerplant Handbook H-8083-32B-ATB Chapter 10 Page 21

10-23 Answer B
The oil temperature gauge line in the aircraft is connected at the oil inlet to the engine. However, during initial testing of an overhauled engine, engine oil temperature readings are taken at the oil inlet and the oil outlet. From these readings, it can be determined if the engine heat transferred to the oil is low, normal, or excessive.
Ref: Powerplant Handbook H-8083-32B-ATB Chapter 10 Page 22

10-24 AM.III.D.K1
Fuel flow on many light aircraft with reciprocating engines is measured
A. with a turbine sensor-based indicating system.
B. using direct flow meters.
C. with a pressure-based flow meter.

10-25 AM.III.D.K4
A manifold pressure gauge is designated to
A. maintain constant pressure in the intake manifold.
B. indicate differential pressure between the intake manifold and atmospheric pressure.
C. indicate absolute pressure in the intake manifold.

10-26 AM.III.A.K9
If only one cylinder is to be continuously monitored for cylinder head temperature, what determines which cylinder is to monitored?
A. The engine manufacturer's maintenance manual.
B. The airframe manufacturer's maintenance manual.
C. The cylinder seen as the hottest during previous tests.

10-27 AM.III.A.K9
When a reciprocating aircraft engine is started, what is the maximum time period to wait for an indication of oil pressure?
A. 15 Seconds
B. 30 Seconds
C. 1 Minute

10-28 AM.III.A.K9
What is the purpose of a power check on a reciprocating aircraft engine?
A. To check magneto drop.
B. To determine satisfactory performance.
C. To determine if the fuel air mixture is adequate.

10-29 AM.III.A.K9
An indication that the optimum idle mixture has been obtained occurs when the mixture control is moved to IDLE CUTOFF and manifold pressure
A. decreases momentarily and RPM drops slightly before the engine ceases to fire.
B. increases momentarily and RPM drops slightly before engine ceases to fire.
C. decreases and RPM increases momentarily before the engine ceases to fire.

ENGINE MAINTENANCE AND OPERATION

ANSWERS

10-24 Answer C
Reciprocating engines on light aircraft use a fuel pressure gauge that is also used for the fuel flow meter. This is because the fuel flow is proportional to the fuel pressure in these systems. Fuel flow is normally measured in gallons per hour. By calibrating the fuel pressure indicator in gallons per hour an acceptable, reliable measurement of fuel flow is obtained.
Ref: Powerplant Handbook H-8083-32B-ATB Chapter 10 Page 22

10-25 Answer C
The preferred type of instrument for measuring the manifold pressure on reciprocating engine is a gauge that records the pressure as an absolute pressure reading. Absolute pressure takes into account the atmospheric pressure plus the pressure in the intake manifold.
Ref: Powerplant Handbook H-8083-32B-ATB Chapter 10 Page 23

10-26 Answer C
While monitoring CHT on all cylinders is advised in order to observe if a particular cylinder is failing, if only one cylinder is to monitored, the one selected is a result of testing on that particular installation of which one runs the hottest.
Ref: Powerplant Handbook H-8083-32B-ATB Chapter 10 Page 23

10-27 Answer B
During warm-up, watch the instruments associated with engine operation. This aids in making sure that all phases of engine operation are normal. Engine oil pressure should be indicated within 30 seconds after the start. Furthermore, if the oil pressure is not up to or above normal within one minute after the engine starts, the engine should be shut down.
Ref: Powerplant Handbook H-8083-32B-ATB Chapter 10 Page 26

10-28 Answer B
Specific RPM and manifold pressure relationship should be checked during each ground check. This can be done at the time the engine is run-up to make the magneto check. The purpose of the power check is to measure the performance of the engine against an established standard.
Ref: Powerplant Handbook H-8083-32B-ATB Chapter 10 Page 27

10-29 Answer C
When performing an idle speed and mixture check, as the mixture control lever is moved into IDLE CUTOFF, and before normal drop off, the engine speed may increase. An increase in RPM, but less than that recommended by the manufacturer (usually 20 RPM), indicates proper mixture strength. A greater increase indicates that the mixture is too rich. If the engine speed does not increase or drops immediately when the mixture control lever in moved into IDLE CUTOFF, the mixture is too lean.
Ref: Powerplant Handbook H-8083-32B-ATB Chapter 10 Page 28

10-30 AM.III.A.K3
If detonation in a reciprocating engine is suspected, the correct action is to
  A. reduce power settings.
  B. lean the mixture.
  C. enrichen the mixture.

10-33 AM.III.I.K1
Which statement relating to fuel/air ratios is true?
  A. The mixture ratio which gives the best power is richer than the mixture ratio which gives maximum economy.
  B. A rich mixture is faster burning than a normal mixture.
  C. The mixture ratio which gives maximum economy may also be designated the best power mixture.

10-31 AM.III.A.K9
Which of the following would most likely cause a reciprocating engine to backfire through the induction system at low RPM?
  A. Idle mixture too rich.
  B. Clogged derichment valve.
  C. Lean mixture.

10-34 AM.III.J.K1
Which of the following will be the result of an induction system leak near a cylinder?
  A. Backfiring
  B. A lean mixture
  C. A rich mixture

10-32 AM.III.A.K9
One cause of after firing in an aircraft engine is
  A. an excessively rich mixture.
  B. an excessively lean mixture.
  C. sticking intake valve.

10-35 AM.III.A.K3
Excessive valve clearance will cause the duration of valve opening to
  A. increase for both intake and exhaust valves.
  B. decrease for both intake and exhaust valves.
  C. decrease for intake valves and increase for exhaust valves.

ENGINE MAINTENANCE AND OPERATION

ANSWERS

10-30 Answer C
The critical point of detonation varies with the ratio of fuel to air in the mixture and can therefore be controlled by varying the mixture. In general, a rich mixture does not detonate as readily as a lean mixture. Thus, the solution if detonation is suspected is to enrich the mixture.
Ref: Powerplant Handbook H-8083-32B-ATB Chapter 10 Page 29

10-31 Answer C
When a fuel air mixture does not contain enough fuel to consume all of the oxygen, it is called a lean mixture. An extremely lean mixture either does not burn at all or burns so slowly that combustion is not complete at the end of the exhaust stroke. The flame lingers in the cylinder and then ignites the contents in the intake manifold or the induction system when the intake valve opens. This causes an explosion known as backfiring which can damage the carburetor and other parts of the induction system.
Ref: Powerplant Handbook H-8083-32B-ATB Chapter 10 Page 30

10-32 Answer A
Overly rich mixtures are also slow burning, therefore charges of unburned fuel are present in the exhaust gases. Air from outside the exhaust stacks mixes with this unburned fuel that ignites. This causes an explosion in the exhaust system. After firing is perhaps more common where long exhaust ducting retains greater amounts of unburned charges. As in the case of back firing, the correction for after firing is the proper adjustment of the fuel/air mixture.
Ref: Powerplant Handbook H-8083-32B-ATB Chapter 10 Page 31

10-33 Answer A
For a given RPM, the power output of an engine is less with the best-economy setting (auto lean) than with the best-power mixture.
Ref: Powerplant Handbook H-8083-32B-ATB Chapter 10 Page 32

10-34 Answer B
Any leak in the induction system has an effect on the mixture reaching the cylinders. This is particularly true of a leak at the cylinder end of an intake pipe. At manifold pressures below atmospheric pressure, such a leak leans out the mixture. This occurs because additional air is drawn in from the atmosphere at the leaky point. The affected cylinder may overheat, fire intermittently, or even cut out altogether.
Ref: Powerplant Handbook H-8083-32B-ATB Chapter 10 Page 33

10-35 Answer B
Valve operation is only correct if valve clearances are set and remain at the value recommended by the engine manufacturer. If valve clearances are set wrong, the valve overlap period is longer or shorter than the manufacturer intended. Where there is too much valve clearance, the valves do not open as wide or remain open as long as they should. This reduces the valve overlap period.
Ref: Powerplant Handbook H-8083-32B-ATB Chapter 10 Page 33, 35

10-36 AM.III.D.K4
At any given RPM, a change in power output can be noted by which engine monitoring instrument?
A. Manifold Pressure Gauge
B. Fuel Pressure Gauge
C. Cylinder Head Temperature

10-39 AM.III.A.K8
When performing a compression check, if low compression is obtained on a cylinder,
A. the cylinder must be removed and replaced.
B. a logbook entry must be made and the value accessed at the next 100 hour inspection.
C. rotate the engine with the starter or restart and run the engine and check the compression again.

10-37 AM.III.A.K8
A hissing sound coming from the carburetor when the propeller is pulled through manually indicates
A. worn piston rings.
B. an induction leak.
C. intake valve blow-by.

10-40 AM.III.A.K8
What is the purpose of "staking a valve"?
A. Checking for proper valve clearance.
B. Dislodge material trapped between the valve and its seat.
C. Realign the valve within its guide.

10-38 AM.III.A.K8
As the pressure is applied during a reciprocating engine compression check using a differential pressure tester, what would a movement of the propeller in the direction of engine rotation indicate?
A. The piston was on the compression stroke.
B. The piston was on the exhaust stroke.
C. The piston was positioned past top dead center.

10-41 AM.III.A.K8
If air is heard coming from the crankcase breather or oil filler during a differential compression check, what is this an indication of?
A. Exhaust Valve Leakage
B. Intake Valve Leakage
C. Piston Ring Leakage

ENGINE MAINTENANCE AND OPERATION

ANSWERS

10-36 Answer A
The cylinders of an engine, along with any type of supercharging, form an air pump. The power developed in the cylinders varies directly with the rate that air can be consumed by the engine. Therefore, a measure of air consumption into the engine is a measure of power input. Together, the manifold pressure gauge and the tachometer provide a measure of engine air consumption. For any given RPM, any change in power input is reflected by a corresponding change in manifold pressure.
Ref: Powerplant Handbook H-8083-32B-ATB Chapter 10 Page 35

10-37 Answer C
Valve blow-by is indicated by a hissing or whistle when pulling the propeller through prior to starting the engine. It is caused by the valve not seating properly and should be corrected immediately to prevent valve failure and possible engine failure.
Ref: Powerplant Handbook H-8083-32B-ATB Chapter 10 Page 39

10-38 Answer C
When performing a differential compression test, turn the engine over by hand in the direction of rotation until the piston is at top dead center. This can be detected by a decrease in force required to move the propeller. If the engine is rotated past top dead center, the 15 to 20 psi from the differential tester tends to move the propeller in the direction of rotation.
Ref: Powerplant Handbook H-8083-32B-ATB Chapter 10 Page 39, 40

10-39 Answer C
Obtaining low compression on the first check of compression check is not automatically grounds for rejection of the cylinder. Debris between the valve face and the seat, for example, could be causing the low reading. If low compression is obtained on any cylinder, turn the engine through with the starter, or restart, and run the engine to takeoff power and recheck the cylinder. If the compression is within limits, continue the cylinder in service.
Ref: Powerplant Handbook H-8083-32B-ATB Chapter 10 Page 40

10-40 Answer B
If low compression on a cylinder found during a compression check is not corrected by cranking the engine with the starter or re-running the engine, the rocker box cover should be removed and valve clearance should be checked. If clearance is within limits, stake the valves by placing a fiber drift on the rocker arm immediately over the valve stem and tapping it with a 1 to 2 pound hammer several times. This is an attempt to dislodge any foreign material that may be between the valve and the valve seat. After staking, rotate the engine with the starter and recheck compression.
Ref: Powerplant Handbook H-8083-32B-ATB Chapter 10 Page 40

10-41 Answer C
Cylinders having compression below minimum specified should be further checked to determine whether leakage is past the exhaust valve, intake valve, or piston. Excessive leakage can be detected (during compression check) past the piston rings by escaping air at the engine breather outlets or oil filler port.
Ref: Powerplant Handbook H-8083-32B-ATB Chapter 10 Page 40, 41

10-42 AM.III.A.K8

An orange band is painted around the barrel of a cylinder. What does this mean?

    A. The cylinder is rebuilt, not new.

    B. The cylinder has been bored to an oversize dimension.

    C. The cylinder is chrome plated.

10-43 AM.III.A.K8

When removing a cylinder from an engine, one must first remove the pushrods. At what position within the cylinder should the piston be to allow the pushrods to be removed?

    A. Top dead center following the compression stroke.

    B. Bottom dead center following the power stroke.

    C. Bottom dead center following the intake stroke.

10-44 AM.III.A.K8

Which of the following problems could be detected by a cold cylinder check?

    A. A defective sparkplug lead.

    B. An out of time magneto.

    C. A carburetor blockage.

10-45 AM.III.B.K5

Compressor field cleaning on turbine engines is performed primarily in order to

    A. prevent engine oil contamination and subsequent engine bearing wear or damage.

    B. facilitate flight line inspection of engine inlet and compressor areas for defects or FOD.

    C. prevent engine performance degradation, increased fuel costs, and damage or corrosion to gas path surfaces.

10-46 AM.III.B.K5

A nick in the metal is found during inspection of an axial flow compressor blade. When assessing whether the damage is repairable, you must consider the location on the blade where it is present. Which section of the blade offers the greatest tolerance for damage repair?

    A. Inboard section, trailing edge.

    B. Outboard section, leading edge.

    C. Fillet section.

10-47 AM.III.B.K5

Turbine engine parts can be cleaned with

    A. emulsion-type cleaners or chlorinated solvents.

    B. mineral spirits.

    C. soapy water and rinsed with clean water.

ENGINE MAINTENANCE AND OPERATION

ANSWERS

10-42 Answer C
Chrome plated cylinders are usually identified by a paint band around the barrel between the attaching flange and the lower barrel cooling fin. This color band is usually international orange. Oversized cylinders are also identified by color coding, but the orange band is reserved to identify chrome plating.
Ref: Powerplant Handbook H-8083-32B-ATB Chapter 10 Page 41

10-43 Answer A
When removing a cylinder from an engine, pushrods are removed by depressing the rocker arm. Before removing the pushrods, turn the crankshaft until the piston is at top dead center on the compression stroke. This relieves pressure on both the intake and exhaust rocker arms.
Ref: Powerplant Handbook H-8083-32B-ATB Chapter 10 Page 41

10-44 Answer A
A cold cylinder check will expose problems unique to that particular cylinder such as worn or broken rings, an intake leak, sparkplugs, spark plug leads, valve clearances, etc. Components which service all cylinders such as magnetos or carburetors, or fuel pumps, would affect all cylinders evenly and would not show up by inspecting individual cylinders.
Ref: Powerplant Handbook H-8083-32B-ATB Chapter 10 Page 43

10-45 Answer C
Accumulation of dirt on the compressor blades reduces the aerodynamic efficiency of the blades with resultant deterioration in engine performance. The efficiency of the blades is impaired by dirt deposits in a manner similar to that of an aircraft wing under icing conditions. Unsatisfactory acceleration and high exhaust gas temperature can result from foreign deposits on compressor components. An end result of foreign particles, if allowed to accumulate in sufficient quantity, would be [fuel] inefficiency and damage to the gas path surfaces of the engine.
Ref: Powerplant Handbook H-8083-32B-ATB Chapter 10 Page 45

10-46 Answer B
While compressor blade damage repair limits are specified by the manufacturer, in all cases it is the outboard sections (leading or trailing edges) where the greatest amount of repair and blending may occur. The inboard stations are more restrictive and the fillet area where typically, only light sanding is allowed.
Ref: Powerplant Handbook H-8083-32B-ATB Chapter 10 Page 45

10-47 Answer A
Turbine engine parts can be degreased by using emulsion-type cleaners or chlorinated solvents. The emulsion-type cleaners are safe for all metals since they are neutral and non-corrosive. Cleaning parts by the chlorinated solvent method leaves the parts absolutely dry. If they are not to be subjected to further cleaning operations, they should be sprayed with a corrosion preventative solution to protect them against rust or corrosion.
Ref: Powerplant Handbook H-8083-32B-ATB Chapter 10 Page 47

10-48 AM.III.B.K5

Which of the following may be used to mark combustion section components exposed to high temperatures?

A. Grease or wax pencil
B. Layout dye
C. Graphite lead pencil

10-49 AM.III.B.K5

When cleaning turbine engine fuel nozzles, loosen carbon deposits

A. only with a stainless steel implement or wire brush.
B. before exposing to manufacturer recommended cleaning fluid.
C. with an approved cleaning product and remove softened deposits with a soft bristle brush.

10-50 AM.III.B.K5

Where do stress rupture cracks on a turbine engine usually appear on turbine blades?

A. Across the blade root, parallel to the fir tree.
B. Along the leading edge or trailing edge at right angle to the edge length.
C. Along the leading edge, parallel to the edge.

10-51 AM.III.B.K3

Turbine blades are generally more susceptible to operating damage than compressor blades because of

A. higher centrifugal loading.
B. exposure to high temperatures.
C. high pressure and high velocity gas flow.

10-52 AM.III.B.K5

When the leading edge of a first stage turbine blade is found to have stress rupture cracks, which of the following should be suspected?

A. Faulty Cooling Shield
B. Over-Temperature Condition
C. Overspeed Condition

10-53 AM.III.B.K5

Initially upon the construction of a 54 blade turbine rotor, blade numbers 1 and 2 are placed in slots

A. adjacent to each other on the rotor.
B. 90° apart from each other on the rotor.
C. 180° apart from each other on the rotor.

ENGINE MAINTENANCE AND OPERATION

ANSWERS

10-48 Answer B
Layout dye or chalk may be used mark parts that are directly exposed to the engine's gas path such as combustion chamber liners and turbine blades and disks. Do not use grease or wax, and never use a lead/graphite pencil because of the possibility of intergranular corrosion.
Ref: Powerplant Handbook H-8083-32B-ATB Chapter 10 Page 49

10-49 Answer C
Clean all carbon deposits from the nozzles by washing with a cleaning fluid approved by the engine manufacturer and remove the softened deposits with a soft bristle brush. It is desirable to have filtered air passing through the nozzle during the cleaning operation to carry away deposits as they are loosened. Because the spray characteristics of the nozzle may become impaired, no attempt should be made to clean the nozzles by scraping with a hard implement or by rubbing with a wire brush.
Ref: Powerplant Handbook H-8083-32B-ATB Chapter 10 Page 50

10-50 Answer B
Stress rupture cracks usually appear as minute hairline cracks on or across the leading or trailing edge at a right angle to the edge length. Visible cracks may range in length from 1/16th inch upward.
Ref: Powerplant Handbook H-8083-32B-ATB Chapter 10 Page 50

10-51 Answer B
Turbine blades are usually inspected and cleaned in the same manner as compressor blades. However, because of the extreme heat under which the turbine blades operate, they are more susceptible to damage.
Ref: Powerplant Handbook H-8083-32B-ATB Chapter 10 Page 50

10-52 Answer B
Do not confuse stress rupture cracks or deformation of the leading edge with foreign material impingement damage or with blending repairs to the blade. When any stress rupture cracks or deformation of the leading edges of the first stage turbine blades are found, an over-temperature condition must be suspected. Check the individual blades for stretch and the turbine disc for hardness and stretch.
Ref: Powerplant Handbook H-8083-32B-ATB Chapter 10 Page 50

10-53 Answer C
Prior to assembly, all turbine blades are accurately weighed and then numbered 1-54 in order of each blade's total weight/moment. As blades 1 and 2 are the heaviest, in order to balance the rotor, they are placed in opposing slots 180° apart.
Ref: Powerplant Handbook H-8083-32B-ATB Chapter 10 Page 52

10-54 AM.III.B.K5
Hot spots on the tail cone of a turbine engine exhaust
   A. indicate a problem in the combustion section of the engine.
   B. can glow red hot and light off any remaining fuel in the exhaust stream.
   C. may indicate damage to the turbine blades or malfunctioning fuel nozzle.

10-55 AM.III.B.K5
Which instrument on a turbine engine will provide a proportional indication to the turbine inlet temperature to determine the energy available to produce thrust?
   A. Exhaust gas temperature gauge.
   B. Engine pressure ratio indicator.
   C. Fuel flow indicator.

10-56 AM.III.B.K1
Which of the following is the ultimate limiting factor of turbine engine operation?
   A. Compressor inlet air temperature.
   B. Turbine inlet temperature.
   C. Burner can pressure.

10-57 AM.III.D.K7
The engine pressure ratio (EPR) indicator is a direct indication of
   A. engine thrust being produced.
   B. pressure ratio between the front and aft end of the compressor.
   C. ratio of engine RPM to compressor pressure.

10-58 AM.III.D.K3
What is the primary purpose of the tachometer on an axial-compressor turbine engine?
   A. Monitor engine RPM during cruise conditions.
   B. It is the most accurate instrument for establishing thrust settings under all conditions.
   C. Monitor engine RPM during starting and to indicate overspeed conditions.

10-59 AM.III.D.K3
In what units are turbine engine tachometers calibrated?
   A. Percent of engine RPM.
   B. Actual engine RPM.
   C. Percent of engine pressure ratio.

ENGINE MAINTENANCE AND OPERATION

ANSWERS

10-54 Answer A
The exhaust section of a turbine engine should be inspected for cracks, warping, buckling or hotspots. Hotspots on the tail cone are a good indication of a malfunctioning fuel nozzle or combustion chamber.
Ref: Powerplant Handbook H-8083-32B-ATB Chapter 10 Page 54

10-55 Answer A
The turbine inlet temperature is proportional to the energy available to turn the turbine. This means that the hotter the gases entering the turbine section of the engine, the more power is available to turn the turbine wheel(s). The exhaust temperature is proportional to the turbine inlet temperature. Regardless of how or where the exhaust temperature is taken on the engine for the flight deck indication, this temperature is proportional to the temperature of the exhaust gases entering the first stage of the turbine inlet guide vanes. A higher EGT corresponds to a larger amount of energy to the turbine so it can turn the compressor faster.
Ref: Powerplant Handbook H-8083-32B-ATB Chapter 10 Page 54

10-56 Answer B
The hotter the gases entering the turbine section, the more power is available to turn the turbine wheel. This increases engine output. However, a point exists when the turbine inlet guide vanes start to be damaged. The turbine inlet temperature and, thus, engine operation is limited by this.
Ref: Powerplant Handbook H-8083-32B-ATB Chapter 10 Page 54

10-57 Answer A
Engine Pressure Ratio (EPR) is an indication of the thrust being developed by a turbofan engine and is used to set power for takeoff on many types of turbine powered aircraft. It is instrumented by total pressure pickups in the engine inlet (Pt2) and in the turbine exhaust (Pt7). The indication is displayed on the flight deck by the EPR gauge which is used in making engine power settings.
Ref: Powerplant Handbook H-8083-32B-ATB Chapter 10 Page 54

10-58 Answer C
Turbofan engines with two spools or separate shafts, high pressure and low pressure spools, are generally referred to as N1 and N2, with each having its own indicator. The main purpose of the tachometer is to be able to monitor RPM under normal conditions, during engine start, and to indicate an overspeed condition, if one occurs.
Ref: Powerplant Handbook H-8083-32B-ATB Chapter 10 Page 55

10-59 Answer A
Turbine engine tachometers are usually calibrated in percent RPM so that various types of engines can be operated on the same basis of comparison. Also, turbine speeds are generally very high and the large numbers of RPM would make it confusing.
Ref: Powerplant Handbook H-8083-32B-ATB Chapter 10 Page 55

10-60 AM.III.D.K3
Which of the following is used to monitor the mechanical integrity of the turbines, as well as to check engine operating conditions of a turbine engine?
 A. Engine Oil Pressure
 B. Exhaust Gas Temperature
 C. Engine Pressure Ratio

10-61 AM.III.D.K3
The abbreviation Pt7 is used in turbine engine terminology means
 A. the total inlet pressure.
 B. pressure and temperature at station No. 7.
 C. the total pressure at station No. 7.

10-62 AM.III.D.K3
What is the first engine instrument indication of a successful start of a turbine engine?
 A. A rise in the engine fuel flow.
 B. A rise in oil pressure.
 C. A rise in the exhaust gas temperature.

10-63 AM.III.D.K3
What instrument on a gas turbine engine should be monitored to minimize the possibility of a "hot" start?
 A. RPM Indicator
 B. Turbine Inlet Temperature
 C. Torquemeter

10-64 AM.III.D.K3
Which are the three primary instruments to monitor when starting a turbine engine?
 A. Exhaust gas temperature, tachometer, oil pressure.
 B. Exhaust gas temperature, fuel flow, tachometer.
 C. Fuel flow meter, tachometer, engine pressure ratio.

10-65 AM.III.B.K4
When starting a turbine engine, a hung start is indicated if the engine
 A. exhaust gas temperature exceeds specified limits.
 B. fails to reach idle RPM.
 C. N1 is normal, but N2 is low.

ENGINE MAINTENANCE AND OPERATION

ANSWERS

10-60 Answer B
Temperature is an engine operating limitation and is used to monitor the mechanical integrity of the turbines as well as to check engine operating condition. Temperature of the gases entering the first stage of turbine inlet guide vane is the important consideration but it is impractical to measure at this point in the engines. Rather, turbine outlet temperature, which is the Exhaust Gas Temperature (EGT), is measured and monitored since it is directly proportional to turbine inlet temperature.
Ref: Powerplant Handbook H-8083-32B-ATB Chapter 10 Page 55

10-61 Answer C
The EPR gauge is instrumented by total pressure pickups since it is a ratio of the pressure at the inlet of the engine compared to the pressure at the outlet. On an actual turbine engine, it compares Pt2 (inlet pressure) with Pt7 (pressure at the turbine exhaust). Therefore, Pt7 is used to mean the total pressure at station No. 7 which is in the turbine exhaust area of the engine.
Ref: Powerplant Handbook H-8083-32B-ATB Chapter 10 Page 54

10-62 Answer C
A successful start is noted first by a rise in exhaust gas temperature. If fuel does not start to burn inside the engine within a prescribed period of time, or if the exhaust gas starting temperature limit is exceeded (a hot start), the starting procedure should be aborted.
Ref: Powerplant Handbook H-8083-32B-ATB Chapter 10 Page 57

10-63 Answer B
During the start of a turbine engine, if the exhaust gas temperature limit is exceeded, a hot start will occur. Exhaust gas temperature is used in many turbine engines instead of turbine inlet temperature. It is proportional to turbine inlet temperature and, although lower, it provided surveillance over the engine's internal operating conditions. So while it is the EGT gauge that is monitored in engines without turbine inlet temperature gauges, it is the turbine inlet temperature that is of concern. Adhere to the manufacturer's start check list and limitations when operating any aircraft engine.
Ref: Powerplant Handbook H-8083-32B-ATB Chapter 10 Page 55, 57

10-64 Answer A
While all engine readings are important, those critical during the starting process are the tachometer to guard against a hung start, the EGT to guard against a hot start, and oil pressure as this is always critical to any engine's health.
Ref: Powerplant Handbook H-8083-32B-ATB Chapter 10 Page 57

10-65 Answer B
A hung start is when the engine lights off but the engine will not accelerate to idle RPM. Therefore, EGT and turbine inlet temperature gauges will show elevated levels but the engine tachometer will not indicate idle RPM.
Ref: Powerplant Handbook H-8083-32B-ATB Chapter 10 Page 57

10-66 AM.III.C.K7
A turbine engine hot section is particularly susceptible to which kind of damage?
- A. Erosion
- B. Cracking
- C. Elongation

10-67 AM.III.B.K1
What is the proper starting sequence of a turbojet engine?
- A. Ignition, Starter, Fuel
- B. Starter, Ignition, Fuel
- C. Starter, Fuel, Ignition

10-68 AM.III.B.K4
What effect does high atmospheric humidity have on the operation of a jet engine?
- A. Decreases engine pressure ratio.
- B. Decreases compressor and turbine RPM.
- C. Has little or no effect.

10-69 AM.III.B.K1
A cool-off period prior to shutdown of a turbine engine is accomplished in order to
- A. allow the turbine wheel to cool before the case contracts around it.
- B. prevent vapor lock in the fuel control and/or fuel lines.
- C. prevent seizure of the engine bearings.

10-70 AM.III.B.K1
Which two engine parameters on a turboprop engine are used to compute takeoff power from the ambient pressure and temperature prevailing at the time of takeoff?
- A. EGT and fuel flow.
- B. RPM and EGT.
- C. EGT and torquemeter pressure.

10-71 AM.III.B.K7
What results if a turbine engine is operated with excessively high EGT?
- A. Damage to the turbine section and/or reduced turbine component life.
- B. Compressor overspeed and associated compressor blade damage.
- C. Lubricating oil vaporization and possible scoring of the main bearings.

ENGINE MAINTENANCE AND OPERATION

ANSWERS

10-66 Answer B
Due to extreme heat, one of the most frequent discrepancies that are detected while inspecting the hot section of a turbine engine is cracking. These cracks may occur in many forms, and the only way to determine if they are in acceptable limits is with the engine manufacturer's service and overhaul manuals.
Ref: Powerplant Handbook H-8083-32B-ATB Chapter 10 Page 47, 49

10-67 Answer B
Always follow the manufacturer's starting checklist step by step when starting a turbine engine. However, the general starting sequence is: 1) Rotate the compressor with the starter; 2) Turn ON the ignition; and 3) Open the engine fuel valve, either by moving the throttle to idle or by moving a fuel shutoff lever to OPEN, or by turning a switch. Thus, STARTER, then IGNITION, then FUEL is the usual starting sequence of a turbojet engine.
Ref: Powerplant Handbook H-8083-32B-ATB Chapter 10 Page 57

10-68 Answer C
Relative humidity, which affects reciprocating engine power appreciably, has a negligible effect on turbine engine thrust. Therefore, relative humidity is not usually considered when computing thrust for takeoff or determining fuel flow and RPM for routine operation of a jet engine.
Ref: Powerplant Handbook H-8083-32B-ATB Chapter 10 Page 59

10-69 Answer A
When an engine has been operated at high power levels for extended periods, a cool down time should be allowed before shut down. It is recommended the engine be operated at below a low power setting, preferably at idle for a period of 5 minutes to prevent possible seizure of the rotors. The mass of the turbine rotor is much greater that the turbine case and the turbine case is exposed to cooling air from both inside and outside the engine. Consequently, the case and rotor(s) lose their residual heat at different rates after the engine is shut down. Without a cool-off period before shutdown, the case, cooling faster, tends to shrink upon the turbine wheels that are still rotating. Seizing is possible.
Ref: Powerplant Handbook H-8083-32B-ATB Chapter 10 Page 58

10-70 Answer C
On a turboprop engine, torquemeter pressure is approximately proportional to the total power output and, thus, is used as a measure of engine performance. The torquemeter pressure gauge reading during the takeoff engine check is an important value. It is usually necessary to compute the takeoff power in the same manner as is done for a turbojet engine. This computation is to determine the maximum allowable exhaust gas temperature and the torquemeter pressure that a normally functioning engine should produce for the ambient air temperature and barometric pressure prevailing at the time.
Ref: Powerplant Handbook H-8083-32B-ATB Chapter 10 Page 59

10-71 Answer A
Some of the most important factors affecting turbine engine life are EGT, engine cycles, and engine speed. Excess EGT of a few degrees reduces turbine component life. The exhaust gas temperature needs to be as high as possible without damaging the turbine section of the engine.
Ref: Powerplant Handbook H-8083-32B-ATB Chapter 10 Page 59

ORAL EXAM

10-1(O).   What is the probable cause of hydraulic lock and how is it remedied?

10-2(O).   What checks are necessary to verify proper operation of a reciprocating engine?

10-3(O).   Explain the checks necessary to verify proper operation of propeller systems.

10-4(O).   What is involved with the correct installation of piston rings and what results if the rings are incorrectly installed or are worn?

10-5(O).   What are some procedures for inspecting various engine components during overhaul?

10-6(O).   What are the procedures for reciprocating engine maintenance as they pertain to overhauling an engine?

10-7(O).   What are some checks necessary to verify proper operation of a turbine engine?

10-8(O).   What are some turbine engine troubleshooting procedures?

10-9(O).   What are some turbine engine maintenance procedures?

10-10(O).   What is the possible problem with an engine that indicates high Exhaust Gas Temperature (EGT) for a particular Engine Pressure Ratio (EPR)?

10-11(O).   What are the typical parameters sought for oil pressure when starting a reciprocating aircraft engine?

10-12(O).   Explain the operation of a temperature indicating system on a turbine engine.

10-13(O).   What is the operation of a turbine engine tachometer?

10-14(O).   How is an EGT System checked for proper operation?

10-15(O).   What is EPR and how is it instrumented on a gas turbine engine?

10-16(O).   What can be done to check the accuracy of a turbine engine tachometer?

ENGINE MAINTENANCE AND OPERATION

ANSWERS

ORAL EXAM

10-1(O).   Whenever a radial engine remains shut down for more than a few minutes, oil or fuel may drain into the combustion chambers or intake pipes of the lower, downward extending cylinders. This is known as hydraulic lock. As the piston moves toward top center in these cylinders, it will collide with these incompressible liquids. Severe damage can be caused. The liquid must be removed to remedy the hydraulic lock and make it safe to start the engine. This is done by removing either the front or rear spark plugs of the affected cylinders and pulling the engine through by hand in the normal direction of rotation. Then the spark plugs are reinstalled and the engine is started.
Ref: Powerplant Handbook H-8083-32B-ATB Chapter 10

10-2(O).   A ground check or power check is performed to evaluate the functioning of the engine by comparing power input as measured by manifold pressure with power output as measured by RPM (or torque) and comparing these to known acceptable values. It also includes checking the powerplant and accessory equipment by ear, visual inspection, and by proper interpretation of instrument readings, control movements, and switch reactions. Fuel pressure and oil pressure checks must verify that these pressures are within established tolerances. A cylinder compression test can be performed if it is suspected that there is a problem with valves, pistons or piston rings. A magneto safety check exposes problems with the ignition system. Idle speed and idle mixture checks can also be performed although these relate more to the proper functioning of the fuel system than the engine itself just as the magneto check focuses more on ignition system integrity.
Ref: Powerplant Handbook H-8083-32B-ATB Chapter 10

10-3(O).   The propeller must be checked to ensure proper operation of the pitch control and pitch change mechanism. The operation of a controllable pitch propeller is checked by the indications of the tachometer and manifold pressure gauge when the proper governor control is moved from one position to another. Each propeller requires a different procedure. The applicable manufacturer's instructions should be followed.
Ref: Powerplant Handbook H-8083-32B-ATB Chapter 10

10-4(O).   Piston rings prevent leakage of gas pressure from the combustion chamber while lubricating the cylinder walls and reducing to a minimum the seepage of oil into the combustion chamber. Worn or broken piston rings can cause excessive oil consumption and loss of compression. Oil blow-by into the combustion chamber can lead to sticking valves, spark plug misfiring, as well as detonation or preignition due to carbonization of the oil. During installation, the rings are place in the proper grooves facing the correct direction according to the engine manufacturer's instructions. The ring gaps are staggered around the piston. They are compressed with a ring compressor to the diameter of the piston as the cylinder is slid down around the piston making sure that the cylinder and piston plane remain the same. As the cylinder is lowered around the piston with a straight, even motion, it displaces the ring compressor as the rings slide into the bore. Rocking or forcing the cylinder over the piston and rings could cause a ring to escape from the ring compressor and expand or it could crack or chip a ring or damage the ring land.
Ref: Powerplant Handbook H-8083-32B-ATB Chapter 10

10-5(O).   There are 3 basic categories of inspection during overhaul: visual, structural Non-Destructive Testing (NDT) and dimensional. The first inspection to be done is the visual inspection. A preliminary visual inspection should be performed before cleaning the parts since indications of failure may often be detected from the residual deposits of metallic particles in some recesses of the engine. Then, parts can be cleaned and visually inspected. Structural inspections can be performed on parts by methods such as magnetic particle inspection, dye penetrant, eddy current, ultra sound, and x-ray as specified by the manufacturer. Finally, using very accurate measuring equipment, each engine component can be dimensionally evaluated and compared to the service limits and tolerances set by the manufacturer.
Ref: Powerplant Handbook H-8083-32B-ATB Chapter 10

ORAL EXAM

10-6(O). Aircraft engine maintenance practices, including overhaul, are performed at specified intervals established by the manufacturer. For an overhauled engine to be as airworthy as a new engine, worn and damaged parts must be detected and replaced. This is done by completely disassembling the engine. Visual, non-destructive, and dimensional inspections are performed. The manufacturer publishes inspection criterion and a new minimum and serviceable dimension for all critical component parts. Parts that do not meet these standards must be rejected for use in the engine. A major overhaul of an engine consists of the complete reconditioning of the powerplant. This includes disassembly of the crankcase for access and inspection/rework of the crankshaft and bearings. It is not a major repair and can be performed or supervised by a certified powerplant technician as long as the engine does not contain an internal supercharger or propeller reduction other than spur-type gears. At the time of an engine overhaul, all accessories are removed, overhauled, and tested in accordance with the accessory manufacturer's instructions.
Ref: Powerplant Handbook H-8083-32B-ATB Chapter 10

10-7(O). The manufacturer's operating instructions should be consulted before attempting to start and operate any turbine engine. Checking turbofan engines for proper operation consists primarily of simply reading the engine instruments and then comparing the value with those known to be correct for a particular operating condition. Be sure the engine and instrument indications have stabilized. Idling speed must be checked (tachometer) as well as oil pressure and Exhaust Gas Temperature (EGT). Engine Pressure Ratio (EPR) measures thrust and is used to set takeoff power. It varies with ambient temperature and pressure. Takeoff thrust is checked by adjusting the throttle to obtain a single, predicted, indication on the Engine Pressure Ratio (EPR) gauge. This can be computed from the takeoff thrust setting curve in the operations manual. It can be done at full power or when the throttle is set at the part power stop. If an engine develops the predicted thrust and if all the other engine instruments are indicating within their proper ranges, engine operation is considered satisfactory. On newer aircraft, performance is a function of the onboard computer. FADEC engines have means for checking the engine and displaying the results on the flight deck.
Ref: Powerplant Handbook H-8083-32B-ATB Chapter 10

10-8(O). Turbine engine troubleshooting should be performed in accordance with the engine manufacturer's instructions. Trouble shooting charts exist to guide the technician. Engine analyzers are manufactured that can assist with calibration and the accuracy of important engine parameter indicators such as RPM and EGT. Follow the analyzer manufacturer's instructions.
Ref: Powerplant Handbook H-8083-32B-ATB Chapter 10

10-9(O). The detailed procedures recommended by the engine manufacturer should be followed when performing inspections or maintenance on a turbine engine. Some common functions include periodic inspection, cleaning and repair of compressor components which can have performance reduction due being dirty and Foreign Object Damage (FOD). Compressor blades, inducers, and guide vanes all may be damaged. The extent of the damage must be ascertained. Repairable damage limits set by the manufacturer must be adhered to and various NDT methods may need to be employed. The possibility exists to rework or blend out damage using stones usually blending parallel to the length of the component. Combustion section inspection and cleaning is very important since the serviceability of the combustion section is a controlling factor in the service life of a turbine engine. Inspection for hot spots, exhaust leaks and distortions can be done without opening the case. After the case has been opened, inspection for localized overheating, cracks, and excessive wear are important. Evidence of FOD can be found even in the combustion section. Hot section inspections, which include the turbine section components, usually are required at regular intervals. Follow the manufacturer's instructions for procedures and damage limits. This is applicable for fuel nozzles, turbine disks, blades, and guide vanes as well as the exhaust section components.
Ref: Powerplant Handbook H-8083-32B-ATB Chapter 10

ENGINE MAINTENANCE AND OPERATION

ANSWERS

ORAL EXAM

10-10(O). The engine is likely out of trim. The accuracy of the EGT gauge/sensors could also be in question and should be checked.
Ref: Powerplant Handbook H-8083-32B-ATB Chapter 10

10-11(O). Oil pressure indication should occur within 30 seconds of start-up. Normal oil pressure indication should occur within 1 minute of start-up or the engine should be shut down.
Ref: Powerplant Handbook H-8083-32B-ATB Chapter 10

10-12(O). Temperature of turbine engine gases entering the first stage turbine inlet guide vanes is the most critical of all engine variables. In many engines, it is impractical to measure the temperature exactly at this point. Relative temperatures that are proportional to this temperature are measured instead. EGT, TGT, TOT, and TIT are all such indications. Accuracy of temperature indication in this portion of the engine is critical because if it is too high, the engine could be destroyed. If is too low, insufficient power will be developed. A series of individual thermocouple probes located around the engine section where the temperature is measured are connected to a gauge on the flight deck. The gauge shows the average temperature measured by the thermocouples. This assists in producing an accurate indication. This indication is so important that testing of the individual thermostats, the indicator, and the entire indicating system is done periodically. An analyzer test box capable of measuring the accuracy of all thermocouple components and the entire system is used.
Ref: Powerplant Handbook H-8083-32B-ATB Chapter 10

10-13(O). Gas turbine engine speeds are measured by the RPM of each turbine-compressor spool and are displayed on the flight deck. Percent of RPM is used rather than the actual RPM so that various types of engines can be operated on the same basis of comparison. Also, turbine engine speeds are very high and percent RPM simplifies monitoring. Some tachometers measure RPM using a rotating tachometer generator that is geared to the engine. The frequency of the generator output is proportional to the engine speed. Another (newer) type of tachometer uses a magnetic pickup that counts passing gear teeth edges, which are seen electrically as pulses of electrical power as they pass by the pick-up. By counting the number of pulses, the shaft RPM is obtained. Clearance between the gear teeth and the magnetic pickup must be maintained for accuracy.
Ref: Powerplant Handbook H-8083-32B-ATB Chapter 10

10-14(O). A calibrated test analyzer unit is used to check the EGT system and components for proper operation. The unit contains heater probes and built-in thermocouples against which the accuracy of the aircraft thermocouples is compared. The analyzer also is capable of checking the continuity of the system and the accuracy of the EGT indicator on the flight deck. Resistance and insulation checks are also made. Follow the instructions that come with the test analyzer unit being used.
Ref: Powerplant Handbook H-8083-32B-ATB Chapter 10

10-15(O). EPR stands for Engine Pressure Ratio. It is an indication of thrust developed by a turbofan engine and is used to set power for takeoff on many types of aircraft. It is instrumented by total pressure pickups located in the engine inlet (P2) and in the turbine exhaust (P7). The indication is displayed on the flight deck on the EPR gauge, which is used in making engine power settings.
Ref: Powerplant Handbook H-8083-32B-ATB Chapter 10

10-16(O). A calibrated test analyzer unit can be used to check the tachometer of a turbine engine. The scale of the RPM check circuit is calibrated in percent RPM to correspond to the aircraft tachometer indicator. The aircraft tachometer and the RPM check circuit are connected in parallel and both are indicating during engine run-up. The RPM check circuit indication is compared with the aircraft tachometer indication to determine the accuracy of the aircraft instrument.
Ref: Powerplant Handbook H-8083-32B-ATB Chapter 10

PRACTICAL EXAM

10-1(P). Given an actual aircraft engine or mockup, appropriate publications, and tooling inspect a reciprocating engine installation and record findings. [Level 3]

10-2(P). Given an actual aircraft engine or mockup, appropriate publications, and tooling inspect a turbine engine installation and record findings. [Level 3]

10-3(P). Given an actual aircraft engine or mockup, appropriate publications, and a bore scope inspect a turbine engine and record findings. [Level 3]

10-4(P). Given an actual aircraft engine or mockup, appropriate publications, and tooling determine the proper crankshaft flange run-out and record findings. [Level 3]

10-5(P). Given an actual aircraft engine or mockup, an airworthiness directive, and required tooling inspect an engine in accordance with the airworthiness directive and record findings. [Level 2]

10-6(P). Given an actual aircraft engine or mockup, appropriate publications, and tooling inspect a turbine engine compressor section and record findings. [Level 3]

10-7(P). Given an actual aircraft engine or mockup, appropriate publications, and tooling inspect a crankcase for cracks and record findings. [Level 3]

10-8(P). Given an actual aircraft engine or mockup, appropriate publications, and tooling inspect a crankshaft oil seal for leaks and record findings. [Level 3]

10-9(P). Given an actual aircraft engine or mockup, appropriate publications, and tooling complete an engine conformity inspection and record findings. [Level 3]

10-10(P). Given an actual aircraft engine or mockup, appropriate publications, and tooling complete an engine airworthiness inspection and record findings. [Level 3]

10-11(P). Given an actual aircraft engine or mockup, appropriate publications, and tooling perform an inspection on a mechanical and/or electrical temperature system and record findings. [Level 3]

10-12(P). Given an actual aircraft engine or mockup, appropriate publications, and tooling perform an inspection on a mechanical and/or electrical pressure system and record findings. [Level 3]

10-13(P). Given an actual aircraft engine or mockup, appropriate publications, and tooling perform an inspection on a mechanical and/or electrical RPM system and record findings. [Level 3]

10-14(P). Given an actual aircraft engine or mockup, appropriate publications, and tooling perform an inspection on a mechanical and/or electrical rate of flow system and record findings. [Level 3]

10-15(P). Given an actual aircraft engine or mockup, appropriate publications, and tooling verify the proper operation and marking of an indicating system and record findings. [Level 2]

10-16(P). Given an actual aircraft engine or mockup, appropriate publications, and tooling replace a temperature sending unit and record maintenance. [Level 3]

ENGINE MAINTENANCE AND OPERATION

QUESTIONS

PRACTICAL EXAM

10-17(P).   Given an actual aircraft engine or mockup, appropriate publications, and tooling troubleshoot an oil pressure indicating system and record findings. [Level 3]

10-18(P).   Given an actual aircraft engine or mockup, appropriate publications, and tooling locate and inspect fuel flow components on an engine and record findings. [Level 2]

10-19(P).   Given an actual aircraft engine or mockup, appropriate publications, and tooling replace an Exhaust Gas Temperature (EGT) indication probe and record maintenance. [Level 3]

10-20(P).   Given an actual aircraft engine or mockup, appropriate publications, and tooling troubleshoot a manifold pressure gage that is slow to indicate the correct reading and record findings. [Level 2]

10-21(P).   Given an actual aircraft engine or mockup, appropriate publications, and tooling remove, inspect, and install fuel flow transmitter and record maintenance and findings. [Level 3]

LIGHT-SPORT AIRCRAFT ENGINES

Types of Light-Sport and Experimental Engines, Opposed Engines, Direct Drive VW Engines,
Maintenance, Lubrication, and Preservation

CHAPTER 11

11-1 AM.III.A.K1
A Light-Sport Aircraft (LSA) means an aircraft, other than rotorcraft or power-lift, that
- A. has a maximum occupancy of no more than four people.
- B. is powered by a single reciprocating engine if powered.
- C. has a maximum takeoff weight not exceeding 1000 pounds.

11-2 AM.III.A.K1
Which of the following statements is true regarding the certification of light-sport aircraft engines?
- A. All light-sport aircraft engines are certified by FAA.
- B. Some, but not all, light-sport aircraft engines are certified by FAA.
- C. By definition, light-sport aircraft engines are not certified by FAA.

11-3 AM.III.C.K1
Who may perform an annual condition inspection on a light-sport aircraft?
- A. Only an FAA certificated airframe and powerplant mechanic.
- B. The owner of the light-sport aircraft who has completed the FAA approved training course for the aircraft in question.
- C. Only an FAA certified airframe and powerplant mechanic with an inspection authorization.

11-4 AM.III.K.K10
Regarding the cooling system of a Rotax 582 engine; to which component does fluid next flow after leaving the cylinder head?
- A. water pump
- B. radiator
- C. expansion tank

11-5 AM.III.I.K13
The fuel system of a Rotax 912 and 914 engine include two fuel pumps with each
- A. connected in series.
- B. connected in parallel.
- C. connected to an independent carburetor.

11-6 AM.III.J.K1
A liquid cooling system is employed on the Rotax 582 series engine. Circulation of the coolant is accomplished by
- A. a ram air driven pump.
- B. the external oil/water dual pump.
- C. an integrated engine water pump.

LIGHT-SPORT AIRCRAFT ENGINES

ANSWERS

11-1 Answer B
A light-sport aircraft is an aircraft that has a single reciprocating engine if it is a powered aircraft. Its maximum seating capacity is no more than two people. The maximum takeoff weight of a light-sport aircraft is no more than 1320 pounds for an aircraft not intended for operation on water; or 1430 pounds for an aircraft intended for operation on water.
Ref: Powerplant Handbook H-8083-32B-ATB Chapter 11 Page 1

11-2 Answer B
The manufacturer of a light-sport aircraft engine ensures the reliability and durability of the product by design, research and testing. Although most of these engines are not certified by the FAA, close control of manufacturing and assembly procedures is generally maintained. Normally, each engine is tested before it leaves the factory and meets certain American Society for Testing and Materials (ASTM) standards. Some engines used on light-sport aircraft are certified by the FAA and these engines are maintained as per the manufacturer's instructions and Title 14 of the Code of Federal Regulations (14 CFR).
Ref: Powerplant Handbook H-8083-32B-ATB Chapter 11 Page 1

11-3 Answer B
The holder of a repairman certificate (light-sport aircraft) with an inspection rating, may perform the annual condition inspection on a light-sport aircraft that is owned by the holder, has been issued an experimental certificate for operating a light-sport aircraft under 14 CFR part 21, section 21.191(i), and is in the same class of light-sport aircraft for which the holder has completed the required training.
Ref: Powerplant Handbook H-8083-32B-ATB Chapter 11 Page 2

11-4 Answer C
The flow of coolant in a water cooled Rotax 582 is from the cylinder head – to the expansion tank to the radiator to the water pump, and back to the cylinder and cylinder head. An overflow bottle is additionally positioned from the expansion tank.
Ref: Powerplant Handbook H-8083-32B-ATB Chapter 11 Page 4

11-5 Answer A
The 912/914 series Rotax engines include two electric fuel pumps connected in series, together serving two carburetors. The first pump in line serves as the main pump. The second is an auxiliary or backup pump.
Ref: Powerplant Handbook H-8083-32B-ATB Chapter 11 Page 6

11-6 Answer C
The cooling system of a Rotax 582 engine is in a two circuit arrangement. The cooling liquid is supplied by an integrated pump in the engine through the cylinders and the cylinder head to the radiator. An expansion tank, radiator, and overflow bottle work together to remove vapor and allow for expansion of the coolant.
Ref: Powerplant Handbook H-8083-32B-ATB Chapter 11 Page 6

11-7 AM.III.H.K5
A breakerless capacitor discharge ignition system such as equipped on the Rotax 912/914 contains five trigger coils. Four actuate the discharge of the capacitors via the primary circuit. What is the function of the fifth?
    A. Provides a backup circuit.
    B. Supplies the secondary circuit.
    C. Counts RPM.

11-8 AM.III.G.K1
What is the recommended fuel/oil ratio for 2-stroke premixed applications on engines without an oil injector?
    A. 40:1
    B. 50:1
    C. 100:1

11-9 AM.III.A.K1
The Rotax 914 engine is a lightweight, four cylinder opposed engine that
    A. is water cooled.
    B. is air cooled.
    C. has water cooled heads and air cooled cylinder barrels.

11-10 AM.III.H.K5
Which statement describes the maintenance requirements of the breakerless capacitor discharge ignition systems as used on most Rotax light-sport aircraft engines?
    A. The system must be checked for clearances and capacitor output every 100 hours.
    B. The system is completely maintenance free.
    C. The charging coils and capacitors must be replaced every 100 hours.

11-11 AM.III.A.K4
A unique manufacturing feature of the Jabiru light-sport engines is
    A. most parts are machined from solid material.
    B. mostly titanium is utilized.
    C. that a great amount of aluminum is used to keep weight to a minimum.

11-12 AM.III.C.K1
If scheduled maintenance of a light sport aircraft engine is specified at every 100 hours, and the maintenance is actually performed at the 10 hour legal tolerance (110 hours) when is the next scheduled maintenance due?
    A. 210 hours
    B. 200 hours
    C. 220 hours

LIGHT-SPORT AIRCRAFT ENGINES

ANSWERS

11-7 Answer C
Two charging coils located on the generator starter supply one ignition circuit each with energy stored in capacitors of the electronic modules. At the moment of ignition, two each of the four coils actuate the discharge of the capacitors via the primary circuit of the dual ignition coils. The fifth trigger coil is used to provide the revolution counter signal.
Ref: Powerplant Handbook H-8083-32B-ATB Chapter 11 Page 8

11-10 Answer B
Most Rotax engines are equipped with a dual ignition unit that uses breaker-less, capacitor discharge design with an integrated generator. The ignition unit is completely free of maintenance and needs no external power. Two independent charging coils located on the generator stator supply one ignition circuit each. The energy is stored in capacitors of the electronic modules. At the moment of ignition, two each of the four external trigger coils actuate the discharge of the capacitors via the primary circuit of the dual ignition coils. A fifth trigger coil is used to provide a revolution counter signal.
Ref: Powerplant Handbook H-8083-32B-ATB Chapter 11 Page 8

11-8 Answer B
When premixing oil, first fill the known amount of two-stroke oil at a ratio of 50:1 (2 percent) into a container containing a small amount of gasoline to facilitate the mix. Then pour the remaining amount of gasoline into the container to achieve the 50:1 ratio. Shake the container thoroughly. Then, with a funnel equipped with a fine mesh filter transfer fuel from the container to the aircraft tank.
Ref: Powerplant Handbook H-8083-32B-ATB Chapter 11 Page 5

11-11 Answer A
Jabiru engines use the latest manufacturing techniques. All Jabiru engines are manufactured, assembled and run on a dynamometer, and calibrated before delivery. The crankcase halves, cylinder heads, crankshaft, starter motor housing, gearbox cover, together with many smaller components are machined from solid material. The sump (oil pan) is the only casting. The cylinders are machined from bar 4140 chrome molybdenum alloy steel as are the crankshaft and camshaft.
Ref: Powerplant Handbook H-8083-32B-ATB Chapter 11 Page 10

11-9 Answer C
The cooling system of the Rotax 914 is designed for liquid cooling of the cylinder heads and ram-air cooling of the cylinders.
Ref: Powerplant Handbook H-8083-32B-ATB Chapter 11 Page 6

11-12 Answer B
Scheduled maintenance of a light sport aircraft engine offers a +/- 10 hour tolerance for when that maintenance is actually performed. However a delay to the limit of that tolerance does not further delay the next scheduled maintenance. Thus, if a 100 hour limit is required, each maintenance remains at that schedule (100 hours, 200 hours, 300 hours, etc,) +/- the 10 hour tolerance.
Ref: Powerplant Handbook H-8083-32B-ATB Chapter 11 Page 16

11-13 AM.III.C.K7
When performing inspections and maintenance on light-sport aircraft engines, whose guidance should be most regarded?
  A. General mechanical standards such as described in FAA-H-8083-32A-ATB are the primary source of guidance.
  B. Published FAA advisory circulars are the primary source of guidance.
  C. The manufacturer's manuals are the primary source of guidance.

11-14 AM.III.H.K5
When performing maintenance on a Rotax light sport aircraft engine, to secure the engine from unintentional operation,
  A. the ignition system must be ungrounded.
  B. the ignition system must be grounded.
  C. the ignition switch must be "Off".

11-15 AM.III.C.K7
When inspecting the magnetic plug in the sump of an engine or gearbox, approximately 1/16 inch of steel filings are observed. What action must be taken?
  A. This is an acceptable amount and no action is needed.
  B. Drain the oil and replace all filters.
  C. Any indication of steel filings is cause to remove and overhaul the engine.

11-16 AM.III.C.K6
Maintenance and inspections on light-sport aircraft
  A. are set up by the owner operator.
  B. are less detailed than with certified aircraft.
  C. must be recorded in the aircraft maintenance logbook.

11-17 AM.III.I.K2
On a light-sport aircraft with two carburetors, carburetor synchronization must be performed as follows:
  A. Pneumatic synchronization first, then mechanical synchronization.
  B. Mechanical synchronization first, then pneumatic synchronization.
  C. Perform mechanical and pneumatic synchronization with the compensating tube connected.

11-18 AM.III.I.K2
In addition to idle speed adjustment during synchronization,
  A. full takeoff RPM must be able to be obtained.
  B. mixture must be checked with full carburetor heat ON.
  C. cruise RPM and mixture must be verified.

LIGHT-SPORT AIRCRAFT ENGINES

ANSWERS

11-13 Answer C
Always refer to the current manufacturer's information as the primary source when operating, inspecting, or performing maintenance on any aircraft engine, including for light-sport aircraft.
Ref: Powerplant Handbook H-8083-32B-ATB Chapter 11 Page 1

11-16 Answer C
Most light-sport aircraft engines require a definite time interval between overhauls. This is specified or implied by the engine manufacturer. Checks and maintenance that are performed should be accomplished in accordance with a maintenance checklist and all actions should be recorded in the aircraft maintenance logbook by the person or company performing the work.
Ref: Powerplant Handbook H-8083-32B-ATB Chapter 11 Page 16

11-14 Answer B
To ensure against an unintentional ignition, the ignition switch should be off and the ignition system grounded. This precaution serves to avoid injuries in case of an unintentional start of the engine such as from hand propping. Remember, as long as the ground cable is not properly connected, the ignition switch is ON.
Ref: Powerplant Handbook H-8083-32B-ATB Chapter 11 Page 5, 16

11-17 Answer B
Mechanical synchronization always is performed first when synchronizing carburetors. Then, the two carburetors are adjusted to equal flow rates at idle by use of a suitable flow meter or vacuum gauges. The compensating tube between the carburetors is typically removed to install the gauges.
Ref: Powerplant Handbook H-8083-32B-ATB Chapter 11 Page 17

11-15 Answer A
Steel chips in low numbers can be tolerated if the accumulation is below 1/8" (3 mm). In the case of unclear findings, flush the oil circuit and install a new filter. Larger accumulations on the magnetic plug require the engine to be repaired and overhauled.
Ref: Powerplant Handbook H-8083-32B-ATB Chapter 11 Page 21

11-18 Answer A
Once the proper idling speed has been established, it is necessary to check the operating range above the idle speed. First, establish that the engine is developing full takeoff performance or takeoff RPM when selected on the flight deck. Then, the setting of the operating range (idle to full throttle) can be checked or adjusted.
Ref: Powerplant Handbook H-8083-32B-ATB Chapter 11 Page 18

11-19 AM.III.G.K6

Prior to an oil level check on a dry sump engine,

    A. motor the engine with the starter to ensure even distribution.

    B. disconnect the ignition switch.

    C. turn the propeller by hand several times to pump the oil from the engine to the oil tank.

11-20 AM.III.A.K9

If a 2 stroke light-sport aircraft engine continues to run with the ignition OFF, a probable cause is

    A. insufficient octane fuel.

    B. an overly lean mixture.

    C. the engine has overheated.

11-21 AM.III.A.K4

In a Jabiru light-sport aircraft engine, what is the integral alternator driven by?

    A. A drive belt.

    B. The reduction gear box.

    C. A flywheel driven by the crankshaft.

LIGHT-SPORT AIRCRAFT ENGINES

ANSWERS

11-19 Answer C
Before checking the engine oil level, make sure that there is
not excess residual oil in the crankcase.
Prior to oil level check, turn the propeller several times by
hand in the direction of engine rotation to pump all of the
oil from the engine to the oil tank. This process is complete
when air flows back to the oil tank.
Ref: Powerplant Handbook H-8083-32B-ATB Chapter 11 Page 19

11-20 Answer C
An overheated 2 cycle engine may continue to run once the
ignition is shut off. A failed ignition switch may also be to
blame. An over-lean mixture or insufficient octane will likely
be the cause of knocking or rough operations at high loads.
Ref: Powerplant Handbook H-8083-32B-ATB Chapter 11 Page 23

11-21 Answer C
An integral alternator provides AC rectification for
battery charging and electrical accessories. The alternator
is attached to the flywheel and is driven directly by
the crankshaft.
Ref: Powerplant Handbook H-8083-32B-ATB Chapter 11 Page 10

ORAL EXAM

11-1(O).   Name some characteristics and types of light-sport aircraft engines.

11-2(O).   How is maintenance recording accomplished on a light-sport aircraft?

11-3(O).   What type of oil system is often found on light-sport aircraft engines and what should be done before checking the oil level?

11-4(O).   In what way does the certified technician deviate from manufacturer's instructions when maintaining a light-sport aircraft engine?

LIGHT-SPORT AIRCRAFT ENGINES

ANSWERS

ORAL EXAM PRACTICAL EXAM

11-1(O).   Light-sport aircraft engines can be classified in many ways. They are usually in-line or opposed in cylinder configuration. Both two-cycle and four-cycle engine are used. Cooling can be liquid-cooled or air-cooled or a combination of both. There is only one crankshaft. Fixed pitch or ground adjustable propellers are used with the exception of an auto-feathering propeller being allowable on a glider. The engines for light-sport aircraft come in various sizes. They utilize various fuels from automobile gas to 100LL– the manufacturer specified fuel is required. Ignition is usually breaker-less capacitor-discharge type. Turbo charging is possible. Some engine are converted automobile engines.
Ref: Powerplant Handbook H-8083-32B-ATB Chapter 11

11-2(O).   Maintenance requirements and recording on light-sport aircraft is very similar to that of aircraf. certified in the standard aircraft category. Manufacturer's checklists and instructions are always used and required. Checklists and work orders for inspections and work accomplished must be recorded and kept in the maintenance records as well as recorded in the logbook. The technician must sign these records. It is the responsibility of the owner operator to store and maintain these records. Execution of service bulletins must also be entered in the logbook.
Ref: Powerplant Handbook H-8083-32B-ATB Chapter 11

11-3(O).   Dry sump oil systems are common on light-sport aircraft engines. Two-cycle engines are often used on light-sport aircraft. These engines use oil mixed with the fuel to lubricate the engine. On some models, the oi. is mixed with the fuel before it is poured into the fuel tank. However, on other models, the dry sump reservoir feeds an oil injection system that supplies the engine with the required lubrication oil. Usually, oil metering is directed in relation to throttle position supplying more oil when engine speed is high. By turning the engine through by hand before checking the oil quantity in the reservoir, residual oil in the system can be returned to establish an accurate quantity level.
Ref: Powerplant Handbook H-8083-32B-ATB Chapter 11

11-4(O).   The powerplant technician must not deviate from the manufacturer's instructions for maintenance of a light-sport aircraft engine. The technician should maintain the aircraft according to manufacturer's schedules and specifications.
Ref: Powerplant Handbook H-8083-32B-ATB Chapter 11

PRACTICAL EXAM

11-1(P).   Given an actual aircraft engine or mockup, appropriate publications, and tooling, inspect a light-sport aircraft engine installation and record findings. [Level 3]

11-2(P).   Given an actual aircraft engine or mockup, appropriate publications, and tooling, inspect the automatic lubrication system on a light-sport aircraft engine. [Level 3]

11-3(P).   Given an actual aircraft engine or mockup, appropriate publications, and tooling, inspect excess pressure valve operation and the cooling system for proper operation and cooling on a light-sport aircraft engine and record findings. [Level 3]

11-4(P).   Given an actual aircraft engine or mockup, appropriate publications, and tooling determine the proper crankshaft flange run-out on a light-sport aircraft engine and record findings. [Level 3]

11-5(P).   Given an actual aircraft engine or mockup, an airworthiness directive, and required tooling inspect a light-sport aircraft engine installation in accordance with the airworthiness directive and record findings. [Level 2]

11-6(P).   Given an actual aircraft engine or mockup, appropriate publications, and tooling check and adjust carburetor synchronization of a light-sport aircraft engine and record findings and maintenance performed. [Level 3]

11-7(P).   Given an actual aircraft engine or mockup, appropriate publications, and tooling, inspect Bowden cables for proper routing, actuation and lubrication on a light-sport aircraft engine and recording record findings and maintenance performed. [Level 3]

11-8(P).   Given an actual aircraft engine or mockup, appropriate publications, and tooling, perform an oil change on a light-sport aircraft engine and record findings and maintenance performed. [Level 3]

11-9(P).   Given an actual aircraft engine or mockup, appropriate publications, and tooling, inspect the magnetic plug on a light-sport aircraft engine for accumulation of metallic chips and record findings. [Level 3]

11-10(P).   Given an actual aircraft engine or mockup, appropriate publications, and tooling, inspect the fuel system pressure control and return lines on a light-sport aircraft engine for proper operation and record findings. [Level 3]

11-11(P).   Given an actual aircraft engine or mockup, appropriate publications, and tooling, perform a frictional torque check in free rotation of the overload clutch on a light-sport aircraft engine and record findings. [Level 3]

11-12(P).   Given an actual aircraft engine or mockup, appropriate publications, and tooling, perform a cylinder compression check on a light-sport aircraft engine system and record findings. [Level 3]

PAGE LEFT BLANK INTENTIONALLY